Gine

Tà's Red Book

The life of Wanda Ferragamo

Electa

contents

4   Introduction
Melania G. Mazzucco

26   **1.** Tà's "Circulars"

42   **2.** Fireflies and Round-Bottomed Dolls

52   **3.** The Shoemaker's Bride

66   **4.** The American Dream

82   **5.** A Telescope for Seeing Far

94   **6.** War Is Never Glorious

104   **7.** Rebuild

142   **8.** Family Life

156   **9.** Prayer

170   **10.** To Work!

188   **11.** How Great It Is To Be Good

198   **12.** Terracotta Pots

210   **13.** Notepads

222   **14.** A Letter to Fiamma

230   **15.** Magic Wanda

246   **16.** Triple-Eared Wheat

256   **17.** Thank You, Tà

Introduction

Melania G. Mazzucco

At the height of his professional career and personal life, Salvatore Ferragamo felt the urge to tell his story in a book, intending it to be an example for new generations and a source of hope. He was following in the wake of great American entrepreneurs such as P. T. Barnum and Andrew Carnegie, who were, in turn, inspired by Benjamin Franklin's example. He also wanted to convey the message that the true legacy of his life was not merely the fashion empire that he had built—and rebuilt—at such cost but an equally precious legacy of morals and values: the power of the will and of dreams, pride in one's work, commitment to talent, the tenacity to get back on your feet when you fall down, trust in innovation and, lastly but most importantly, the centrality of love and family. His autobiography, *Shoemaker of Dreams*, written in English for an English-speaking public with the support of a famous duo of ghost writers known as Douglas Warner, was published in 1957 by George G. Harrap & Co. in London; for some reason, it was only translated into Italian in 1971 by the Florentine publisher Sansoni.

A spell-binding epic tale of an ingenious, humble emigrant from Italy's south (one of twenty million Italians who left their country) as well as the story of an ambitious, visionary self-made man, *Shoemaker of Dreams* captured his life forever, transforming it into legend.

Wanda Ferragamo left no autobiography. When her grandchildren asked her to write her memoir, she would reply with a question: "Why? I haven't done anything remarkable or worth writing about." And yet, as the decades passed, the remarkable nature of her life must have become apparent even to her. And it was certainly recognized by society at large, as evidenced by the many awards she received: Cavaliere della Repubblica Italiana in 1987, an O.B.E. in 1995, Cavaliere di Gran Croce al Merito in 2004. Only toward the end of her very long life (she died aged 97) would she recount it, either in response to journalists and biographers in interviews and documentaries or on her own initiative, in letters and "circulars" intended for her grandchildren. Indeed, unlike her husband, whose manual skills and practical genius concealed an unexpected talent for storytelling, Signora Ferragamo had always been a prolific writer of notes, letters, handbooks, tips, even recipe books. But the educational and "testamentary" intent that was implicit in Salvatore's narrative ended up overwhelming Wanda's story. Maybe she had too many commitments—despite her age, she was still the pillar of the business and of her family—or maybe her wish to tell her story was not as strong as her desire to remain in the shadows. Throughout her life, she had sheltered behind the figure of her husband, even when he had become an angelic, evanescent shadow. In order to write about yourself, you have to be willing to reveal yourself, something that she was ultimately not prepared to do. As a result, her autobiography remained fragmentary, unfinished, and then interrupted for ever by her death in 2018. And only then did her granddaughter Ginevra Visconti gather together all of these materials, along with other eminently private writings, working with great dedication to transform them into the book that you are about to read.

The personal and professional story of Wanda Ferragamo is like a thread running through an inextricable tangle of myth, legend, society chronicle, family and corporate memoir. We can attempt to historicize it by dividing it into three acts apparently corresponding to the three traditional stages of a woman's life—daughter, wife and mother, widow. This is because a woman could never just be herself, she had to be and do what her relationship with others (family, society) prescribed. But today, as we explore the weft and warp of this extraordinary life, we become aware of its continuous shift from the norm, even though concealed and sometimes denied. This strategy, which may have initially been unconscious, is what allowed Wanda to attain unexpected goals and to leave behind the protective shadow of her beloved husband to become a beacon for women in the twenty-first century.

The daughter of Doctor Miletti (1921–1940)

Salvatore Ferragamo's autobiography begins with Wanda. Indeed, the dedication on the first page reads, "To Wanda / for whom I searched the world / and whom I found in the / village of my birth." She is announced as the destination of the protagonist's journey, as the fairytale princess who is the reward awaiting the hero at the end of his vicissitudes. In fact, she does not make her entrance until Chapter 18 (the fourth from last), "War, Marriage, and Persecution."

On June 10, 1940, Mussolini put an end to Italian neutrality by declaring war on France: Ferragamo, the eleventh of fourteen children, who had been working since he was 9, found himself with no job. His Florentine warehouses contained five thousand pairs of shoes intended for the British and American markets that could no longer be shipped. His workers were called to war and he could no longer import materials from abroad. Salvatore, who specialized in making high-quality luxury footwear, was hardly going to start making boots for soldiers. At the age of 42, he found himself with nothing to do. He decided the time had finally come to find a wife, as his relatives had been urging him to do for some time. He had left Bonito for America in 1915, returned to Italy in 1927, and decided to settle in Florence. But like all emigrants, he wanted to look for a wife in his hometown.

So he set off for Bonito. Perched among the mountains of Irpinia, Bonito was only a few hours' drive from Naples, where Salvatore was staying with his mother and two sisters. Italy may have been at war, but the front was still far away and there was no shortage of petrol. While he was having lunch with his

uncle, Father Alessandro, who now lived in his family's humble house, they received a visit from the local podestà, Fulvio Miletti, whom Ferragamo knew because he was the village doctor. Miletti wished to speak with Ferragamo, who was a generous donor to the poor of Bonito. However, Salvatore was unaware that this money rarely reached those most in need, so Miletti suggested organizing a more efficient donation system. Given that their conversation promised to be protracted, Ferragamo invited Miletti to stay for lunch. The podestà refused his offer on the grounds that he had recently lost his wife and was still in full mourning: in 1940s southern Italy, tradition was respected. Ferragamo expressed his regret.
He had known Giovanna Pellegrino, who was a loyal customer of his before he emigrated to America. When he left, Giovanna still owed him the money for two pairs of shoes. Although he had asked his mother to collect the debt, she did not dare ask the doctor's wife for money and the shoes were never paid for. Ferragamo had not forgotten the debt (and in his memoirs makes sure we also know about it) but did not mention it to the podestà. Instead, he accepted Miletti's invitation to come to his home at eight that evening to continue their discussion.

Why go? He was supposed to go back to Naples and this unforeseen event overturned his plans. He could not really have been that interested in organizing these donations. And yet, inspired by the infallible, almost prophetic instinct that had always guided him, he canceled his return journey.

The scene that took place in his family home that summer morning is like an anthropologically accurate X-ray of the customs, traditions, and prejudices of an Italian village in 1940. Let's leave their names aside for now and consider them in terms of social roles.

We have an emigrant who has returned to Italy after making his fortune in America, settling in Florence rather than in his hometown, which offers no future for his business; following a series of ups and downs, including a bankruptcy, he has now become one of the country's leading entrepreneurs. But he will never be able to hide his lowly origins. In Bonito, he was a shoemaker, the most despised of the artisan crafts because it dealt with the least noble part of the human body, the foot. He came from a family so humble that collecting a debt from someone belonging to a higher class was an unthinkable act. As Mozart had observed, Italy was still a "sleepy country." And money alone would not subvert the hierarchy. In 1884, when Edmondo De Amicis returned from his journey to Argentina, he criticized his country's lack of social mobility (or the "social elevator" in sociological jargon), the powerful economic driver that was transforming the American continent. But not Italy. In the Italian "colonies" of Rio de la Plata, he had met emigrants who had become entrepreneurs and eminent citizens in the New World who had no intention of returning to their homeland. When asked why, they replied that their fellow villagers would always consider them to be landless day laborers, the beggars they formerly had been.

Then we have Uncle Alessandro, who is the parish priest of Bonito. He comes from the same humble family as the shoemaker, but since the church is still the heart of every Italian village, his entry into the clergy has somewhat improved his social standing.

And then we have the podestà, the supreme municipal authority in Fascist Italy, who will always belong to the class of the notables by dint of his birth and political will. Furthermore, Fulvio Miletti was also the town doctor. Together with the lawyer, the priest, and the marshal of the Carabinieri, he is one of the stock characters in every provincial theater. Naturalist literature from Italy and elsewhere in Europe (just consider Flaubert) is full of such examples. Although he treats Salvatore with respect, the podestà does not allow him to forget their difference in status: indeed, Doctor Miletti is not really in full mourning but in half mourning, because his wife died the previous year. The real reason for his refusal to stay for lunch is to make the "humbler" man come to him and not the other way round.

Wanda, the doctor's daughter, was not there and had not even been mentioned. Salvatore had forgotten about her existence altogether: she was born in 1921, when he was on the other side of the ocean, and was still a little girl when he visited Bonito in 1927. And yet she was the predestined one and Salvatore's recognition of this was immediate and definitive. After meeting her at her father's house and hearing her pronounce a few quick words of welcome on the steps, he murmured to his sister—in English so as not to be understood—that this was the girl who would become his wife. As Ferragamo tells it, his visit to the podestà ends with a "comedy." Having resolved the matter of the donations in just a few minutes, Salvatore tried to prolong his visit and captivate the daughter while her father clearly wished to get rid of his guest. Miletti brushed off Salvatore's many questions, answering in monosyllables and making no attempt to hide his reluctance to entertain the "cobbler." Ferragamo cleverly steered him into his home ground by forcing him to talk about feet. Doctor Miletti may have thought he knew everything about anatomy, but Ferragamo wanted to illustrate his theory of the perfectly fitting shoe. He asked Wanda—who had so far played only a decorative role—to take off her shoe then held her foot in his hand. Wanda, who had a hole in the toe of her silk stocking, blushed in embarrassment.

The tone of the narrative moves from comical, almost crude realism toward that of a fairytale. Here is a man kneeling before a standing girl, holding her foot in his big laborer's hands, handling it with infinite delicacy. The Disney movie had yet to disseminate the film version throughout the entire world (it was only made in 1950) but every child knows the story of Cinderella—in the sugar-coated version of Perrault or the gory version of the Grimm brothers, while the Neapolitans would probably have been more familiar with Basile's variant. Shoes play a magical role and exercise a strong attraction both in traditional fairy tales and in the modern fables by Andersen, himself the son of a cobbler. Talisman, gift, instrument of freedom, movement, and redemption, sexual symbol but also a curse, in that shoes are the objective correlative of our deepest self. In this updated re-interpretation of Cinderella, the prince does not require the assistance of a chamberlain to place the girl's foot in the glass slipper in order to recognize her: he does it all himself.

And yet—as Andrea Vianello points out in his *Storia sociale della calzatura*—the comedy staged by Ferragamo in Miletti's salon is less innocent than may appear at first sight. From Roman times onward, through the Middle Ages and until the Revolution, there was an enormous difference between a bare foot and a shod foot. Slaves, servants, and peasants are barefoot, and prostitutes reveal their feet: the nudity of skin or the transparency of stockings are a sign of sexual availability.

And heels are an almost diabolical temptation. For centuries, preachers have thundered against women who artificially increase their height by wearing heels, altering the proportions of the human body established by God. The cobbler holding the girl's bare foot in his hands, making her dream of a pair of shoes with heels, ended up revolutionizing the entire world. He may not have known it yet, but the power now lay in his hands.

According to Salvatore's account, he sent Wanda a bouquet on the following day and declared his love to her, obtaining her consent. She in turn warned him to be careful not to make any false moves with her father who disapproved of the match and would do everything in his power to discourage this enterprising, mature suitor. Little did Doctor Miletti know that Salvatore's uncle had already introduced him to Meneca, Wanda's housekeeper, who was willing to help them. As if in a commedia dell'arte (the two lovers preferred to evoke the more noble *Romeo and Juliet*), she was to become their trusted messenger, carrying their billets-doux and their notes organizing chaste secret encounters. Although Meneca would sometimes withdraw discreetly, Salvatore had to virtually abduct Wanda in his car before mass in order to embrace her. The podestà reacted by sending his daughter away from the village.

Why was Doctor Miletti so opposed to their relationship? Despite their age difference and Ferragamo's hulking laborer's physique, he was an excellent match for an 18-year-old daughter to marry. Salvatore was a considerate, brilliant man with a kind smile and a huge fortune—he even established a workshop producing uppers in Bonito. But he was still just a shoemaker. In the end, though, the suitor's insistence wore down the podestà's resistance and on November 9, the two love-birds finally married in the church of Santa Lucia, Naples. Their wedding night in Sorrento was lit by the flashes of the Allied bombing of the port of Naples. After their brief honeymoon on the Amalfi Coast, the two newly-weds made their way to Florence, settling in the villa Il Palagio on the Fiesole hills, in a fairytale "castle" where they lived happily ever after.

That's it. At least, this is Salvatore's version. Given that his autobiography would become a sort of Gospel for Wanda—who consulted it, like an I Ching, at critical moments of her life, seeking answers to her doubts, advice on her dilemmas, endorsement and guidance in the professional decisions she had to make—it should correspond to Wanda's version. She refers to her encounter with Salvatore in various interviews, memoirs, letters, and in *Tà's Red Book*, with a narrative that both coincides and diverges from his. What we need to do now is try to change our perspective and point of view by entering the mayor's residence on Via Roma and transforming ourselves into an 18-year-old girl.

Wanda had never left Bonito, the village to which Salvatore returned after thirteen years spent traveling and discovering the world, struggling and suffering. She had never traveled further than Naples, never left Campania. The last of six children (two of whom died in childhood), she grew up in a prosperous family, typical of the bourgeoisie of southern Italy in the early twentieth century.

Her father was a learned professional man, a philanthropist (he treated the poor free of charge), a deeply religious practicing Catholic, who shone in society and in female company (women who found him handsome would come all the way from the provincial capital to be visited by him), courteous to his wife but strict, authoritarian, and cold with his children who were not allowed fun, tears, or any display of emotion. Mostly absent (he received his patients in his surgery but also made home visits, traveling to farmhouses in his barouche), he so rarely played with his daughter that 80 years later, she would still remember the time when he listened to her dolls' hearts with his stethoscope after returning home from work one evening. He was the undisputed master of the household, laying down its rules.

Her mother was sweet and patient, loving and caring (even though her favorite was her son Silvio), a superb cook, and perfect housewife. Beautiful, refined, elegant. She yearned for distant high society but was happy to read about it in the press. A conservative like her husband, she was scandalized when Edward VII gave up the English throne for a divorcee. She resembled the sophisticated heroines who were imprisoned in the stifling and smothering contemporary Italian novels and films.

Wanda was brought up in the Catholic faith and taught to respect authority, to be obedient, devout, and aware of her intended future as a girl from a good family. She was educated till the age of 8 at home by governesses from the neighboring towns—the public primary school was only for poor children who would attend for just two years—and then at Istituto Magistrale "Mater Dei," a boarding school in Naples where she prayed and studied French *comme il faut*. She learned to cook, as befitted her future role as housewife, and to play the piano, as befitted her bourgeois social status. In brief, she was equipped for the sole purpose of her life: marriage, to be decided by her father at the right time.

A predictable life, punctuated every Thursday by *La Semaine de Suzette*, a French magazine with brightly colored illustrated stories, comics, childish romances, monologues, puzzles, patterns for dolls' clothes, and recipes. But even this was a controlled form of escapism because her father had given her the subscription to help her learn French. It may have been a privileged life, but one already touched by suffering: in 1938, she lost her brother Silvio in a tragic accident (he fell into a well while playing football and the rotten beams crushed his skull) followed a year later by her mother, who never recovered from this loss. An 18-year-old orphan, Wanda was familiar with the hierarchy, with the rituals and hypocrisies of society.

She was not supposed to meet her father's guest even though she would certainly have known about his arrival. In Bonito everyone, even the greengrocer, was talking about the visit of Signor Ferragamo from Florence. And Florence, seen from the perspective of Bonito, was a capital of elegance and good taste—Italy's autarkic Paris. Wanda would probably have gossiped about him with her cousin. After all, Ferragamo made shoes for movie stars, and the movies were possibly the only form of recreation that girls from her class were allowed to indulge in, since there was no theater or opera house in Bonito.

Salvatore was admitted to the house by the maid. Encouraged by her excitable cousin, Wanda goes downstairs to meet him, hoping to make a good impression. She wants to seem informed about fashion. So—in her version—she does not address him hurriedly, inviting him to come upstairs to wait for her father, as in Salvatore's version. Instead, she makes a casual remark, "You must be the famous Salvatore Ferragamo." Ferragamo replies modestly that he was unaware of being so famous. She insists, praising him for his contribution to the elegance of women. Then immediately regrets her words, which are based only on hearsay. She knows nothing about fashion—there is not a single dress shop in Bonito—and if their conversation were to continue, she might expose her ignorance. Ferragamo would discover that she is just a flighty—though fairly emancipated—girl from the provinces. She is saved by her father's arrival.

But she ends up being exposed anyway. Because she has a hole in the toe of her silk stocking and her foot is nothing like Cinderella's. She wears a size 7, like the Ugly Stepsisters. There is a popular belief (not shared by Ferragamo who classifies women by their shoe size: Cinderella, smaller than size 6, Venus, size 6, aristocrat, a 7 or larger) that ladies have small lily-like feet and that large feet are a sign of lowly origins. Has the magic vanished? Was the coach just a pumpkin? Ferragamo promises to make her a pair of shoes of just the right size.

Wanda makes no attempt to downplay her father's opposition to this relationship and provides us with the true reason for this. He had always used the figure of the shoemaker as a demeaning bogeyman. When she was 16, she had once dared to use eyeshadow; her father forced her to wash her face then threatened to wed her to the "first cobbler to ask for her hand in marriage" if she persisted with such frivolous behavior. Wanda does not hide her doubts regarding the insistent courtship of someone who is not only a virtual stranger, but considerably older than she is; someone who sends her not a bouquet but an entire hothouse of tuberoses the day after his first visit (she had to press into service every vase in the house); someone who sends her a note via her maid asking when they can meet again, and in the following note already claims to love her, saying that he will only withdraw if she rejects his offer of marriage.

She describes how she schemes with Meneca to organize meetings with Ferragamo behind her father's back and does not conceal her fear of how he might react (she places her father on a pedestal and wishes neither to disobey nor disappoint him). Nor does she hide the confusion and uncertainty of her own feelings. She even ends up asking for advice from the wife of one of her brother's teachers. The teacher's wife advises her to follow her heart: "Do you love him or not?" When he returns to Tuscany, she sends him a postcard with the words "Pensando a te" (Thinking of you). As soon as he receives it, he sets off for Bonito and asks for her hand in marriage.

She also reports an episode that Salvatore was too discreet to mention. Indeed, Doctor Miletti only agrees to his proposal after receiving irrefutable proof of the standing achieved by the "shoemaker." The love that he has declared for his daughter is not enough. So Ferragamo sends a car to Bonito to pick up the podestà and take him to Florence, where he shows him the elegant Palazzo Spini Feroni near the Santa Trinita Bridge, home to his company headquarters, followed by his newly acquired holiday home, a beautiful villa at Forte dei Marmi. Not just the mayor's equal, the shoemaker is clearly worth much more. Only then does Miletti give in and grant him his daughter's hand.

When they arrive in Florence after their honeymoon, he stops his Alfa Romeo in Piazzale Michelangelo to allow his young wife to admire the beauty of the city and the view. Another rite of passage, as if to say, "All of this is now yours." Then he takes her home to Il Palagio, the "imposing Renaissance villa" on the hills of Fiesole overlooking Florence. She is left speechless, incredulous and enchanted by such beauty. Even overawed. After all, she is not even 19 years old (her birthday is the following month); she is on her own, in an unknown city among strangers. But she receives a warm welcome from his mother and sisters (they all live together, according to the tradition of patriarchal families), an affection unknown to her, and she soon settles into the villa and into her new life, without any further hesitation. So, in her own account Wanda portrays herself as an obedient daughter and the object of another's love. When in actual fact, it was her will that steered events. Her freely given consent. Her choice.

The "sublime womb" of my dreams: wife and mother (1940–1960)

The last mention of Wanda in Ferragamo's autobiography is when she hides in the cellar with him and the children during the Allied bombing of the Fiesole hills. Afterwards, Wanda is included in the subject of every sentence, implicit, inseparable, as vital as one of the body's organs. Whenever he uses the first-person plural "we," Salvatore is including her. This grammatical fusion is the highest praise that this husband can give his beloved wife, who would go on to become the pillar and driver of his existence until the very last day of this existence.

Footage from home movies shot in the villa gardens around 1940 shows Wanda, plump and smiling, domestic and yet regal in her furs, running across the lawn or going up the entrance staircase. With her is Salvatore's mother. Elderly, humble, somewhat "ancient." The difference between the two women, born in the same place, Bonito, just a generation apart, could not be more striking. Wanda, self-confident and radiant, boasts the outfits, jewelry, and hairstyles of a star of a White Telephone film (a cheerful, natural Alida Valli with a Mediterranean look), while her mother-in-law is a timeless country woman with a wrinkled face, sturdy body, and uncertain, modest smile. As Salvatore moves from one woman to the other, his devotion to them causes the hand holding the movie camera to shake ever so slightly. The entrepreneur, the genius, is soft-hearted. There is no doubt that from 1940 onwards, his life was dedicated to his wife.

Wanda describes the years of her marriage as an oasis of happiness that not even the war could ruin, at least for a while. No longer distant flashes of light seen from the balcony of a hotel on the Amalfi Coast, the war is drawing closer and closer to their door and beginning to threaten their wellbeing (the business has practically come to a standstill). Nonetheless, World War II coincides with the most thrilling period of her motherhood. Her children are born in swift succession, following the natural rhythms of female fertility: Fiamma in 1941, Giovanna in 1943, and Ferruccio in 1945. Wanda takes care of her little girls and of her husband—whom she only sees at lunchtimes, when he takes a couple of hours break from his work. She runs the household and manages the staff, an army of maids, cooks, gardeners, butlers, and nursemaids. She is surprisingly good at this because as her mother told her, *si tu sa fa, sa pure cummannà* (if you know how it is done, you know how to order it done). Her daily purpose is to make her husband's life easier—his business has come to a virtual halt due to the war and this embitters him; to ensure that the house is always neat and tidy; and to make sure that a delicious meal is always waiting for him when he comes home. Because—as she would later tell her granddaughter Ginevra—a "husband must come home to rest and recharge his batteries, not to worry about household matters." She is not really affected by the problems in the outside world—such as the Italian military defeats in 1941 and 1942 and the worsening living conditions for civilians. In fact, rationing did not really touch the Ferragamo family: they managed to produce most of their food on their land, which was as fertile as the couple. It was not until September 8, 1943, when Florence was occupied by the Germans, that History interrupted their idyllic life.

Wanda is resting upstairs when she hears a commotion telling her that German troops are at the door. They have driven their trucks through the open gates and are now at the entrance to the villa, which they intend to turn into their army HQ. They order Wanda to leave with her children. She has no choice but to obey, but first calls her husband (who is in Florence) to come and save her. Yet again, she portrays herself in her account as a fragile woman in need of help.

Ferragamo rushes back to the villa where he is interrogated at gunpoint by an officer (someone has informed the Germans that the owner of the villa is an American spy). He tries to convince the officer that he is just a shoemaker and shoe salesman, and begs him to let his wife and children stay. The officer agrees to his request and Salvatore agrees to give him the shoes left in stock, which have remained unsold because of the war. In exchange, the Ferragamo family must also provide lodgings for thirty or so people from the surrounding area who have been forced to give up their homes to billet German soldiers. Wanda is not really aware of their presence and years later, looking back at that time, she could barely remember them. She devotes all her energies to keeping everything running in peace and harmony, even if they are occasionally forced to hide in the cellar during bombing raids: she looks after the girls, organizes their supplies, and reigns wisely over her invaded kingdom.

But the Germans are still holding the Gustav Line and the war reaches a deadlock: the Allies suspend their advance and start bombing relentlessly. Wealthy Florentines are barricaded in their villas in the surrounding hills while all the others struggle for survival in a starving city that is attacked 25 times and bombed 7 times; the sirens sound at least 325 times. Some Florentines join the Resistance and more than 700 civilians die beneath the rubble. At Il Palagio, they are safe from the sufferings of the besieged city. Salvatore does not return to Florence and remains at the villa to comfort his family with his presence. In her account, Wanda does not draw attention to her husband's problems—he was arrested twice by the Germans on spying charges. Nor does she mention the searches carried out by both the Fascists and Republicans, who were convinced that weapons or food were hidden in the villa. Or the real risk that Il Palagio might be blown up, when demolition squads placed mines in preparation for the German retreat (once again danger was averted thanks to Salvatore's diplomatic skills). The extent of the destruction caused by the retreating German troops would only become apparent to her later. However, when the Germans blew up the bridges over the Arno on the night of August 3, 1944, she was shaken by the thunder of the explosions and distressed by the destruction of the lovely Santa Trinita Bridge, just a few yards from Palazzo Spini Feroni.

The only episode on which they both dwell at length in their accounts took place after the war had ended—Florence was liberated on August 11, 1944—in the frenetic months after the Liberation. On August 3, 1945, Ferragamo is arrested by the order of the CTLN (the Tuscan National Liberation Committee). The partisans accused him of collaborating with the enemy. He had made shoes for Donna Rachele, Claretta Petacci, and Eva Braun, therefore he must be a fascist. Meanwhile the Republicans reasoned that as he has made shoes for the Queen of Italy and for the Savoy princesses, he must therefore be a monarchist. Wanda is eight months pregnant and can play only a limited role in the negotiations for his release, contacting those able to help but without really being able to get around or appear in public. This was a nerve-wracking period for Wanda because this was a time of reckoning in Italy and of executions after summary trials. Ferragamo was the object of envy and his enemies may have wanted to use this opportunity to get rid of him. This was a tragic time for the couple—Salvatore in jail, Wanda alone in the hills. Yet both of their accounts are very matter-of-fact. Ferragamo minimizes the risk because he believes there is no need to "dig up the past and dwell on all that hatred."

He successfully defends himself from his accusers, saying that he is "just a shoemaker who knows nothing about politics." In his account he describes how, after obtaining his release, he returns to the ruins of what was formerly a flourishing business, as Italy embarks upon reconstruction. Wanda, on the other hand, recalls with relief Salvatore's return from prison, accompanied by a CTLN official who was there to protect him from a lynch mob. And she remembers the date of his release— September 8—because it coincides with the birth of their third child and first son, Ferruccio. She attributes this act of providence to her faith: God has listened to her prayers, begging him not to bring her son into the world while his father is still in jail.

The 15 postwar years of reconstruction are "marvelous": Ferragamo gets the company back on its feet, expanding into foreign markets and growing the business all over the world. Wanda is happy in her role as wife and mother. She moves among the cream of Florentine society—many of her friends come from old noble families—and accompanies her husband on his business trips (in September 1947, she boards the *Queen Elizabeth* ocean liner on her first trip to America where Salvatore is to receive an award from Neiman Marcus for his "invisible sandal," becoming a fervent admirer of the States). She appears in photos in glossy magazines at the side of her illustrious husband as he receives prizes from industrialists and chairmen or contemplates radiant Hollywood stars wearing his latest creations. Dark-haired, green-eyed, bejeweled, extremely elegant and always smiling, she is the perfect image of a 1950s wife. A model of inspiration in the joy that appears on her nicely rounded, contented face.

In the meantime, she has three more children (Fulvia in 1950, Leonardo in 1952, and Massimo in 1957). This time, she calls upon the services of wet nurses, selected by her husband and father in Ciociaria according to time-honored fashion: based on the shape of their breasts and the abundance of milk flowing from them. She is the "sublime womb" of her husband's dreams, as he describes her in the handwritten dedication to his autobiography, which was published in the year their youngest son was born. Wanda organizes parties for the children, teaches her teenage daughter dance steps, plays with the dogs; she oversees the farm work and honey production in the country estate purchased in 1955; she supervises her older children's studies and the behavior of the English nannies responsible for the younger children—replacing them frequently because they are never up to scratch; kindly and firmly, she passes on to her children the same values that she and her husband had received from their own parents. They are taught that privileges must be earned: she applies a reward system based on money and affection, and the children receive a modest allowance on the basis of their school reports. They are expected to always behave properly, to tell the truth, to respect their elders, to take care of their appearance, and to remember their manners. Years later, she would compare looking after children to running a railway. It is the duty of parents to ensure that the train, station, and platform are well maintained and to leave children free to express themselves without going off the rails. In short, she carried out her mission as a woman.

At the same time, these years as the wife of an entrepreneur and mother of six children can also be seen as an apprenticeship—or "training ground," in the words of Ginevra Visconti. By running a complex household like Il Palagio—along with the Viesca country estate—taking care of everyone, rewarding them while making demands, and supervising the work of a staff of 12 people, without even delegating the choice of fruit to place on the table at lunch, she was developing her innate tendency to control that would prepare her to manage a far larger organization. However, she did not realize this just yet. She had unconsciously absorbed a male-focused patriarchal vision of the world whereby domestic work is not true work. Aged nearly 90, she would continue to say, "I had never worked a day in my life before then."

The Cavalier Ferragamo (1960–2018)

Salvatore Ferragamo fell ill on his return from a trip to Australia in 1958, which was a commercial success because it opened up the Australian and then the Asian markets in the south-east of the globe where Ferragamo still dominates today. Weak and tired, after a restorative break in Capri that had failed to improve matters, he agreed to take some tests. The diagnosis left no hope: liver cancer. He had surgery, but it was

too late. He survived for three more months before dying on
August 7, 1960, aged just 62. Wanda was only 39 and totally
unprepared for this loss; during his illness she always tried to
appear optimistic, hiding her fears so as not to worry the
children or sadden him. Now her entire world had fallen apart.
She had never even contemplated life without Salvatore, who
had been her beacon and guiding light for the past twenty
years. Wanda was grief-stricken. Her oldest daughter was only
just 19, and her youngest child not even 3. The business was
built entirely around the figure of its creator, and now the light
had gone out. Everything that Salvatore had built up—for her
and with her—would be lost. She would have to sell up. How
could she possibly run the Ferragamo business? She knew
nothing about "financial and economic organization," about
sales, distribution, administration, production, or
management. And she was a woman. Apart from Coco Chanel
and Estée Lauder, who had both created their own companies,
how many women in the world were running a business?
In Italy, not a single one. The dream was over.

The young widow needed some time alone to give herself up
to her despair. She left the children at home—she did not want
them to see her so distraught and insecure—and hid out in a
hotel in Vallombrosa, a short distance from Viesca. But her
despair did not last long. Her husband may have been dead,
but she still felt his presence in her and close to her. He had
two dreams. To expand the Ferragamo market: not just shoes
but "a House of Ferragamo" clothing women from head to toe.
And to involve his children in the company, so that it would
grow, generation after generation. She knew that she was born
to make Salvatore's dreams come true, not to destroy them.
She had become the "means" to bring them about. She needed
to transform the joy that she had received from her husband
into energy. Wanda used a military term to describe the
moment when she forced herself to recover: "I began to fight
my battle against depression."

On her return to Florence, she acted with the same
determination as the 18-year-old girl who wrote "Thinking of
you" on a postcard, thereby determining her fate. "Thinking
of you," she decided not only to inherit Salvatore's business but
also his dreams. It proved to be a transformative decision:
"I was a lioness, full of strength and determined to take on the

world." When the factory reopened after the August bank holiday, the employees, suppliers, clients, workers, and estate agents were all left open-mouthed. Signora Wanda had decided against selling. Instead, she would be taking over as the new director of the House of Ferragamo.

She took possession of her husband's office in Palazzo Feroni, going there every morning. From that day on, she would rule the House of Ferragamo with the same iron fist in a velvet glove as the Ferragamo family. With the same rules, the same principles, the same aims. Control of every tiny detail, from raw materials and production to stores and staff. Respect for tradition and willingness to innovate—new techniques, new materials as well as new products, new lines, and new markets. She listened to her staff and was receptive to their advice, but, ultimately, she alone made the decisions, as if possessed by the spirit of her husband (she needed to believe this in order not to seem too daring, either in her own eyes or those of the world). She could be as naive or shrewd as circumstances demanded, stubborn, and always authoritative.

Year after year, she went on work trips, often crossing the Atlantic (the first was to New York in 1961), holding meetings with collaborators and accountants, clients and suppliers, representing the company, socializing in order to maintain and build relationships. She rubbed shoulders with queens both on and off the throne, she received the respects of movie stars; gone were the days in which she was jealous of Katharine Hepburn, Rita Hayworth, Ingrid Bergman, Greta Garbo, or Marilyn Monroe. She lists these beauties as lepidopterists do butterflies—after having caught and pinned them.

One by one, just as their father had hoped, their children joined the company. The first was Fiamma, who, after her father's death, created the first collection based on his designs and thereafter became brand ambassador in the U.S. After her came Giovanna, Ferruccio, who devoted himself to administration, and Fulvia, who came up with the fabulous silk scarves. Then they were followed by the younger siblings. Ferragamo was now producing bags, leather goods, fragrances, silk accessories, and even had a range for men.

Wanda reigned from Palazzo Feroni and from Il Palagio, surrounded by employees, secretaries, and relations: her daughters, then her sons, got married and multiplied like bees. She devoted the same attention to her 23 grandchildren as she once did to her own children, selecting their babysitters as she once had her children's English nannies. She wrote to them when they were far away. She took on the role of teacher, and preacher. The family geography exploded from their point of origin in Bonito, and the Ferragamos became scattered all over the world. Wanda kept in touch with them through her letters, her "circulars," and peremptory invitations on their return ("blunt" is the word that Ginevra uses to describe them). The threads may be infinite but at the center of the web was always Wanda, who continued to weave together everyone's lives. Perfectionist, obstinate, she charmed them with her care, with the sharpness of her observations, her ability to remember birthdays; she intimidated them with her unpredictable mood swings, her outbursts that could reduce even adults to tears, and harsh reprimands. She pursued her mission—that of passing on the values that had brought Salvatore, then her and the whole family to success—with an almost religious zeal and with the pedantry that she had inherited from her father. She might deny it to outsiders, but she knew well that she was an example for her family, and wished to be one for her descendants. Her need to control things—something she could not always do because of the distances involved—would run riot and the obsession with rules that she shared with Doctor Miletti was unleashed in the form of rules of conduct (her father had written a list of rules guaranteeing longevity), guides to survival, etiquette rules, and lists of the fundamental principles of life and business (innovation, tradition, integrity). She even found the time to send letters to ministers and MPs, advising them to ensure that school children are told the stories of Leonardo Del Vecchio and Angelo Rizzoli, both self-made men like Salvatore Ferragamo, who can teach them to follow their dreams.

In this vertical life—a trajectory constantly moving upwards—there was no room for tiredness or melancholy. No regrets for the choice made in 1960, for the huge burden of responsibilities that she took onto her shoulders. It is only by reading between the lines that we realize the price that she paid for these dreams. Making them come true came at a cost. Fulfilling Salvatore's dreams, making them her own to the point that she *turned into* him meant she would never have another life partner. Wanda, who always reminded her daughters and granddaughters to be professional without giving up their femininity, has had to give up her, relegating it to mere appearance: elegance, outfits, trimmings. Being the head of a dynasty that has expanded all over the world meant spending weekends in her "fairy castle," surrounded by domestic staff, but alone. There is no success without sacrifice.

But this is a lesson that Signora Wanda never committed to paper. Doctor Miletti's daughter would have been punished for showing her emotions and even in her late nineties, she still felt obliged to suppress them, keeping her inner self under lock and key just as she did with everything in Il Palagio and Palazzo Feroni. You will look in vain for any signs of letting go in these pages. All of her emotions are devoted to those twenty years spent at the side of an exuberant, sentimental man who could be loved with abandon. Salvatore evoked in her only tangible memories of tenderness as she described missing his big hand holding hers. Everything else is detachment. She would reserve all of her pride for the company, never for herself; and she brought a dignified restraint to both her affections and to her sometimes terrible sufferings—her beloved daughter and ally Fiamma, as well as Ginevra's mother Fulvia, both died before her. Placing the pain under lock and key, in fact. In her final words, she said that love is everything. As in fairy tales. But she formulated this dogma like a procedural code.

Wanda left the task of bridging this gap to the next generations. And as she weaves together her grandmother's memories with her own, Ginevra, who is so different from Wanda yet so similar in her emotional restraint, in her down-to-earth approach to the story of a unique family and her refusal to turn it into a saga, infuses the myth with a new intimate light, revealing that she is certainly equal to this task.

*

*Great love stories still exist. To the very end,
my grandmother Wanda remained deeply in love
with my grandfather, Salvatore Ferragamo, the
"shoemaker of dreams."*

*I was not lucky enough to meet my grandfather in
person, but I know him both from the pages of his
autobiography and, most vividly, from the stories about
him that my grandmother never tired of telling. After
his untimely death, she kept his memory alive every day.
She made herself the narrator and witness of his life
story and of his work, of his teachings and his dreams;
and she made remembrance of them and him the mission
of our entire family.*

*Drawing strength from her love for her departed
husband, my widowed grandmother, known to us 23
grandchildren (and to us alone) as "Tà," presided with
determination and courage over—and, indeed, dedicated
her whole being to—the company that he created.*

*For more than fifty years, she would rise at dawn with
the same steady resolve to carry forward her husband
Salvatore's project. With enviable self-discipline, she
would neatly make her bed, read the newspapers, cut out
the most interesting articles, write down some considered
observations, organize her thoughts, dress with care, and
finally arrive punctually in the office before everyone else.*

*She worked from a room in Palazzo Spini Feroni, the
company office in her beloved city of Florence. Between
presiding over and attending meetings, fielding and
making telephone calls, and making decisions, she
always tried to find a moment's peace to write down*

useful counsel for us grandchildren. She would send her notes to us all at the same time, safe in the knowledge that her words would be preserved between the leaves of the "Red Book." A carefully customized copy of this book (essentially a collector's album), which was supplemented by a second, third, and fourth volume, was given to every one of the 23 grandchildren. Tà's idea for the Red Book was that it would contain the letters she sent us over the years, and would therefore be filled with thoughts, notes, memories, lessons from real life, and information about the company, all seasoned with affectionate, practical advice.

Each new letter was added to the Red Book, which thus became a testimonial of Tà's deep commitment to the principles of beauty and excellence, which she sought to create in her own life and inculcate in her family and in her company. The Red Book tells the story of a marriage and a family united by a shared dream. It tells the story of a company that, step by step, with perseverance but without compromise, has prospered and grown while rising to the challenge of supporting the traditions of Italian quality and craftsmanship.

These letters capture Tà's energetic character, Faith, common sense, and far-sightedness while also chronicling the stages of her personal and professional life as a woman and business leader.

I want to share what she taught us so that her wisdom may also touch the hearts of many others. I want the story of my grandparents to be read as an encouragement to people to stay the course and to keep their faith, whether it be in their country, their family, their work, or in the truth of Love (a word she always capitalized). In every letter, Tà exhorted us to remain true to ourselves. Little did we realize at the time how uniquely privileged we were to have such an exceptional grandmother, who was always so mindful of the young people around her, for she knew the future lay in their hands.

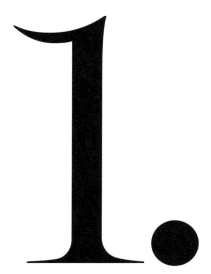

Tà's "Circulars"

A solitary Federal Express package was waiting for me on the front table of my Buenos Aires apartment. Shining through the large windows overlooking the monkey puzzle trees of Plaza Alemania was a bright beam of sunlight that seemed to fall directly onto the waiting parcel. I could never have imagined that this would be just the first of a constant stream of such packages. It was November 2008, and I had been living in Argentina for four years with my husband and two children.

Sitting on the squeaky parquet, I tore open the package, my curiosity magnified by the fact I received few packages in the post back then, as most of them would get held up at customs as a result of the restrictive policies of the Kirchner government. I sensed it was something important. The weight and size suggested catalog, or perhaps a picture frame. Driven by mounting curiosity, I attacked the top of the package with a pair of scissors. Inside was a large, elegant leather-bound burgundy volume, with my name and surname inscribed on the spine in golden letters: Ginevra Visconti. It was more a photograph album than a book in that it had transparent adhesive sheets, except that it contained no photographs. I stood up and placed the book on the table, surprised and intrigued, but none the wiser, until out slipped an envelope containing a typewritten letter on headed paper bearing the name Salvatore Ferragamo S.p.A. I recognized Tà's unmistakable signature, the final À marked with an accent as strong and decisive as Tà herself. Now it seemed that the beam of sunlight was illuminating the letter. Excitedly, I began to read: "My dear grandchildren, I am writing to commend into your safekeeping this Red Book into which you can put the various missives that I shall be sending you, and whose meaning you will understand better as you grow older. Look after it because I will be sending plenty of letters for inclusion in its pages. Cherish this book, because my words will stand you in good stead for your future life and work. Hugs, Nonna Tà."

It was the eldest grandchild Gaetano who first wittily dubbed the letters "Tà's circulars" in reference to the rather corporate approach Tà took to her communications, to their officially headed notepaper, and to the categorical imperatives that Tà loved to proclaim in them.

It was not the first time that Tà had sent a letter addressed to her grandchildren. For some time, she had been wont to make her presence felt in the lives of us 23 grandchildren, now living all over the world. But the contents of that FedEx parcel were not just any old "circular," such as a careless grandchild might mislay or, worse, throw out. This particular letter arrived with its designated place of conservation: the Red Book. Each grandchild received a customized copy by post, their name and surname clearly stamped in bold characters.

I opened the windows, bathing myself in the sweetness of the moment and the jasmine-scented warm spring air. My eye glimpsed the violet of the jacaranda trees coming into timid bloom behind the monument at the center of the plaza, and I was reminded again of how similar it seemed to European parks. Until the sight of the Rio de la Plata flowing in the distance quickly brought my wandering mind back to where I now lived in the southern hemisphere. I would have loved to show Tà my panoramic view of the immense city that day by day was becoming ever more my home.

There was only ever one Tà in the world. As for her odd nickname, it dates from the time her grandson Gaetano was learning to talk. She became a grandmother at 43 and, feeling too young to be called *nonna* (granny), she decreed that Gaetano should call her *zia* (aunt).

"I tried, but I just couldn't get him to pronounce the Z properly. I still remember his little mouth from which the same sound always came out: Tà. Job done! Tà made a perfect replacement for *nonna*, I felt. More than fifty years later, this nickname is still being used, now by your children... There sure are a lot of you... As it is hard to find time for each one of you, this is the best way to make sure you are all up to date about the family and the company. The Red Book is a really clever idea."

This is what she told me when I visited her in Florence sometime after receiving the book. She was glad that I appreciated the gesture and reiterated the importance of preserving the documents she would be sending. It was February and, despite the bitter cold that normally bothered her, we went into the garden and walked alongside the wall overlooking the road to Maiano. From here, Florence can be seen in all its glory, beautiful in every season of the year. I invited her to visit me in Buenos Aires. She smiled, seeming glad that I had made the offer, though I knew very well that she would never take a break from her work.

"It is very important to me that the Red Book be kept in good order. It is a testimony to be passed on to future generations. It will be a practical way of filing the letters. When they arrive, all you have to do is put the latest into the next blank page, and, hey presto, job done!" she said, miming the gesture with her big hands.

Although she had a very busy email address from which she would write and respond in a flash, the letters destined for the Red Book never arrived electronically. Tà knew that if they had a physical presence, the letters would need to arrive by post.

"Having something in your hands that you can touch, whose value you can feel, is a different sensation, don't you think?" she said, moving her fingers as if they held a sheet of paper.

Before leaving for Argentina, I stopped by her office to say goodbye with my children Ottavia and Leo. She was sitting behind her huge antique table, which had once been Salvatore's, in the large room of Palazzo Spini Feroni, leafing through a pile of papers all neatly stacked in order of urgency. Her face took on a look of deep concentration as she sagaciously selected from among the documents and perused the notes or articles she had collected; it would assume an expression of repugnance if someone tried to interrupt her at her work, and of satisfaction when she fulfilled an important obligation. Tà carefully analyzed each paper before turning it into a blunt message intended for us. Under the gaze of our immortalized younger selves in the photographs on the high walls of her office, Tà seemed to look at us one by one before choosing which page would end up in our respective Red Books.

Her face lit up when she saw the children at the door. Ottavia and Leo entered shyly, intimidated by the imposing boiserie but intrigued by the collections of objects in glass display cabinets. They approached Tà to give her a kiss. "My dearest darlings, just look at how beautiful you are," she exclaimed, planting her pink-lipsticked lips on their plump little cheeks. She immediately made them sit down and, raising her voice a little, told Giulia her secretary to fetch a little present for them. Giulia arrived with a quilted canvas handbag and a small tie, in which the children were only relatively interested. So Tà took out pencils and paper. Once she saw the children happily occupied, she proudly showed me the letters ready to send to us. Passing to and fro between her office and the next room where her patient secretaries worked were messages that Tà would write out in longhand, so that they could be typed up on the computer, printed out, placed in the right envelope, and finally sent to our various addresses far and wide around the world.

When it was time for lunch, she hurried us in the direction of the dining room, briskly locking the door of her office, which she did every time, as if it were a safe. It might not have been an actual safe, but it was certainly a treasure trove of wisdom.

"Without values, even the most comfortable existence loses all its meaning. We are happy only when we feel gratified to have achieved something in which we strongly believe, perhaps at the cost of considerable sacrifice," she wrote in one of the first letters she sent for inclusion in the Red Book.

The words "strongly believe" encapsulate the secret of her glamorous yet well-adjusted life. Determination, consistency and perseverance, combined with a fair dose of stubbornness, are what made Tà the special person she was. When she got it into her head to do something, she would press on with it, without a backward glance, no matter how much effort it took. Her own life was a string of continuous challenges, of objectives to pursue, of goals always to be reached.

The name shown on Tà's birth certificate is Wanda Miletti, but for most people she was Wanda Ferragamo, the lady of fashion, the business leader from the "Made in Italy" world of craftsmanship, honored by her country as a captain of industry, or Cavaliere del Lavoro to use the official title: she was the chairwoman of the company. With a blend of humility and farsightedness, she called herself Salvatore Ferragamo's wife.

Wanda Miletti was born in 1921 in Bonito, a hill village of just over two thousand inhabitants on the border between the provinces of Avellino and Benevento. This area, an expanse of mountains dotted with hamlets and farmhouses, is at the heart of the seismically active district of Irpinia, which lies at the end of the Apennine mountain chain. I never knew much about Bonito other than that it was my grandparents' hometown and therefore the legendary place where Grandfather Salvatore made his first pair of shoes.

It was there that Tà and Grandfather first met, and it was there that their love had blossomed and bloomed. "To Wanda for whom I searched the world and whom I found in the village of my birth, and to all those who must walk," reads the dedication on the first page of the autobiography Grandfather wrote shortly before his death. All her life, Tà continued to look for and find inspiration in his words. "When I don't know what my next step should be, I open Grandfather's book. You should do likewise," was her advice to us whenever we were stuck for a solution to a problem.

Out of ignorance and superficiality, I had never bothered to find out anything else about Bonito until one day in May 1994, when I was at university, an unexpected item was added to my schedule. Tà had organized a trip in which the entire family was under strict orders to participate without fail. Destination Bonito. And when Tà said "without fail," she meant it. There could be no defections. Like the adolescent I was, I huffed and puffed against the imposed schedule and the various constraints, but, in reality, I felt a strong pull toward that world that belonged to me, far though it was from the Milanese scene in which I wallowed, too lazy to break free. The village, spoken of at home as if it were almost a hallowed place, is where my lineage comes from. Bonito is the opening chapter of a marvelous story about a family and its business.

One or two foolhardy defectors aside, all 40 or so of us, uncles, grandchildren, and cousins turned up. We formed a company under the command of Tà, who was as tireless as ever, but more excited than I had ever seen her. Here she felt at home. All of a sudden, she became more indulgent, more forgiving. Tender, even. Perhaps being in Bonito afforded her the luxury of going back in time to become a child again.

After landing at Naples airport, we boarded a coach that drove us miles and miles through a countryside made up of farmlands, Dominican monasteries, and timeless towns with mosaic floors, until, reaching the end of the only road left, it deposited us at our destination. Waiting for us in the house of our maternal great-grandfather, in that cul-de-sac, that "dead-end with no hope of expansion" (which is what our Grandfather called Bonito before he became world famous), was a welcoming committee of cousins and relatives of whose existence I was barely even aware. In the large blossoming courtyard of a typical manor house, traipsing timidly around an ancient Roman fountain, we made interesting discoveries about our backgrounds and bonded with our new-found cousins and with each other. Just as Tà had planned.

More than twenty years have now passed since that trip, yet I am still stirred by deep emotions when I call it to mind. Everything had been designed to further Tà's mission which was, as it always had been, to keep the family together.

As I flew over the Atlantic back to Buenos Aires, and southwards into the opposite hemisphere, which always gave me a feeling of disconnection, a deep melancholy stole over me as I thought of the family and its bonds, the remote landscape, and the legendary place where the fascinating story of my grandmother began.

Her father, Fulvio Miletti, a severe man of great moral rectitude and high moral standards, was the podestà of Bonito and the district doctor. I think it is fair to say that Tà's esteem for him bordered on the excessive. I have often wondered whether her idolizing of her father had to do with the internalization of certain "macho" beliefs, or whether it was simply—and understandably—a question of idealizing the person who brought her up after she lost her mother while still a teenager.

The Miletti family enjoyed a prominent position in the little village. Originally from Venice, they settled in southern Italy in the seventeenth century. An archive record shows that in 1671, a Miletti who ran a newspaper, *Giornale di Venezia*, married a Cassitto belonging to a noble family from Ravello. Some traces of our ancestors are to be found in the records relating to the anti-Bourbon revolutions in Naples during the Risorgimento (the Italian struggle for unification). It was probably owing to the complexities of the political situation that the Milettis migrated south.

Tà never let the fact of being born in a poor village diminish her self-assurance one jot, not even when she found herself, as she often did, in the company of queens, princesses, and noblewomen. The culture and values she inherited from her family formed the bedrock of her moral and spiritual serenity.

Grandfather Salvatore used to classify women by the size of their feet. Anyone under size 6 was a Cinderella, a size 6 was a Venus, and a size 7 and up was an aristocrat. Tà, with her ample 39-size shoe was in good company with the aristocrats. Certain that true nobility did not depend on titles, she was open-minded and curious about other people. She loved getting to know and surrounding herself with all sorts of different people, as long as they shared her practical values.

When my son Leo was born, Tà invited me to spend the summer vacation in her beautiful house in the pine forest of Roccamare, near Grosseto. I was very fond of the place, having spent part of my childhood there, familiarizing myself with its every nook and cranny. We spent most of our time on the beach, in the shade of a cabin where the children met and played for hours. That summer, the group of children was joined by Amalia, a blonde and very light-skinned girl. She was the eldest daughter of Queen Maxima of the Netherlands, an Argentine by birth with whom I had several acquaintances in common. A lovely affinity arose among the members of the group and we spent a good part of the vacation in each other's company. One evening, shortly after Tà had arrived in Roccamare to spend a few days with us, we invited Maxima, her husband the then Prince Willem-Alexander, and their daughters to our place for dinner. Tà was happy to make their acquaintance, first of all because Queen Juliana of the Netherlands had been a very good Ferragamo customer, and, secondly, because Maxima's story awakened a certain sense of fellow feeling in her. She welcomed them on the terrace in the shade of the maritime pines that gave off the "balsamic" scent she liked so much. Her Sri Lankan butler, in a perfect white jacket with gold buttons, served chilled white wine while Tà regaled the company with fascinating tales about her husband and distributed the finger-food delicacies she had had made in Florence beforehand so as not to arrive unprepared. A middle-class Argentine woman, without a drop of blue blood in her veins, Maxima won Tà over with her authenticity, humility, classiness and intelligence, just as she had won over the hearts of the people of the Netherlands. She had what Tà considered true style.

When Tà spoke of families that she considered worthy of esteem, including her own, she would exalt their concrete achievements and honorable conduct. Her mother Giovanna was a homemaker, an excellent cook, and a patient and understanding wife—fitting qualities for a married woman in the southern Italy of the time. She had been a wise administrator of the family wealth during the years in which her husband, my great-grandfather, had been away fighting in World War I. Giovanna had proved herself very skilled at maintaining the web of social relations that ensured the people of Bonito remained well disposed and grateful to the whole family, especially her husband, who always carried out his vocation as a doctor "with deep Faith in our Lord."

Tà was the youngest of six children, two of whom had died at an early age. She grew up with Tullio, Silvio, and Flora, her elder siblings. The popular saying goes that the youngest child is the most astute and smart, and Tà sure seems proof of the truth of this claim. I have never known a person sharper than her—her clear-headed and resolute attitude could charm or flummox in equal measure.

Her moral and intellectual upbringing was undoubtedly shaped by her father. I knew him from photos to have been a tall, elegant man with a stern look hidden behind a manicured black mustache. Tà described him as principled, uncompromising, very strict, and not inclined to let himself go emotionally.

"He did not allow me any of that easy familiarity you now enjoy with your dads. I feel almost envious when I see you laughing and joking around with them. That was not granted to me. Only once did he give me a big hug. I must have been 6 years old, and in the presence of various family members I began to cry, saying that everyone loved my brothers and that nobody loved me. Dad hugged me to show me his love, and I realized then whom I should turn to in case of need."

Loved by everyone in the village, her father possessed a dignity and generosity that shone through Tà's stories. With his children, however, he could be unbearably harsh. She still remembered a telling episode from her childhood, when on a rainy winter evening her father had come home late and very tired after spending days on his rounds. She watched her dad as he, wet and cold, took off his boots, and she imagined him alone, in the rain and in the dark. On impulse she ran toward him, but her father brusquely waved her away, saying that girls would do well not to be too sentimental. Tà froze in her tracks.

At 16, like every teenager, Tà once applied eye shadow that she had received as a gift from one of her schoolteachers, young Neapolitan women who seemed elegant and modern compared to those of Bonito. To the young Tà, however, they looked like high-society sophisticates, cosmopolitan ladies whom she wanted to emulate. So, one fine day, Tà arrived home wearing eye shadow. Her father's reaction was terrible. To his conservative mind, it was inconceivable that a 16-year-old girl from a good family should go around wearing cosmetics. Pointing a threatening finger at her, he declared that he would marry her off to the first shoemaker who asked for her hand. It was the worst thing he could have said to a teenager with a romantic attitude. At the time, being a shoemaker, a cobbler, was the lowliest of professions. And yet... just three years later, that is exactly what happened: her father gave her in marriage to the first shoemaker who asked for her hand. "And what a shoemaker!" Tà recalled with an affectionate laugh.

I can sometimes still hear that laugh of hers. When she allowed herself moments of mirth and tenderness, she would loosen up and her good mood became infectious. Not that Tà was always in good humor—on the contrary, she was well known for her mood swings. But when she laughed, she laughed till she cried. It was irresistibly infectious. Nor did she hold back, even though she took every opportunity to preach the virtues of equanimity. A demanding perfectionist, intolerant and stubborn, she would sometimes get irritated by trivial details, not to mention more complex problems. Over the years she had become less ferocious, but her famous outbursts of temper could sow terror everywhere. She must have inherited some of the dark sides of her father's character.

Making up for the rigidity of her father was her sensitive and loving mother, whom Tà remembered with immense nostalgia. She used to cite her mother as an exemplary woman, who combined excellent skills as a housewife with an imaginative and curious mind. She was full of dreams, inquisitive, and well informed about the facts of the world. She loved music and took particular care to make sure Tà learned to play the piano well, this being one of the necessary accomplishments of a proper bourgeois upbringing. In those days, girls' education barely touched upon subjects of general culture and focused instead on cooking and dressing well, with a view to marriage. Tà eventually forgot how to play the piano, but not how to cook. The best recipes I know I learned from her, some of them handed down from her mother. Every day in Bonito a chestnut and chocolate cake or else a sponge cake with whipped cream was prepared, including for the children of the village. The Milettis had the good fortune to be supplied with fresh food from farmers who preferred to pay in kind for the doctor's visits. It was the same in the kitchen of Il Palagio, the house where Tà had lived since her arrival in Florence; here the basic ingredients, sugar, fresh eggs, coffee, and ricotta were never lacking, along with oil from her olive grove and herbs and spices from her garden. Tà used fresh ingredients to cook simple and healthy dishes. She loved cooking, and her cooking reflected her character; so, while she cherished authenticity and simplicity, she also pursued refinement and novelty. She took great care with presentation as well as preparation. As an aesthete, she rejoiced in the beauty of the china, the silverware, the table linens and the centerpieces. Conversely, she could be absolutely intolerant of what was not to her liking—be it food, objects, or people.

Whether at home or in the office, where she dined during the day, she never used the same table setting. Her table was decorated with flowers, another of her passions, and was always colorful, carefully arranged, elegant, vivacious. Blessed with an infallible memory, she could recollect the provenance of every single object, which she looked after with care because, as she put it, "each has its own story."

"I bought those glasses with Salvatore in Capri, and, you know, they are no longer available... I bought that tablecloth in Paris with Fiamma, but these people..." (referring to careless servants) "they ruin things by throwing them in the washing machine. They just do as they please, no-one has taught them any better; but even if you try to teach them, they never learn. And these placemats! We bought 24 of them that time with Chiara in New York. There are 16 left. Who knows what they did with the others..."

She snorted impatiently. In my mind's eye I can still see her standing there, irascibly opening and closing cupboards in her office in Il Palagio as she spent some of the few free moments that she allowed herself in the day organizing dinnerware sets and glasses, linen and silverware, unable to help herself from complaining bitterly about her incompetent staff, who were always a source of vexation for her.

Il Palagio, the large mansion on the hills of Fiesole where Tà had arrived as a young wife with her husband Salvatore, will forever remain a treasure trove of memories for me, beginning with the kitchen, which was a veritable theater of distinctive sensations, smells, and sounds. It is a large room and, unlike the other rooms, which preserve their Renaissance character through antiques and period objects, the kitchen of Il Palagio is modern and fully equipped. A large French door with a six-teenth-century grille overlooks a courtyard where Tà had the dogs locked up when they were not roaming the woods around the villa. She loved the dogs, but "only in the garden: that's where they belong." She complained about the (very common) habit among family members of keeping dogs at too close quarters. An entire generation of Italian wolfhounds and pointers with long pedigrees used to press their noses up against the glass door of the kitchen waiting for caresses and leftovers, much to the delight of us grandchildren when we were young kids.

When I was a little girl, a visit to Il Palagio in Fiesole was an event for me and my sisters. We would arrive by car or train from Milan, crumpled and suffering from travel sickness, but always excited. We knew that waiting for us was a large garden where we could play freely with the dogs and with our cousins, James, Salvatore, and Vivia, Uncle Ferruccio's children, who lived in the house next door. After we had passed through the large mansion door (which used to open too slowly), we were ti-died up and our hair was combed back into shape. Once the formalities of the polite greetings were over, we, with the com-plicit approval of our mother, would make a dash for the garden. We would jump down from the low walls to land in front of the hothouses full of roses, run up to the little house in the woods, then back down again to find the dogs in the courtyard next to the kitchen. Bea, the irreplaceable nanny of all the Ferragamo family, would be waiting for us with abundant refreshments made from all-natural ingredients. From her office, Tà issued orders for the preparation of slices of toasted Tuscan bread with fresh tomatoes with a splash of freshly milled (and therefore rather zesty) olive oil. The kitchen table was never without a block of seasoned pecorino covered with a white cloth, and no-one passing through the kitchen could resist cutting them-selves a slice.

In one of the first "circulars" destined for the Red Book, Tà underscored how important it was to feed children with com-pletely wholesome foods. She advised her granddaughters who were already mothers to give the children tomato bruschetta by way of a snack. My mother was happy to take her advice to heart. On school trips, I would open my packed lunch of bread, butter and anchovies, and envy the delicious-looking snacks of my schoolmates. But in the end, I fell so much in love with the taste of that oil that I could not give it up and, for 11 years, I used to carry suitcases full of Tuscan olive oil back with me to Argentina.

Ricotta and spinach dumplings, melon risotto, ciambellona, pineapple cake, chocolate and almond cake (*torta caprese*) and sweet fritters (*struffoli*) were just some of Tà's favorite dishes.

"Your grandfather used to call our dining room 'the cathe-dral' because it was where we all congregated. We taught your parents to say grace before a meal. At Easter, we used to lay out all the dishes on the table and have Don Giulio come and bless the food. It was a beautiful occasion. We have lost the habit of thanking God for our food. Instead of thinking so much about diets, it would be better to think about how lucky we are always to have something to eat."

Shortly before my wedding, she gave me an inquisitorial once over with her eye and, evidently taking in my measurements at a glance, declared in a tone of annoyance and disapproval: "You are too thin." From when we reached adolescence, Tà had kept a close eye on us granddaughters, advising us time and again to eat well, "because a woman's body shape is important, especially for her mental health." I remember vacations in Capri where she tempted us with flourless chocolate cakes (*capresine al cioccola-to*), a specialty of the island, outsized pieces of buffalo-mozzarel-la, and delicacies of all kinds, always served under her peremp-tory gaze.

Tà was a gourmand who could not resist intervening directly in the kitchen. It was her nature to be a fastidious perfectionist. Armies of Filipino, Sri Lankan, and Polish staff have come under her strict command. Not all of them managed to keep up with her exacting demands.

Whenever she spent a weekend in Fiesole, she would take the opportunity to invite a few grandchildren to dinner.

"Some of you have things to do in one place, others in another, with the result that I am left to spend Saturdays and Sundays on my own. And to think that there are so many of us! What is a large family for? How can it be that no-one ever stays in Florence? How over-busy you all are!" Basically, she just liked to grumble: the truth is that she always, invariably, had company at the weekend.

One Saturday evening she managed get a full complement of grandchildren around the dining table. That was the time she taught me how to make Tarte Tatin. I had asked her for advice on a business matter that was worrying me. She hauled me into the kitchen and, with me watching, set about preparing the dish. Annetta, a slender and quiet Polish girl who outlasted most other members of staff in her employ, stood fearfully next to her, passing her the ingredients and watching in absolute silence. I watched Tà's plump hands confidently and rapidly crumble the butter, the glitter of her rings disappearing under a cloud of flour. With the same determination with which she had attacked the pastry making, she delivered instructions to me without missing a beat. She sliced apples and emphasized the importance of humility in work; she put the tart in the oven and offered me practical and terse advice on how to deal with my problem. Now whenever I think of a Tarte Tatin, I imagine it filled with good counsel as well as fine ingredients.

Tà knew how to savor the most important things in life. She did not waste time in pointless socializing; she ate healthfully and went to bed early. Yet her days were anything but boring or monotonous. If you asked her what was her secret for staying in shape, she would emphatically spell out her response, letter by letter and syllable by syllable: " W-O-R-K and E-QUI-LIB-RI-UM." She often cited, by way of example of what not to do, a friend whom she had once invited to stay.

"She worked like crazy and ate absolutely nothing. Not even here, where she had come supposedly to rest, did she manage to relax. She ran around the house with a full cup of black coffee and a cigarette in her mouth. One day, she came crying to me, saying she didn't understand why she was depressed, and that she wanted to see a doctor. She was utterly clueless! She didn't need a psychiatrist; what she needed was some judicious equilibrium."

Tà was adamant about eating well, not smoking, and getting enough rest. How many times she criticized our dietary fads... How many times we sprayed ourselves in perfume before visiting her just to hide the smell of cigarettes... I still have a note she wrote to me one summer to thank me for spending a few days with her. I must have been very agitated at the time, for she wrote: "My advice is: learn how to relax, don't try to do too much."

Tà knew each of us much better than we thought, which is why her "circulars" always came with a purpose and a point.

"I see everything, I write down everything, I stick my nose in everywhere. All it takes me is five minutes to figure out what is wrong in one of our stores," she once told a journalist who had asked her what her role was in the company. It was the role she played best, both at work and in the family.

Fireflies and Round-Bottomed Dolls

Firefly, firefly, come here for a treat,
For you shall have king's bread to eat,
Food for a king, food for a queen,
Firefly, firefly, make yourself seen...

Tà had learned this nursery rhyme as a child and it came back to her when she was in a good mood. She sang it with her brothers when they were eating al fresco on summer evenings.

Until the age of 8, neither she nor her siblings attended a regular school; governesses came from neighboring towns to give lessons to them at the home. Only later did Tà study at Pia Casa d'Istruzione e Lavoro in Ariano di Puglia (a secondary school) followed by the Istituto Magistrale "Mater Dei," a boarding school in Naples, along with her sister Flora. She remembered those years as being one great big waste of time.

"We studied, ate, prayed, and went to bed. The same routine day in, day out. These were some good things, no question about it, but the restrictions taught me nothing about the intricacies of life," was her verdict on her school years.

She had a predilection for literature and French, a language that she considered elegant and essential for social relations in Europe. To help her with her French, my great-grandfather gave her a subscription to a weekly French magazine for girls, *La Semaine de Suzette*. Tà eagerly looked forward to each new issue, for the magazine contained not only illustrated texts and stories but also tips, ideas, and instructions on making dolls' clothes, along with recipes and many other topics that piqued her curiosity.

"I was really keen to read my French, which has caused me to appreciate how important it is to structure learning around what the student is interested in. If something is fun, it is much easier to learn. Keep this in mind for the education of your children," she counseled us.

I remember how happy she was when I brought her two large binder volumes containing the issues of *La Semaine de Suzette* from the 1940s and 1950s that I had found at an antiques market in Buenos Aires. They were supposed to be a gift for her, but she convinced me to hang on to them because they would help Ottavia enjoy learning French. So I brought them back to Argentina. Not that Tà had given up reading in French! The arrival of the magazine *Point de Vue* was one of the highlights of her week. She would look carefully through the pages, pausing to look at the shoes and clothes being worn by European celebrities and princesses, and gobbling up all the press stories about them. Weddings and parties offered a further opportunity for her to develop new style ideas, of which she was never short.

Tà loved the French language and spoke it with a charming grace that verged on affectation, as if she were playing a part. I liked listening to her when, in French, she repeated the conversations she had had with the Baroness de Rothschild, her idol of refinement, class, and good manners. When Tà acted out a conversation, it was as if the Baroness were in the room with us or as if we were watching a scene from a film. Actually, Tà's own life, of which she was the undisputed protagonist, would make a good movie.

Apart from her dull boarding school years, Tà's childhood and most of her adolescence were untroubled; she was basically carefree until, quite suddenly, tragedy struck. Silvio, her beloved brother, two years her elder, was killed in an accident. It was an extremely painful first experience of bereavement.

"Oh my, how beautiful he was with that athletic body... he looked like an actor," she said of her lost brother when telling her stories.

The accident happened when Silvio was playing football with friends. The ball landed on a well that was covered with rotten wooden planks. When he went to retrieve it, the planks gave way under his weight. He fell and fatally hit his head. All efforts to revive him were in vain. He was dead before his parents arrived on the scene.

The tragedy, which left a deep mark on the family, had been preceded by a premonitory dream. The night before the accident, our great-grandmother had dreamed of a rotten piece of meat. In those days (it was 1938), the custom was that when a bull died it would be brought immediately to the slaughterhouse so that its meat could be sold at a good price. Tà's family had bought meat of this sort. The entire town turned out for Silvio's funeral. People busied themselves with helping the family with various tasks, and the piece of meat was left in the pantry. My great-grandmother remembered it only a few days later, but by then the meat really was rancid, as she had seen it in the dream.

For Tà, dreams, divine signs, superstitions, and coincidences were not anomalies, they were part of the fabric of her world. She always advised us to pay heed to our instincts. She trusted her own so much that she wove it into her daily routine. When facing a weighty decision, many in the family used to turn to her as if she were an oracle. They could be sure of a wise and practical answer, which Tà would invariably present as having been "dictated from above." I do not think I have ever known anyone who placed so much trust in her own faith as she did.

"When I lose hope or confidence, I pray to our Lord, and I turn to Salvatore to illuminate my path. Even from up there he has always helped me."

Tà claimed that throughout her life, her husband had guided all her choices, even after his death. To anyone who congratulated her for managing the Salvatore Ferragamo company, raising six children, and piloting the company to a stock market listing, she would reply: "Me, I did nothing; it was all Salvatore's doing."

In the Miletti household the loss of Silvio brought about a crippling sadness. Tà's mother never got over the loss of her son. She aged suddenly and never found peace of mind again. One year later, in 1939, she followed her son to the grave.

"I lost my mother just when I needed her most." Tà was overcome with emotion every time she remembered her. The death of loved ones was a tragic constant in her life. I find it hard to acknowledge that Tà, with her strong and determined personality, always so sure of herself, had gone through so much pain. She lost her brother when he was still a child; she lost her sweet and kind mother; she lost her beloved husband; and then she lost two of her daughters: Fiamma, my aunt, and Fulvia, my own beloved mother, who preceded her by a few months. Tà did not like to talk about her sorrow. It was her way of protecting herself and it allowed her to keep going despite the pain.

In his "Conversations in Jerusalem," Cardinal Martini states that strength and confidence come from positive childhood experiences. For me, this confirms that Tà's childhood gave her an edge. Even when grumpy, she was never despondent. When she was in a bad mood, she would let fly at whoever happened to be close by, then immediately recover her composure. Whenever she fell, she would bounce up again, like one of those old round-bottomed dolls that rights itself as soon as you push it over. She saw the silver lining in every cloud and, even in the worst situations, she could set aside any negativity and focus on what was good and constructive. Tà firmly believed in the hand of Providence, which would come to her aid in the toughest times.

In March 2006, while I was living in Argentina, I was forced to remain immobilized in bed for four months with two broken vertebrae as a result of a bad fall from a horse. Tà's comforting words reached me via email.

"My dearest Ginevra, you can imagine how sorry I was to learn about the accident that has caused you to be laid up immobile for several months. But as the consequences might have been so much worse, we should thank Providence for saving us from an even more disagreeable outcome. You have all our sympathy as you spend this period of suffering. Be patient, for it will pass. My thoughts also go to Andrea and the kids. Give them a special hug from me. We look forward impatiently to your recovery. We will shower you with gifts, but only as long as you promise not to go gallivanting around on horseback anymore. You must protect your life, your family, the wellbeing of your children and husband, because they are the most important things. They repay us mothers with joy and serenity of mind. A big, big, big, beautiful hug from your Tà."

A few weeks later I received a beautifully wrapped package. I had little doubt about where it came from, so when they brought it to the bedroom where I was confined, I opened it with great curiosity. I recognized the parcel as being from the Pagliai silverware store in Florence: an elegant blue box, tied up with a white satin bow. Inside the box was a solid silver doll, wrapped in white tissue paper. I pulled it out slowly. It had a heavy, round base, and a red ribbon tied around the neck. It was a round-bottomed doll: a reproduction of those ancient roly-poly toys that can be made to wobble and make a tinkling sound as they do so. Clearing a space among the painkillers and vitamins, I placed the doll on the nightstand and looked at it in amazement. I gave it a little nudge and spun it around several times, listening to the metallic sound it made. The weight of the silver on the wood enhanced its heavy materiality and presence. I began to play with it, watching with pleasure as the doll fell over with each push only to return to a perfectly upright position. While looking at my reflection on its rounded surface, I noticed an inscription engraved on the back: "Find your balance again and continue along the straight road of principle and righteousness that has been shown you. Nonna Tà."

I was doubly amazed thinking of the 23 round-bottomed dolls arriving at the house of each of my cousin at the same time. I thought about the weight of the inscribed words, which sounded almost intimidating, and their multiple meanings. Surely, I thought to myself more than once, it was no coincidence that I should have received the doll just as I was about to start walking again, almost as if it were a metaphor. I thought about premonitions, and pondered the fact that in the days before the accident I had had several dreams of falling from a horse, but had paid them no heed. It occurred to me that to receive life lessons is actually a great luxury, and that we should waste no time in applying the wisdom they teach. Most of all, I thought about how my grandmother was an absolute phenomenon.

I called her immediately on the phone, sure that I would find her at home because it was dinner time in Italy. I wanted to tell her how much I appreciated the gift, and talk about the thoughts to which it had given rise. Annetta, her maid, answered the phone and went to fetch Nonna Tà from the kitchen. I could hear the quick little steps running down the tiled-floor corridor that connects the service area to the salons in Il Palagio. In one corner, on a small table flanked by two antique wooden stools, was the telephone, and, next to it, an address book and pen. It was there that Tà settled down every time she received a phone call. On the other side of the line, the footsteps grew louder and more definite as Tà's heels clacked on the floor. I remembered that the worst time to call her was before dinner because her fluctuating mood was particularly susceptible to hunger and fatigue. She dismissed me in a few words, and I promised myself to call her back at a better time.

I looked at the doll again. It seemed to be telling me not to yield to the nostalgia that was threatening to overwhelm me at that tough time in my life. The doll was a gentle caress and a deliberate gesture of love delivered to me from a distance of 14,000 kilometers.

The doll now lives with me back in Milan, where I have been for the past eight years. She sits on my desk keeping me company. I placed her close to the photo of Tà and my mother, both pictured smiling at work. I like to look at them doing what united them, working together: two invincible and immortal women.

The doll cannot be put into the Red Book, but it is no coincidence that I always find it near me, turning and making its vibrant tinkling sound. Actually, there are now three dolls in our house since my children also received one each. It has become a familiar object, whose recondite meaning is known only to an honored few. I prod the toy and listen to it tinkle back at me, its little bell like an alarm to remind me that falling over is easy, the trick is to bounce back up immediately.

"I never expected you to be perfect. Making mistakes is an unavoidable part of life, but if you have a firm moral grounding, you will be able to correct your mistakes and restore your balance, just like the doll I gave you," Tà wrote in a letter that reminded me of a story about a different doll, one from Tà's childhood. When her father came home from work in the evening, he would sometimes indulge Tà in a game of make-believe. Before he had a chance to set down his doctor's bag, Tà would ask him to visit her dolls. Dolls were a luxury in those days, and playing with them was her favorite pastime as a little girl. Her dad would then take his stethoscope and recite his part, which ended with the excellent news that the dolls were all as fit as a fiddle.

After her mother's death, Tà's father, Fulvio, inevitably became the anchor in her life. He lived a long time and remained an important presence even into adulthood. He belonged to a special generation of doctors who had trained at the University of Naples. They all adhered to certain sound philosophical principles, including a strong belief in the value of education. My great-grandfather was also a very handsome man, visited by many ladies from nearby towns and villages under the pretext of a cough or the flu. He made sure to visit the homes of those who were sick and in straitened circumstances. In spite of their lack of financial wherewithal, these patients would insist on paying him. In order not to embarrass them in front of relatives, he would take the proffered money with one hand, and slip it back under the mattress with the other.

"He was an extraordinary man in so many ways," Tà often used to say. "From him I learned three fundamental values: self-discipline, dedication, and respect for others."

My great-grandfather was a hard worker who never put off a medical visit to the next day. The people of the town loved him. The *piscuni* in the garden of his house are tangible proof of their esteem. If I hadn't seen the *piscuni* on that visit to Bonito, I would not have been able to understand what they were. The

local peasant farmers were very poor and subsisted on the produce of a few hectares of land. They cultivated every little parcel of
ground they had. Often when tilling and hoeing the earth, they
would come across slabs made of rock and marble, which in the
local dialect were called *piscuni*. These precious structural remains from ancient Roman times were nothing other than a huge
nuisance for them. Knowing, however, that their doctor was a
man of culture, every time they came across a *piscuno*, they would
bring it to him as a sign of gratitude and respect. Over the years,
the garden in Bonito filled up with precious pieces of antiquity. It
was a veritable museum, with urns, fountains, and statues scattered all over the place. My great-grandfather, who had a powerful sense of allegiance to the Italian State, mentions his collection
of *piscuni* in his will: "Always remember that this gallery contains
pieces of the Roman Empire of which we are the only guardians.
They are not our property, for they belong to the Italian State and
are therefore untouchable." When Tà settled in Florence, her father did not allow her to transport even one *piscuno* to her garden
in Fiesole. The garden in Bonito still contains the entire magnificent collection, which includes a statue of Hippocrates and a head
of Jupiter that is very similar to the one in the Vatican Museums.

Another invaluable legacy that Tà boasted of having received
from her father was the gift of religious faith. Great-grandfather
was a very religious man who found no difficulty in reconciling his
scientific work with his beliefs. He used to say that any man who
witnesses the birth of a child cannot but believe in God.

"He was a humble person. He went to church alone, where he
would sit in a corner pew. People invited him to come forward, but
he would say he did not feel worthy enough to stand before God.
He was genuinely modest."

So Tà described him. Yet to judge from the accounts of other
family members, his inflexibility could be hard to take, and his
severity was off-putting.

Great-grandfather loved to write down his musings on all sorts
of subjects, which Tà kept and collated into a book, which she titled
Pensieri e parole di Fulvio Miletti (The thoughts and words of Fulvio Miletti). Of course, each of us grandchildren was delivered a
copy at our home address. When I started reading it, I immediately

realized how monotonous it was, but I plowed on anyhow. As I read on, it occurred to me that the thoughts expressed in it were a recapitulation of the beliefs that had informed Tà's upbringing, beliefs that she was anxious to keep alive among us.

Faith and equilibrium: these were the two values inherited from her father that became the pillars on which Tà built her life. Religious faith runs deep in southern Italy and Tà was convinced that her faith had particularly protected her, and she saw it as a gift.

"It has always been a wonderful support for me... Maybe it is not given to us to know more, but Faith is a great and beautiful thing."

My great-grandfather's book does include one section that touches my heart because it forms the basis of one of Tà's circulars for the Red Book: "The Ten Rules for a Long Life" is, as the name implies, a list of ten simple, enduring rules that Tà has passed on to us just as they were written: point by point, in strong and clear terms:

1. Look after your body, but look after your soul even more.
2. Think and act with the serenity of a philosophical mind.
3. Find a wise and prudent spouse who will complete you.
4. Cultivate constancy of method in your activities.
5. Work hard but do not overstretch yourself.
6. Be frugal in diet, but detoxify and strengthen your body with vitamins and plenty of milk.
7. Prevention is the best defense against disease.
8. Do not smoke and do not abuse drugs.
9. Avoid the dangers of the road.
10. If you have inherited a long life expectancy from your ancestors, do not abuse this gift.

Throughout her life, Tà remained true to the very letter of these ten commandments written down by her father in Bonito more than a century ago. Even now they seem oddly relevant. Tà wanted to transfer his thoughts to us grandchildren directly as they were, without any rhetorical affectation, purely with the intention of protecting us.

The Shoemaker's Bride

After returning from a month's holiday in Uruguay, which is where we used to spend the summer vacation when we lived in the southern hemisphere, I came back to a pile of mail, mostly bills and Christmas cards, in the midst of which was a new "circular" from Tà. Inside the envelope was a photocopy of a hand-written letter vigorously titled "1957 Wanda!" This time, the letter had an engaging and absolutely captivating tone. I felt transported back to the Italy of the late 1950s, to the day when Grandfather Salvatore, in his bold slanted handwriting, had written these words:

"The opening of a new year of work begins with the arrival of this first volume, which divulges a little bit of my journey. You were also there in my dreams, there before you even existed. You are an inseparable part of my life, and, beyond that, you shall always be the sublime womb of my dreams."

This was the message Grandfather Salvatore wrote to Tà on the copy delivered to her of his just published autobiography *Shoemaker of Dreams*, which he completed shortly before his death. Over the years, this book became Tà's Gospel, a "sacred" text and now a source of inspiration for us all.

One morning, walking down the long Avenida Libertador leading to the newsrooms of *La Nación*, where a few months previously I had started a journalism internship, I was seized by anxiety over a professional quandary. I had to write a piece on a venerated Argentine artist concerning whose past, however, I had discovered certain dark things. My editor-in-chief insisted that I investigate these aspects and highlight them. I felt very uncomfortable. I decided to call Tà for advice. In Italy it was nearly eight, and I interrupted her while she was in the library, sitting in her leather armchair, ready to watch the evening news. She came to the phone out of breath, tired from the day's work, and did not draw out the conversation. Sternly, she advised me never to write anything "bad or negative," but to focus instead on possible solutions and on the words of my interviewee, who was bound to have answers for the questions I had. Before hanging up, she told me to consult my grandfather's autobiography. I was a little disappointed. I had expected more precise advice from Tà, as that was what she generally gave me, but the conversation at least enabled me to appreciate the full significance of Grandfather Salvatore's moral values for Tà: they were her articles of faith, her credo.

Speaking of credo and moral values, I remember one of the first letters we received for the Red Book, which featured the "Credo of J. D. Rockefeller," a text to which Tà often referred.

"I believe in the supreme worth of the individual and in his right to life, liberty, and the pursuit of happiness. I believe that every right carries with it a responsibility; every opportunity an obligation; every possession a duty. I believe that the law was made for man and not man for the law; that government is the servant of the people and not their master; that the world owes no man a living but that it owes every man an opportunity to make a living. I believe that thrift is essential to well-ordered living and that economy is a prime requisite of a sound financial structure, whether in government, business or personal affairs. I believe that truth and justice are fundamental to an enduring social order. I believe in the sacredness of a promise, that a man's word should be as good as his bond; that character—not wealth, power, or position—is of supreme worth. I believe that the rendering of useful service is the common duty of mankind and that only in the purifying fire of sacrifice is the dross of selfishness consumed and the greatness of the human soul set free. I believe in an all-wise and all-loving God, named by whatever name, and that the individual's highest fulfillment, greatest happiness, and widest usefulness are to be found in living in harmony with His will. I believe that love is the greatest thing in the world; that it alone can overcome hate; that right can and will triumph over might."

Tà fully subscribed to the principles of this philosophy. She had found her own personal credo in her husband's project, the pursuance of which became the main object of her existence. Whenever she was recounting the story of their life together, her lively, small but elongated green eyes used to dart back and forth behind the serious glasses she wore, and would shine with a special light as she theatrically narrated the events, captivating her audience.

In the summer of 1940, Grandfather Salvatore visited Bonito, from where he set off to Naples in the company of one of his sisters with high expectations of finding a wife (a detail that Tà was not to learn until much later). While in Bonito, Salvatore and his sister joined their uncle for lunch, Don Alessandro, who was the local parish priest. Hearing of their arrival, Tà's father, Fulvio, went round to Don Alessandro's house to broach a delicate issue with Salvatore. Salvatore, who was undoubtedly the most famous person ever born in the village, had for some time been generously donating money to the less well-off. But Fulvio knew that some people were making inappropriate use of the money. Salvatore invited him to join them at lunch, but he refused because he had entered a period of mourning during which he could accept no invitations. He was recently bereft of his wife, and he was a stickler for tradition. He reciprocated by inviting Salvatore to visit him in the late afternoon.

"That informal invitation changed my whole life," Tà was happy to tell a journalist from a famous Italian magazine who had asked her about the first time she met her husband.

I try to imagine her as a teenager in southern Italy 80 years ago, as an 18-year-old girl who was "a bit ignorant and emancipated," as she defined herself in that same interview. That evening, she could never have imagined that the person on the other side of the door knocking to be admitted was the famous shoemaker of dreams, the man who would become her husband. Tà never missed an opportunity to tell us every delectable detail of their meeting, and as a child I loved hearing her tell this story.

"Father was late, held up by a patient, and I was at home with a cousin and a maidservant. When the knock came on the door, my cousin ran excitedly into my room to tell me someone had arrived from Florence, and that I was to receive him. For us southerners in those days, Florence was a magical city, famous for art and fashion. The thought that someone from Florence was visiting Bonito stirred up great excitement; it wasn't something that happened often. So I mustered up my courage and went to open the door, assuming the airs and graces of a woman of the world—ridiculous antics by a girl who had never been outside Campania." I imagined her flustered but determined to make a good impression by reverting to her innately theatrical attitude. She descended the stairs as if making a stage entry. She saw a charming man and an elegant lady waiting by the front door: Grandfather Salvatore and his sister. Tà came forward with a nonchalant smile, and introduced herself as Doctor Miletti's daughter. "You must be the famous Salvatore Ferragamo," she said with a certain coquetry, to which he answered promptly: "I didn't realize I was so famous!" Tà, still playing the part of woman of the world for all she was worth, replied: "Congratulations on the magnificent contribution you have made to female elegance." It was not the sort of reply he had been expecting. He asked Tà how she managed to be so well informed (for he knew quite well that Bonito was hardly the center of the universe). She replied that she had read all about it in magazines. This was a shameless lie, for fashion magazines did not reach the village, and she had no clear idea of who he was. She had overheard a few conversations about his fame, but she was certainly never going to admit that what she knew about him she had learned from the greengrocer. Tà accepted his compliments for her perspicacity, all the while desperately wishing Grandfather would change the subject. She saw him whisper something in his sister's ear, in English, a language that Tà did not understand at the time: "This girl is going to be my wife." I have always suspected that by dint of character and determination, Tà had the power to make her dreams come true.

With a good dose of shrewdness and savoir-faire, Tà had her guests take a seat in the living room. Fortunately, at that moment her father returned to interrupt the conversation. "If it had gone on, Salvatore would have soon realized that I didn't know anything at all about fashion, and I would have cut such a foolish figure," she said, widening her eyes as if still worried at the prospect.

The meeting between Salvatore and our great-grandfather did not last long, but Tà liked to emphasize that Salvatore never stopped looking at her, constantly appealing for her opinion and trying to extend his visit. At a certain point in the proceedings, Salvatore asked Fulvio for his doctor's opinion on the anatomy of the foot and, to everyone's surprise, bent down to examine Tà's foot. Tà gasped; there was a moment of embarrassment. Back then, stockings were made of silk and ripped easily, which is how we get to the sweetest part of the story.

"As soon as Salvatore took off my shoe, out popped my beautiful big toe peeking out from a large hole in the stocking. I turned as red as a beetroot and didn't say a word." Grandfather, gentleman that he was, pretended not to notice and just asked her what her shoe size was. He then made her stand up and, demonstrating his command of the subject, illustrated his theory on the anatomy of the human foot and its relationship to a correct fit. He explained to Tà that the shoes she was wearing were too small. "The foot has to be free to move and the arch of the foot must fit properly in the shoe. Never wear short shoes!" he told her. Tà, embarrassed, came up with the excuse that it was difficult to find shoes of her size—in fact, she just wanted to make her feet appear smaller than they were. Such was the fashion of the time. Many women caused themselves considerable problems with their feet just to appear elegant.

Taking leave of them at the end of that first meeting, Grandfather Salvatore promised Tà a pair of custom-made shoes. Tà was impressed by him and by his promise. When she realized her father was impressed, too, she was delighted. The next day, contrary to his plans, Salvatore drove to Naples in his gray Alfa Romeo. "He wasn't a person with many vices, but he had a weakness for beautiful cars, and the convertible Alfa with the red leather seats was his favorite." In Naples, he went to a florist and returned to Bonito with a gigantic bunch of tuberoses for Tà, accompanied by a note in which he said that he had been very taken by her and wanted to see her again. They filled all the vases in the house with those magnificent tuberoses, which, not coincidentally, remained her favorite flower forever.

Tà thanked Salvatore with a note in which she warned him that her father would not easily accept their age difference. She was 18 and he was 42. They would therefore have to meet in secret.

In the Miletti home worked a girl called Meneca, who accompanied Tà everywhere. Just like in the story of Romeo and Juliet, or so Tà's romantic memory has it, Meneca acted as the go-between for my grandparents, ferrying their letters back and forth. Salvatore was completely set on marrying Tà, who was both flattered and intimidated. She was not yet sure she wanted him for a husband, but she understood that he was a special man whom even her father respected. There were more flowers, more courting, and more letters, all conducted with the utmost discretion. They went out together a couple of times and, although unable to spend time alone in his company, Tà came to see more and more every day what a wonderful person he was. Soon it was time for Salvatore to leave Bonito and return to work. Before leaving, he kept his promise and gave Tà a beautiful pair of shoes, the first of more than two hundred that he would create for her. They were made of black suede, with a small heel; the shiny upper leather had a scaly pattern, like the skin of a fish. It was a true work of art. "With those shoes on my feet, I felt like I was flying," Tà recollected dreamily.

When Salvatore left, Tà's father Fulvio was made aware of what was going on. His reaction was fierce. Tà remembered him imperiously and categorically telling her: "No, no, and no again. It is completely out of the question. The age difference is too big. You'll end up on your own looking after a bunch of children." Yet another premonition that came true.

Salvatore took a canny approach to the situation. First, he allowed some time to pass, then he invited Fulvio for a visit. He sent an elegant car to pick Fulvio up and take him to Florence, where he showed him everything he had created with his work. Salvatore then took him to Forte dei Marmi to show him the villa he had bought on the seafront, and, in that beautiful setting, finally spoke to him about his intentions with Tà. Won over, Fulvio dropped his objections.

Now the problem was Tà. She was very young. She could not work out in her own mind whether she loved him or not, though she enjoyed his company and was attracted by his magnetism and intelligence. She knew little about him and had no idea what it meant to be in a relationship with a man. She particularly missed her mother, who would have been able to give sage advice. So Tà confided her doubts and fears to the wife of her brother's teacher, with whom she had struck up a friendship. Reassured by her, she sent Salvatore a postcard with a view of Bonito, on the back of which, above her signature, she had penned three simple, courageous words: "Thinking of you." With that postcard, she signed off on the script of their love story. When the postcard reached Florence, Salvatore was at his beach villa. It therefore came first into the hands of his sister, who immediately rushed out to bring it to him. That very same day, Salvatore set off for Bonito to ask for Tà's hand in marriage.

They were married a few months later. "I was no longer afraid of anything, for in my heart I knew what kind of person Salvatore was, and I was right." Once again, she had been helped by her instinct, bolstered in this case by her deep faith in the sanctity of marriage, a sacrament that was part of her supreme credo.

Tà spoke to us on many an occasion about marriage. Whenever any of us girls was getting married, sure enough an imperious Tà letter would arrive by post. The men were spared such missives, the implication being that marriage was really a matter for women. When the first of the grandchildren was getting married, we all received a letter in which was written:

"Message for young brides: I am constantly thinking of your happiness, which I hope is what life holds in store for you. I want to share some cautionary thoughts with you. In the early days, marriage is a wonderful and euphoric experience. Bit by bit, things cool down and consolidate. Some difficulties will arise and need to be dealt with (this is absolutely normal and happens to everyone), but it is precisely at this moment that the union is strengthened and the couple begins to perceive its validity and solidity. This is what gives the couple a mutual sense of assurance as they bring up a family. The husband will have the necessary resolve and strength to deal with his work and whatever difficulties it might cause as long as he finds support, understanding, comfort, and love in his family. I assure you that all this is the greatest good on earth. So, my beautiful girls, a good and joyful life has been placed in your hands. Protect it with all your might." She was crystal clear on the subject, and she repeated the admonition to me when I called to say I was getting married. She was the only person not to be taken aback by the impetuousness of my 21-year-old self; quite the contrary, she was bursting with enthusiasm and joy. For her, as for many women of her generation, marriage was not just a sacrament but the principal object of a woman's life. In July 1997, three months before I got married, she wrote me a letter that I occasionally find myself rereading.

"My dearest Ginevra, your mother gave me your wedding invitation yesterday morning. Last night, in the peace of my house, I finally read it, and it brought me immense pleasure. It moved me a great deal. When you little girls were born, I used to wonder would I ever see you married. We mothers immediately think about that, because marriage is an important goal in a woman's life. One stage of life draws to an end, and another very important one starts. You must meet marriage with joy, enthusiasm and serenity, but also treat it with great seriousness. Sound and solid foundations are laid for the new family in the earliest years of the union. Fortunately, your upbringing and the principles inculcated in both you and Andrea provide you with a rich and valuable moral patrimony that you must never lose and whose worth you must never undervalue. These principles stem from sacrosanct concepts that shall always be valid wherever you go and wherever you are. Remember that in the life of a man, the woman plays a decisive role. She may do so quietly, as long as it is with love and understanding. We shall have opportunity to speak about this in person. A thousand best wishes, Tà."

So when I went to visit her in Capri that August, she put me on my guard about some things, but remained intransigent on what she saw as the woman's role. "She is the true guardian of a sound marriage," a concept she reiterated in another letter (addressed to all her granddaughters), when Vivia got married.

"A new chapter in your life is opening up. You are erecting a new building to enshrine the most beautiful thing in the world: Love. Love is pivotal to human existence; it must be at the center of all your efforts and precautions; it must be your foremost concern, for it will also be the reason for self-denial in the name of protecting all that is good. I refer to the good that gives you the strength to live, fight, and overcome moments of bitterness so that your children may grow up healthy in body and strong in spirit. Inside this edifice of love, you shall build your family. Your home shall be a nest where your husband, returning after a hard day's work, may find warmth, rest, joy and tenderness. A real wife is also a bit of a mother. Salvatore always used to tell me that being at home with me enabled him to recharge his batteries so he could go back out to fight with renewed vigor and resolve. How much Salvatore taught me! And how much we owe him! Let us always remember him, and he will continue to guide us."

Tà kept all Salvatore's letters to her in a special album in the library of the villa. They were so precious to her that she knew some of them by heart. When Grandfather went to Australia, Tà once told me, he used to write home to her every day: "I am so keen to get back home. I dreamed of you last night, and I didn't want to wake up because I knew it was a dream and that if I woke up you wouldn't be there anymore. It makes me so happy to know you are always in my heart. I thank God for this gift, and I ask you to thank Him too. Thank Him for all we have. We must recognize that He has given us even more than we asked for." While Tà was repeating these words aloud, it again occurred to me my grandmother had met a truly special man. "What plenitude Salvatore gave to my life. He was always so kind, enthusiastic and devoted. To be in receipt of his love was a blessing. Even now it seems impossible to me that he no longer exists. I still feel him close by me every day."

I have often reread the letters. Times have changed and marriages today are very different from then. The roles have become confused, along with, alas, the nature of mutual relations. Nowadays, women do the same work as men and struggle to be mothers to their children, let alone mothers to their husbands. Conversely, the husband is no longer the head of household nor, consequently, the object of his wife's devotion. This is one of the many reasons why marital breakdowns have become so common. People read how-to books, or visit a couple's counselor to save their marriage, if it can be saved. The rules have been thrown out the window, so chaos prevails. Yet those few little words spoken by Tà, so judiciously balanced and commonsensical, resonate in my mind every day, occasioning many a reflection, many an anxiety, but also many a hope. Surely all the goodness and love that Tà received from her husband enabled her to fill the emptiness that her mother's death had left in her.

It was her father in person who was in charge of making the arrangements for the wedding gowns. Being well turned-out was a constant preoccupation in Tà's life. She extended the preoccupation to her children and grandchildren—there could be no peace until she saw everyone "properly turned-out." For Tà, being well dressed was a rule of life, but also a form of personal respect, first learned from her father and then from Salvatore.

"When we got engaged, your grandfather always used to compliment me on how I was dressed, which delighted me because I knew his business involved very elegant and refined women."

Tà used to buy her outfits at the local dressmakers', who copied patterns out of magazines. She remembered one with particular fondness, a soft fabric dress with a touch of tulle and a row of black buttons. Grandfather absolutely loved it. She wore it the first time they officially went out together, when they went to Naples to have lunch with Fulvio at Giuseppone al Mare, a restaurant at the foot of Posillipo hill. "What an incredible moment," Tà used to say with a note of nostalgia, a tender tear falling from her eye. With the help of Salvatore's sister, she had her wedding dress made by the Finizio boutique in Naples (the only store of its kind at the time), along with the wardrobe necessary for the honeymoon: a travel dress, a day-wear dress, a leisure dress, and a pair of evening dresses.

"My bridal dress was made of heavy, plain white silk that fell in a straight line from the shoulders and ended with a long train. The shoes, made by Salvatore, obviously, were of white satin, with a slightly raised heel and a small bow." Tà would give detailed descriptions, gesturing with a certain vanity as she recalled how she had looked.

In one of the rooms of Il Palagio, displayed on a large table that runs the entire length of wall, are the photographs of all the weddings of our family. Standing out from the others is the one photo in black and white showing Tà standing next to Salvatore, smiling, radiant, young and naturally beautiful. They married in the church of Santa Lucia in Naples on November 9, 1940, five months after their first meeting.

"As my father walked me down the aisle to give me away to Salvatore, I could feel the presence of my beloved mother. At that very moment I remembered a particular episode from my childhood. I was a very active and restless child: I was forever running, playing and dancing about. I never stood still. One day, my mother came up to me and told me that soon she would have to buy me a new pair of shoes because I had worn them all out. Jokingly, she added that what was needed was a whole shoe factory just for me. Without even meaning to, she was predicting my actual fate. I thought of her smiling up there at seeing me as a bride to one who was not only a wonderful man, but also the greatest shoemaker in the world. I am positive that people who have lost their mothers at an early age as I did receive a special blessing and protection that helps them when they need it most.

I've seen it happen many times. It is a kind of sacred compensation, which probably comes from that higher order which is not revealed to us, and we cannot fully understand. In my case, I'm sure it was my mother's blessing that made me meet Salvatore."

The wedding was marvelous in spite of the difficulties of the country, which had just entered the war. More than one hundred friends and family turned up from all over Italy to celebrate the newly-weds. The wedding banquet was held at the Hotel Excelsior, overlooking the sea. In the late afternoon, Tà and Grandfather left for Sorrento on the coast, the first stop on their honeymoon. Tà remembered that looking over the bay from the terrace of the hotel in Sorrento, they could see the bombs falling on Naples. The Allies had begun bombing on November 1, 1940. She remembered the frightening sound of ambulance sirens and the blasts of the explosions. Salvatore tried to comfort her by telling her to imagine they were fireworks for their wedding, but they both knew very well that was not the case.

The honeymoon was short. After Sorrento, they visited Amalfi, where they stayed at the Hotel dei Cappuccini, in the garden of which Salvatore discovered the feijoa, an oval, sweet-tasting fruit with a green peel that is unknown to most people. The garden in Fiesole now grows several specimens of the plant, which Grandfather was able to import.

"On our way to Florence, the two of us happier than ever, I began to understand properly who my famous husband was. He was an incredible man who would reveal to me an entire world of which I knew nothing, a world in which places such as the United States could exist. From that moment on and forever after, he was the rock of my life."

The American Dream

"America is a great country that has given us so much!" Tà frequently voiced this opinion of the United States, a nation to which she felt true gratitude and held in high esteem. I saw Tà particularly moved when she received a communication from Capitol Hill telling her that the American flag had been flown at the White House on June 5, 2009 to commemorate the birth of her husband and to honor his name. The following year, on December 18, 2010, the flag would be raised again, but this time in honor of her.

We were in Roccamare having breakfast in the shade of the pines when Tà told me how fond she was of the United States for the opportunities it had afforded not only Grandfather, but all the family and the company. She told me about her many trips, most of them to New York, one of her favorite cities, first as Grandfather's wife and later as a representative of the company. In an apartment in the Olympic Tower, which is where she lived when in the Big Apple, Tà mulled over and worked out new ideas and corporate strategies that she would then inexorably apply as soon as she returned to Florence.

After coffee, she enjoined me to relax on the red chaise longue and to enjoy the delicious scent of the pine forest, the peace, the chatter of the cicadas, and the sound of the nearby sea, and thus stymied my fond plans of going down to the beach for a dip. "Breathe," she ordered me. "The pine has a balsamic perfume, and you need it to feel good all winter" she told me, as if this were news to me. With the curt and despotic tone that she used on such occasions, she forestalled any reply I might have made with a command: "And now just shut up for a moment."

I remained in enforced silence, spying on her from time to time out of the corner of my eye. She wanted to rest, or maybe just a moment to think. She closed her eyes and struck a creative pose that I found fascinating. I was sure she was ruminating over some idea that would come out of the blue. Indeed she was, for a few minutes later, she opened one eye and said to me: "Later let's go to Punta Ala to look for some écuelles. The ones we had were delightful. I can't believe there are only six left. I bought 18 of them because I know that afterwards you can never find the replacement when a piece of a set gets broken." In a tone of menace that chilled me, she added: "But from now I am not going to lend this house to anyone."

Which is why I spent a blazing hot July afternoon traipsing around after her in a shopping center in Maremma, on the hunt for soup tureens, her precious écuelles. I followed in silence, carrying her light bag, which always contained the essentials (wallet, keys, pen and fuchsia-pink lipstick). I watched as she strode briskly on, heedless of what she felt was superfluous, comfortable inside her white linen pants and confident in her elegant classically shaped summer wedges, "which we should start making again for the good of everyone's feet," she declared with a resolute air. I watched as her discerning eye sifted through the window displays, rapidly separating the beautiful from the ugly, while also curiously examining the new. Every so often she would complain of the heat, and lightly run her hand over her fine hair, which was still perfectly coiffured despite the mugginess. She walked in and out of stores with very clear ideas of what she wanted, and was pretty outspoken with her expressions of approval or disapproval. She did not rest until she had hunted down just the right sort of écuelle, which she used that same evening to triumphantly serve pumpkin soup, the apotheosis of that unforgettable afternoon spent trudging behind my almost 90-year-old grandmother.

A few weeks later, on my return to Argentina, I received my letter for the Red Book, enclosed with which was a copy of the flag-flying certificate from the White House.

"Dearest ones, I am quite positive that nations of the world that prosper best are those that, even amid a thousand difficulties and problems, find time to honor ordinary people who have spent their lives contributing to industry and employment. In this regard, and with this premise, I inform you that I have just received a communication that on the Capitol Hill, the White House has flown the American flag in honor of Grandfather. I was deeply moved by this gesture. All of us, especially the little ones who are setting out on their journey, must carry forward this name, and we must be in no doubt that work can be the source of immense rewards that are also a moral acknowledgment of the effort and hardship it can entail. I am attaching the certificates relating to the above, which should be placed in the Red Book. A loving hug to all of you. Nonna Tà."

For Tà, the United States was the most civilized country in the world. Rightly or wrongly, she considered it a magical place where dreams come true. After all, it was there that Grandfather's career took off. It was there that the "shoemaker of dreams," born in 1898, achieved the success that still enables us to walk the paths of life in comfort.

Grandfather Salvatore was the eleventh of 14 children. He was born into a new Italy, a country that had unified a little more than thirty years earlier, but was still in very parlous condition, especially in the south where farming provided the only means of subsistence. Educational opportunities for children were restricted to a few years of elementary school. Few had access to secondary education; fewer still to university. Parents usually made sacrifices to enable their first son to study, in the hope that, with a decent job, he could then support everyone. Accordingly, Grandfather's elder brother, Agostino, was the only one of the 14 children in the family to go to university. The

Ferragamo family had pinned all their hopes on Agostino's talent and serious-mindedness. Sadly, weakened by the efforts of his studies and poor nutrition, he died of pneumonia a few months after graduation. Apart from the desperation of losing their son, the Ferragamo parents found themselves in dire economic straits. There was no more money to allow another child to study, so the only solution, in Italy, as in many other European countries, was emigration.

America was the land of opportunity. By 1907, when Salvatore was 9, seven of his brothers had already gone to look for work in the United States. Separation was a tragedy for the families of the time, but sadly there was no other choice, as is unfortunately still the case today in too many countries around the world. Salvatore, still too young to emigrate, remained in Bonito with his parents and younger siblings Elio, Giuseppina, and Rosina. He had just finished his third year of elementary school but already saw that he needed to find some way of boosting his family's low income.

Tà recalled that Grandfather had always been fascinated by shoemakers and footwear. "He spent his free time in the workshop of the town shoemaker (the one to whom my father had threatened to marry me!). When he told his parents that he wanted to learn the shoemaker's craft, they discouraged him and tried to persuade him to follow a more respectable career. Even among the poorest peasants, the shoemaker, the "cobbler," was considered the poorest of professions. So Salvatore was sent to work in a tailor's shop, but soon they realized he had no aptitude for the work. They sent him to the town barber, but he was not much of a success there either. Then they sent him to the carpenter's, where he went just twice. There was nothing to be done. Your grandfather wanted to be a shoemaker. It had become his ruling passion and there was no way to change his mind. Despairing at his obtuseness, Salvatore's parents gave in and sent him to the cobbler's shop. It was a godsend for him. He sensed that there he could finally make his dream come true. He soon had the opportunity to prove that his passion was justified. Once a year in Bonito's church children received their First Communion; it was a sacred moment as well as the most important social event in the village. Rosina, Salvatore's six-year-old younger sister, was preparing to receive the sacrament along with her sister Giuseppina. All girls were formally required to wear white shoes, but the ones they had inherited from their older sisters were now very worn, and there was not enough money to buy new shoes. The youngest children had to make do with hand-me-downs from their elder siblings; if the clothes and shoes were not in good condition, they simply went without. Salvatore's mother searched all over town for shoes to borrow, but to no avail. The night before Communion Day, she went to bed sadly, trying hard not to think about the next day and about how her little girls would receive the holy wafer without white shoes. Salvatore resolved to act. Unbeknownst to his parents, he went to the shop of Luigi Festa, the shoemaker with whom he had begun to work, and asked to take home a large white canvas, cardboard, tacks, glue, two lasts, and some necessary tools. Then he returned home and waited until everyone had gone to bed. When all had fallen silent, he slipped quietly into the closet below the stairs, and, working at a small bench, began to make his first shoes, the ones that would fill his little sisters with joy and his mother with pride in front of the whole town. In his autobiography, Grandfather confessed that he had never made a pair of shoes before, but felt as if a powerful force were guiding him in his task, as if he had always known how to do it, as if he had learned all this in a previous life and was now simply remembering how to do it.

In a letter for the Red Book, entitled "Supernatural Perceptions," Tà speaks of this "knowledge from above," an idea to which she was very devoted.

"Sometimes you have the feeling that your good and healthy instincts are by your side, like helpers sent from the Beyond. And when you get this feeling, you can be sure that the best way of keeping your helpful instincts alive is to follow the path that leads to goodness. If you stray from this path, you distance yourself from these helpful instincts, and then, well, either you abandon them, or they abandon you!"

But let's return to that night. At four in the morning, probably awakened by the tapping of the hammer, Salvatore's father went downstairs to find him at work. He stood still in silence for a few moments, watching his son. From the corner of his eye, he saw small white shoes sitting on the shelf. He told Salvatore it was very late and that he should get some sleep. But the boy was too excited. His father's stern gaze was daunting, but his work was not done yet; he wanted the shoes to be ready to wear when his sisters woke up. And so it came to be that the following day, Rosina and Giuseppina were to enter the church wearing their beautiful, new, white shoes. The shoes became the talk of the town that day (as well as the episode in the story of Grandfather's life that Tà narrated most frequently): hadn't Mrs. Ferragamo been just now going from house to house in a vain attempt to borrow shoes? So, everyone was now wondering, where had those marvels come from? Excited, proud, and herself amazed, our great-grandmother Antonia explained that her son had made them, and that he had been up all night doing so.

I was reminded of Ottavia's First Communion in a colonial-style church in Buenos Aires on a sunny November day. More than a century later and on the other side of the globe, my daughter entered the church wearing a pair of white *Varina* ballet flats, a classic, cherished Ferragamo model that has become globally popular.

From that Communion Day on, Salvatore's parents set aside their reserves and supported their son's apprenticeship at the workshop of Luigi Festa. So Salvatore returned to the shoemaker to learn the trade that would define his destiny.

"Keep this in mind also for your children. Have faith in them and in their abilities, but remember that a trade is best learned from the bottom up. To begin with, Salvatore had to resign himself to the job of picking up cobbler's nails from the ground and straightening them out with a hammer so that they might be used again. He alternated this tedious chore with babysitting Festa's children when he was busy with more important jobs. Your grandfather was a humble person, but he put his all into everything he did. He knew then that he was learning the trade of shoemaker, and he wanted nothing more. This is the mentality to which we subscribed as a couple and inculcated in your parents, and I hope that you will pass it on to your children, which you will, won't you?" Tà said, raising her voice and accentuating these last words with a frown, as was her wont whenever she was issuing us with a warning.

Tà was sincerely convinced that starting at the bottom and working your way up was the secret to competitive success. In one of her "circulars" for the Red Book, she told us that she and Grandfather had decided to get the children working in the trade as soon as possible by sending them, aged 13 or 14, to spend a month every summer in the factory carrying out simple jobs, such as boxing footwear and checking inventories. They received a small reward, a couple of liras, which was a smart way to teach children to respect work and enjoy the satisfaction of earning money by doing a job properly. Grandfather, like Tà, was of the firm opinion that the three-month summer vacation from school was far too long.

Tà was always last to go on vacation in the summer. There was no way to get her away from work. At the end of August, she would always be the first back in the office. In another letter she wrote: "Some remarks concerning the vacation period just gone. Yes, I rested my mind a bit, but I found that laying off my work, interrupting my schedules, and allowing my concentration to slacken put me off the place where I was staying, so I'm happy to be back at my desk. Work gives me a reason to live, it's my mission. And, most of all, work is a tribute to my beloved Salvatore. Enjoy getting back to it, all of you. Hugs. Nonna Wanda."

Her message was not only meant as a dig at us, an enjoinder to get back to work or to make ourselves busy and productive. This is how she genuinely felt about work. It was as if she could enter a state of grace only when she was at work and therefore proceeding along the path marked out for her by her husband.

Salvatore was only 10 years old when his father died. By the side of his deathbed, he had vowed to look after his sisters and mother. By then he was already making shoes for the ladies of Bonito, including Tà's mother, and everyone appreciated them for their quality and aesthetic refinement. Two of the townspeople, namely the pharmacist and the schoolteacher, stepped up as important helpers in Grandfather's life. Concerned for the condition of Salvatore's family following the death of his father, they encouraged him to leave Bonito for Naples where he could perfect his trade and earn better money. Grandfather took their advice and spent several grueling years in Naples before returning to Bonito. But the result of the venture was that, in 1912, at the age of just 14, Salvatore had already opened his own shop employing six workers, all older than him. Except for the boy who collected the nails.

The ladies around town soon realized that Grandfather's shoes were as good as those sold in the boutiques of Naples, Bari, or Avellino. When Salvatore's brother Alfonso returned from the United States to visit their mother, he was very impressed by Salvatore's success, and suggested that he emigrate to America. He knew that his brother's shoes would sell for more in America. And so it came to be that, in late March 1915, a few months before Italy joined the Great War, our not-yet-17-year-old boy, just like more than five million other young Italians in the early years of the twentieth century, followed his destiny and left his native land in search of a better life overseas. In addition to the emotional wrench of emigration, the voyage from Naples to New York Harbor was a nightmare.

"Salvatore had bought the cheapest ticket, two hundred liras (about thirty euros today), for a berth in a cabin for six. But the conditions were intolerable, not even fit for animals."

Tà was moved to sorrow whenever she thought of Salvatore at so tender an age on his sea voyage. By way of documentary evidence of his experience, she sent for inclusion in the Red Book a copy of the certificate of the American Immigrant Wall of Honor, which reads: "Salvatore Ferragamo came to the United States of America from Italy joining the courageous men and women who reached this country in search of personal freedom, economic opportunity, and a better future for their families."

The way Tà tells it is that when Grandfather disembarked at New York Harbor, he found himself lost. His sister had gone to meet him, but so long a time had passed that she did not recognize him. Not speaking English and making do as best he could, he made his way alone to Boston.

"When his sister saw him at the front door, she was astounded. She had not recognized him at the port because she had not been expecting an elegant young man of such class and style, already the signature characteristics of your grandfather at the age of 17. The customary practice among the poor from whom he came was for the younger children to wear clothes, shoes, and coats handed down from their siblings, whereas Salvatore had used his first savings to buy himself a small number of new outfits. He had gone to a boutique in Naples and bought a rust-colored gabardine coat with a fur collar and a walking stick with a celluloid case. While in Naples, he had been mocked several times for his rustic appearance; so, as he faced the future that awaited him in the New World, he embraced the idea that clothes maketh the man."

I leave it to the reader to imagine Tà's excitement at the discovery in 2006 of another of Grandfather's patents, this one registered in 1921 by the American Patent Office, one of the 368 to have been rediscovered.

"It is yet more proof of his exceptional creative vision," she told us in a letter. "Only yesterday, we discovered on an American site that, at the age of 23, Salvatore registered a patent for an apparatus similar to his 'leg-traction device.' The thought that such a talented person should still be present in our lives so many years after his death moves me very much."

Of the history of Grandfather's immigration to America, Tà has kept meticulous record: letters, awards, certificates, articles, patents, and an especially meaningful document, Salvatore's first passport, faithful replicas of which she had made and sent to us. A copy of the passport is now kept in each of our Red Books.

Grandfather stayed in Boston for a short time. His family in America had found a job for him in a shoe factory in the hope that it would be to his liking, but he could not bear to stay even a day there. He couldn't stand to see machines mass-producing shoes that were all the same, made without any distinctive elements, without any human workmanship, without delicacy, to all of which he attached foremost importance.

"He was not a production line worker, he was an artisan shoemaker, and wanted to remain so," Tà always said by way of underlining the value of manual skill and craftsmanship.

Grandfather then decided to move to California and join his brothers who lived near Santa Barbara. Secondino was a carpenter and Girolamo a tailor. Alfonso, the brother who had convinced him to emigrate, proposed him a series of jobs, one of which would turn out to be the opportunity of a lifetime.

Alfonso used to iron and press set costumes for the American Film Company in Santa Barbara. Many of the silent films of the time were made there before the industry moved south to Hollywood. The wardrobe supervisor hired Grandfather to make cowboy boots for the stars of westerns, which were a very popular genre at the time. Boots always presented problems of size, fit, and design; they took a long time to make and were never quite right. The wardrobe supervisor was pleased with Grandfather's work, and with the fact that he stayed on set to fix and finish the boots on the spot. Wearing boots that were finally a comfortable fit, the actors were likewise appreciative. When the actors were happy, the directors no longer had to put up with their complaints and could do better work. Cecil B. DeMille once told Grandfather that the Far West would have been won far sooner if only they had had boots like his.

Grandfather began making the costume footwear for other films, as well as for actors such as Douglas Fairbanks, who would later become a good friend. For many films, such as *The Thief of Baghdad* and *The King of Kings*, he created very special shoes that have entered the annals of fashion history: the kidskin pump with painted dots, the suede shoes with the raised toe, and later the *Rainbow* sandal with the multicolored wedge that he made for Judy Garland. Hollywood actresses began to order made-to-measure shoes from him. This marked the inception of his stunning relationship with the most famous stars of the day, a relationship that has survived even though the generations of actresses and actors have changed several times since. No-one ever before had made shoes that were so innovative in design and at the same time so comfortable to wear. He was obsessed with quality and made sure every time that every shoe was a perfect fit.

When he had arrived in America, it was without a word of English. He realized at once that he had to learn the language as a matter of priority. He mastered it quickly and was therefore soon able to audit anatomy courses at the University of Los Angeles, where he deepened his knowledge of the human skeleton, specifically the structure of the bones of the foot and how they work in relation to the rest of the body. It was during his anatomy studies that Salvatore made a breakthrough discovery that was to revolutionize how he made his shoes. He carried out trials in which he demonstrated that the weight of the body bears down directly on the arch of the foot from where it is distributed to the heel. He realized that the entire weight of the body was borne by a section of the foot that measured barely a few centimeters. He therefore decided to add a reinforced arch to the soles of his shoes. His customers soon noticed the huge difference in quality between his shoes and those made by others. He had invented a shoe that was not just innovative in design but also extremely comfortable to wear. A crowd of actresses soon gathered around him. When the film production company moved from Santa Barbara to Hollywood in 1923, Salvatore took over a store in Los Angeles that quickly became a tremendous success. It was called the Hollywood Boot Shop and soon attracted a large number of enthusiastic customers, eager then as now to emulate their favorite movie star. Salvatore got to know many stars, such as Joan Crawford, Gloria Swanson, and Rudolph Valentino, and became fast friends with some. His fame and business took off.

His main problem now was finding workers with the necessary craft skills that his artisanal approach demanded. He could find no-one he considered up to the task. After spending a long time searching for artisans in Boston, New York, Philadelphia, and Chicago, he decided that the best solution was to look among the shoemakers of Italy with their centuries of experience. So in 1927, after 13 years in the United States, he returned to Italy. In Genoa, Naples, Rome, and Turin he met several local artisans, but, although very skilled at leather work, they did not have the mental elasticity to change their way of working to suit his innovative ideas. Only in Florence, cradle of centuries-old craftsmanship, did he find workers who understood and appreciated his methods. Grandfather designed like the beginner he was, creating on the go, working all day long at the shoe last, and producing patent after patent. He needed cutters and fitters to turn his designs into proper models, and found the artisans he was looking for in Florence, which is why he chose to set up shop there. Tà was also of the opinion that Florence was the soul of Italian craftsmanship, which is why the company retains its headquarters in the city.

Grandfather planned to return to the United States once he had set up and begun manufacturing operations in Italy, with the idea to sell to department stores in America and around the world. But the Wall Street Crash of 1929 derailed his plans and had a catastrophic impact on his business. As the Great Depression took hold, luxury items were the first to be cut out of people's straitened budgets. Sales collapsed and his dream seemed to come crashing down with them. But Grandfather was not the sort of person to accept defeat. That is not who he was. He took out loans to keep himself afloat, but eventually could not keep up with the high interest charges and, in 1933, his company was placed in compulsory receivership by the Court of Florence. That was a turning point. He knew that many people depended on him; nor had he forgotten the promise made to his father to look after his mother and his two sisters and their families. Furthermore, he had prepared several young people for the profession for whom he now felt responsible, evincing a conscientiousness and honesty that Tà always held up as exemplary.

"A long time afterwards, I asked him whether he had been afraid, to which he replied that, no, the road he had to follow had never been so clearly visible to him as then. Even so, he spent many a sleepless night, during which, as he confessed to me, he had been visited by revelations. First and foremost, he told me, he felt sure of himself because, though he had lost his money, he had not lost his talent. Secondly, his manufacturing knowledge was now far more advanced than at the time of the Crash. He knew he could count on the skill of his craftsmanship to get back on his feet. His shoes would continue to be made by hand: no machine would be included in the production of an Original Ferragamo, which has remained our basic premise."

Grandfather resolved to pay off all his debts and never again have recourse to any capital other than his own. All future growth of his business would be self-financed and the company would continue to cultivate direct relationships with its customers. He realized that he had to stop relying solely on exports, because they were one of the very causes of his difficulties. When the Great Depression caused export sales to slump, he realized he simply did not have enough customers in Italy to make up for the shortfall. So, he resolved then and there that half the company's output would be destined for the Italian market. Finally, he understood that his company needed a name and a head office that would be worthy of it and so, several years later, he bought an elegant atelier to serve as his workshop.

By putting these decisions into effect, he got his business back on its feet. He began by successfully fulfilling an order for three pairs of shoes for one of the most beautiful and elegant ladies in Florence, who had already bought shoes from him in New York, and who in turn introduced him to other ladies. In a short time, he had built up a large new clientele. Piece by piece he reassembled his business according to the big picture he had in mind. He opened several footwear stores in Italy and started exporting again. Little by little, he was able to pay off all his debts.

All this was taking place in the Italy of the 1930s: the political situation would soon explode, culminating in the ascent of Benito Mussolini to power, which was to have monumental consequences for the whole world and led to the inevitable imposition of sanctions on Italy.

As a result, Grandfather lost not only export sales once again, but also the possibility to procure the best materials, which were reserved for military use. The unavailability of fine leathers and of the steel shanks needed for arch reinforcements caused him huge production problems. When materials of sufficient quality were lacking, he faced a quandary. If he used the low-grade metal available, the arch support in the shoe would bend and break, which would be an utter disaster because the supported arch was his signature technique, on which his name and reputation rested. He could never have settled for making shoes of inferior quality.

So he had recourse to his innate creativity, with the result that the pressure of these difficult circumstances pushed him into developing what became his most famous models. He began to use raffia, a fiber originally from Madagascar, with which he was able to manufacture shoes for years. For evening footwear, he concocted an even more ingenious solution: cellophane instead of unobtainable silk and satin. Tà's story about how Salvatore was struck by inspiration after buying a box of candies has stuck in my mind.

"As he was unwrapping one, he looked closely at the cellophane and began to unroll it between his fingers, turning it into a strip. He noticed how brightly it shone in the light, and pulling at it, he saw it was resistant to force. He immediately intuited that this was the material he needed, so he ordered it in large quantities. He then cut the cellophane into long strips and inserted gold and silver embroidery, which added an extra shimmer effect. In place of the fine leather he had been using for applications and detailing, he deployed the intertwined cellophane strips he had made. His innovation was so popular and became so famous that he continued to use it and its many variations for years. The end of the war did not kill the appetite of the great French fashion houses, which continued to order these wonderful evening shoes for their collections. Hearing Salvatore tell me these stories, I was always awestruck by his intelligence and resourcefulness. He always took the positive view. His attitude taught me that any obstacle might really turn out to be an opportunity. Instead of losing heart and giving up, he was enthused by the challenge of having to work things out in a new way. This is what we now call thinking outside the box. A beautiful product can come from the most unexpected of sources, from humble materials such as cork or even from discarded candy wrappers."

Grandfather accrued a loyal clientele made up of some of the most prestigious women in the world, including members of the European aristocracy, and the wives of famous industrialists.

By 1938, Grandfather's economic position seemed finally to have stabilized. He had exited bankruptcy and his business had expanded from Europe to America. The name Salvatore

Ferragamo joined other top-tier Italian fashion houses exporting luxury products around the world. The stores were much
sought-after and very popular. The workshop in Florence was
located in a magnificent medieval palace, namely Palazzo Spini
Feroni, built in 1289 in front of the Santa Trinita Bridge over the
Arno. Palazzo Spini Feroni remains the company's headquarters to this day.

"Salvatore fell in love with the building at first sight. Chance
and good fortune came to his aid. After a tiring and complicated
to-and-fro with the sellers, he managed to buy the building,
move all company operations into it, and rent out the rooms he
did not need. Having found an elegant location for the company,
he now set about finding a house in which to take up private residence. He had very clear ideas about how the house of his
dreams should be. It needed to be southward-facing to catch the
sun, and it had to be located outside the city so that he could
unwind and restore his energy at lunchtime and after work. He
also wanted a plot of land to cultivate, which remained one of
his favorite pastimes. The house also had to be large, because he
would bring his mother and his sisters to live there with their
families, just as he had promised his father."

Tà told me about Grandfather's house-hunting one summer
afternoon as we were sitting in the garden of Il Palagio admiring the view that took in all Florence. "It was here that I, as a
young bride, arrived in November 1940 after our honeymoon.
Before we went to the house, Salvatore took me to Piazzale Michelangelo to show me the panorama of Florence. It was my first
view of the city that was to become my home for so many years,
the city I now love. I was in ecstasy over its beauty and enchanted by its history, which I only knew through schoolbooks at that
stage. Salvatore pointed out Palazzo Spini Feroni in the distance
to me, then, on the other side of the hill, "Villa Il Palagio," our
new home. Never in my life had I experienced an emotion such
as I felt at that moment."

5.

A Telescope for Seeing Far

As a child, I was always excited whenever I took the road to Fiesole that gently wends its way uphill from Florence through sloping groves of olive and cypress. Of course, a visit to Tà's place at Il Palagio, the country villa that is the beating heart of my family, was never a question of casually dropping by. The visitor was naturally expected to arrive well turned-out and with hair suitably brushed. It was also to be preferred that the visitor did not speak out of turn or talk too much. Whether as children or as adults, we never lost our fear of Tà's verdict on our appearance, and the first few moments of her appraisal were always critical. Even so, visiting her was always a happy occasion. I returned from every visit with my consciousness expanded. Whether visiting as a child shyly clutching my mother's hand or visiting as a fretful adult, I would leave feeling heartened, freshly enthused, and armed with wise advice. At Il Palagio Tà received visitors in surroundings that were beautiful beyond imagination. I loved her large, tidy, welcoming house; I loved the framed photographs, artifacts and collections that told the family history; and I loved the large garden brightened by roses, peonies, hibiscus and, at the back, a thick woodland of ancient trees.

Family legend has it that Grandfather found Il Palagio without the help of real estate agents by standing in Piazzale Michelangelo in Florence with a pair of binoculars focused on Fiesole and its surrounding area, picking out the hillside villas one by one until he found the one he was looking for: an island surround by green, not too far from the city, and with a large park in front that afforded a magnificent view of Florence. He wanted a house that would allow him to disconnect from work, for he knew that if the house were too near the workshop, he would always come home late. He fell in love with the villa at his first visit and, thanks also to his characteristic doggedness, eventually managed to buy it after long-drawn-out and difficult negotiations.

It was there, in that villa in its superlative setting, that Grandfather taught Tà to love not just Florence but also the natural world, in which he had always had a lively interest. In the garden, he proudly set up a telescope to which, mainly on summer evenings, he used to bring his young children so that they could together look up at, and wonder upon, the marvels of the firmament. The children used to line up to look at the stars and have them explained by Salvatore, who was genuinely attracted to the study of astronomy.

In June 2011, a letter from Tà was delivered with an invitation to dinner to inaugurate a new telescope that she, keen to revive these memories, had bought for us grandchildren. Sadly, I never experienced one of those evenings in person, but I still have the photograph Tà enclosed with the letter showing Grandfather with my aunts and uncle as children, their illuminated gazes turned up to the heavens.

"I like the idea of kindling in you an interest in astronomy, for it helps you understand the greatness of Creation, before which we must bow our heads and pray, and keep it in our hearts. It is a nice coincidence that I have bought a new telescope on the fourth centenary of its being invented by Galileo Galilei." As always, I thought to myself, Tà never leaves anything to chance.

I stood for a while looking at the black and white photo. Aunt Giovanna is looking into the telescope, Aunt Fiamma is smiling while striking a pose, and Uncle Ferruccio, his nose sticking up in the air, is still too short to reach the instrument. Seated behind them in the flower-filled garden of Il Palagio, elegant and beautiful, Tà is being served coffee. The photograph caused me to consider that Grandfather was far-sighted in every sense of the word, and that he really knew a lot about both kinds of stars, not just those of the firmament.

The "shoemaker of the stars," as he was nicknamed, had always been surrounded by the divas of Hollywood: Greta Garbo, Paulette Goddard, Ava Gardner, Lauren Bacall, Claudette Colbert, Sophia Loren, Silvana Mangano, Audrey Hepburn... We granddaughters have often wondered how Tà must have reacted to Grandfather's spending most of his time surrounded by splendidly attractive women.

In an interview with *Corriere della Sera*, she confessed that Salvatore's past did indeed excite considerable feelings of jealousy in her. It was a torment to think of Ingrid Bergman, Katharine Hepburn, Rita Hayworth, Bette Davis, with their fairytale feet, ankles and legs, before which Grandfather knelt as he tried his shoes on them. In that interview, she pulled out the pumps with size-11 high heels that Marilyn Monroe had worn in *Some Like it Hot*. Tà told the reporter that she had traveled the world looking for them, and had spent a fortune on retrieving nine pairs of the shoes Salvatore had made for Marilyn. Accompanied by Uncle Massimo, in 1999 she bought her first lot of shoes for 50,000 dollars at an auction at Christie's in New York. Uncle Massimo's memory of the event is of Tà sitting in the front row anxiously raising her paddle every time the bid price went up, without even waiting to see if anyone was bidding against her. Her enthusiasm cost her dear as they ended up paying far more than expected for the shoes.

Grandfather got his ticket into the world of cinema through the good offices of Mary Pickford and Joan Crawford. Returning to Italy after 12 years in America, it seems that he brought with him two giant poster photos of these two actresses that had once been displayed at his Hollywood store, along with two other life-size photos of Greta Garbo and Jean Harlow. Both of the giant posters featured a dedication, "To Salvatore with love," a message that did not please Tà, who, in a fit of jealousy, came up with an idea that has remained legendary ever since.

"One day, Salvatore returned for lunch only to find me gone. He asked our butler where I was. The butler, knowing what I had done, had to suppress a smile. Since he never took me to the cinema or the theater, I had placed a cardboard actress at each of the places around the dining room table and left a note: 'Have you had your fun? Well, stay with them for lunch.' It was an attack of jealousy partly justified by the fact that I was always big and pregnant while he spent all of his time with these slender-bodied women..."

The story does not end there.

"At that very moment, the parish priest of Maiano, Don Paolo de Töth, came to our house and was very taken aback to see that gallery of *femmes fatales*, with their low-cut dresses and cigarette holders between their lips. Salvatore told him to pay no heed, explaining that I was in the throes of a jealous fit. In the wake of that episode, Alessandro Zullo, our long-standing butler, seeing that the giant poster pictures were a bone of contention in the family, threw them out with the garbage. And now every time I organize an exhibition, be it in Palazzo Strozzi, the Victoria and Albert Museum in London, the Sogetsu-Kai Foundation in Tokyo, or the Los Angeles County Museum of Art, I really regret getting rid of them!"

When Tà arrived in Florence, it was as a married woman who was also little more than a girl. Back in those days, the custom was that a woman would enter her husband's house as a married woman, not as a young lady. So it was for Wanda.

"As Salvatore was driving from Piazzale Michelangelo and up the narrow streets of Fiesole, he noticed that I was a little nervous. It was a perfectly normal thing for me to be, for I had no idea what sort of new life lay before me. But he quickly set my mind at ease by telling me about his family, about how they would take me in with love, and how there were many people who would help me settle in. I was happy to hear his reassuring words, for I knew I had much to learn and that my new role would take some getting used to. When we reached the top of the hill, Salvatore pointed out Il Palagio, an imposing residence, bathed in the light of the setting sun. I was dumbstruck. I simply couldn't believe my eyes. As we passed through the gate I gazed in amazement at the broad facade of the villa. He parked his Alfa Romeo at the bottom of the terraced garden leading up to the front door. I could feel smiling and curious looks upon me from all around as I got out of the car. Salvatore's mother and sister, who were to continue living with us for a year, embraced me warmly and immediately made me feel at home. As soon as I got a chance to look around, I found myself utterly bewitched by the incredible view, not only of the city but also of the surrounding hills. It is a view of whose beauty I never grow tired."

Weather and work schedules permitting, Tà always paid a visit to the garden before sunset. After a tour of inspection of her beloved roses, she would sink tiredly into the large red and white cushions and silently contemplate the immutable beauty of the city stretched out below her.

"For more than 70 years I have thanked God every day for this vista, for all those moments of sublime beauty that allow me to unwind and think in peace."

When you visited Tà in her garden, she would from time to time ask you to stay in silence so that she might sacralize those moments of contemplation during which she would also marshal the multitude of thoughts that had occurred to her over the day. One of the thoughts to emerge from her contemplations arrived in the form of another of her missives for the Red Book.

"Unless we become better people and more honest in our intentions, we shall be overwhelmed by evil. We ask God for the Grace to become better, more generous, and ready to lend a helping hand to those in need. It is our duty of course, but doing so will also improve our peace of mind and our conscience."

Every July, Tà organized a family reunion to celebrate the many birthdays that fell in that month. We would meet there for an aperitif and enjoy the sunset over the city. Not even after her children had left Il Palagio forever did she think about moving out. In that huge house with its lofty ceilings and thick walls, with large wrought iron railings over the windows, Tà lived alone for many years in rooms that remained unchanged. The careful and respectful upkeep of the rooms was not just a way of keeping the memories alive, but also a gesture of love and gratitude toward the man who first brought her to that villa.

"I had never seen such a big house. The front of it was immense. It looked like a fairytale castle. When I entered, I saw that each room had been furnished with scrupulous care, with beautiful fabrics, silverware, and porcelain. Salvatore proudly showed me every corner of the house and I fell in love with it from the very first moment. Twelve domestic staff worked in the house including a cook, waiting staff, a driver, a gardener, and a farmer who took care of the small farm that belonged to the property at the time. I soon learned to manage the staff well and give the right sort of orders for the optimal running of the household. I have my mother to thank for imparting to me this axiomatic truth: *Si tu sa' fa, sa' pure cummannà* (If you know how it is done, you know how to order it done). I found that a very valuable lesson that helped me in running the house."

One of Tà's gifts was her unparalleled ability to give orders, the result of which was evident in her homes, which she loved and managed with almost obsessive care. Perhaps her house management was training for the corporate management to which, when called upon to perform, she applied the very same methodology.

"A house reflects the people who live in it, the love you put into things. The house is like a person. If you don't show discipline and love, everything falls apart," she told me a few days before I got married. "It is important for a husband to be able to return to a harmonious household where everything is ticking along just as it should. Disorder in the home breeds chaos in the family. The husband needs to be able to come home to rest and recuperate from work; he should not have to concern himself with chores, which are your responsibility. If something has gone awry, try to fix it by yourself, or else choose the right moment to talk to him about it," she recommended, as if foreshadowing episodes from my future.

A house is the shared dream of a married couple, as well as the foundation on which they build their family. To turn a house into a home, both husband and wife need to work together on choosing its décor and furnishing. It must become a place of peace and rest for everyone. Speaking personally, my experience of our warm, bright Buenos Aires apartment was that I felt at home from the moment I set foot in it. It was located on the top floor of a French-style building in the very central and leafy Palermo district of the city. We had plenty of help, including a day porter and a night porter, which meant I could come home from the office at any time without feeling in danger. I would drive the car directly into the garage and take an elevator from there to the house. Certain conveniences like this are often an effective way of making sure no-one in the family is left feeling disgruntled, but an ideal home has to be the result of everyone working together.

"Salvatore's coming home from work was a hallowed moment in my day. We had precious little time to spend together, so I steered well clear of dull housework talk. Lunch and dinner were the only moments we had for ourselves. After lunch, we would walk around the garden for a while, then he would rest for a while before returning to work. I would not see him again until evening. At first, I was intimidated when the cook appeared in the dining room and asked me to set the menu of the day and issue instructions for making it. Bit by bit, though, this task became one of my delights. My affectionate mother-in-law and sister-in-law helped me feel not alone, including during the war, when we were all a little isolated from everything up there in the hills."

The organizing of lunches and dinners became a joyful pursuit for Tà, who dedicated herself in person to choosing the menus, be they for a dinner at home, a lunch in company, or a gala with hundreds of people. Nowadays, images of her decoratively laid out tables would unquestionably be all over social media networks.

"I see it as a beautiful tribute paid to those seated at the table, whether guests or not. Even when I eat alone, I like the table to be beautifully laid. I have all these flowers in the garden to choose from for the table. When I arrived at Il Palagio, I found fine porcelain tableware and tablecloths of every sort and for every season completely at my disposal. Setting the table was a pleasure, was fun."

I still remember a lunch at Tà's in the middle of January at which I found myself delighted by the freshness of the flowers in the center of the table, accompanied by pomegranates, some whole, others halved to reveal their glossy red insides. Over the years I never saw a table set twice in the same way, which justifies the amount of cupboard space devoted to dinner sets and glassware in her large office, along with table linens of every color, material, and pattern. Like an artist with her tools, she used these items to compose irresistibly inviting and creative table displays. From every trip she made, Tà returned with some sort of piece of tableware. In any one of her homes, she could set a table fit for a king.

Through Grandfather, Tà became acquainted with ladies of great distinction, class, and learning. Two such were the wife of the ambassador of Romania, Princess Ginori Conti, and Countess Clelia de Marinis, of whom she grew particularly fond.

"I met her soon after my arrival. Although I was very proud of my family origins, I still felt like a provincial girl, and it was hard to feel at my ease in a refined city such as Florence. Salvatore had been introduced into Florentine society where he was now known, and the people with whom we socialized were all older than me."

Clelia was Tà's first Florentine friend, and became a kind of teacher and mentor. Her husband, Count Tammaro de Marinis, was a famous collector and bibliophile.

"Clelia had a truly fabulous way of doing things and entertaining people. They lived in a magnificent house near us in Fiesole. Whenever they invited us for dinner or lunch in the early days of our friendship, I used to feel intimidated by so much elegance. I studied every little detail of their arrangements: what flowers they used, how they set the glasses on the table, how they served the bread. I wanted to learn as much as I could so that I might do the same in our house. I wanted to imitate Clelia because she seemed like the perfect hostess. Both she and her husband admired Salvatore and were our great friends. Before the war, they had hosted Churchill and Chamberlain, and were close friends with Maria José di Savoia, the queen of Italy.

During the war, the philosopher Giovanni Gentile was killed by a group of partisans right in front of the gates of their villa."

As fate (or another curious coincidence) would have it, years later Aunt Giovanna would marry Giovanni Gentile, the eponymous grandson of the philosopher, who was a sweet-natured, even-handed and generous man, regarded as a solid and exemplary figure by all the family who enjoyed the unconditional esteem of Tà.

"Even during the war, Grandfather was busy at work, but he still wanted us to enjoy our new city together. I used to pick him up at the office, and we would walk around the Old Town. How we enjoyed that! Florence is a city full of treasures; its people are very cultured, but also ready and willing to help. Salvatore found himself surrounded by Florentine artisans who, like him, were trying to keep going a proud tradition that was declining generation by generation. I shall never forget my first visit to the Uffizi, the first time I saw Michelangelo's *David*, the cloister of San Marco, the Medici tombs, and the church of Santo Spirito. Wherever you look in Florence is a feast for the eyes and food for the soul. No more than a small city, really, yet the cradle of so much talent and genius. It seemed almost predetermined that Salvatore should likewise end up living and making his dream come true here."

Tà's last thoughts were dedicated to "her Florence," to which she wrote a letter that was read out on the day of her funeral, as she had instructed. I have entered the letter in the Red Book even though Tà is no longer here to remind me to do so. Nothing moves me more than this letter of thanks that my grandmother penned to the city that had opened its arms to her. Nothing surprised me more than her decision to write a farewell letter... to a city.

"Florence, my final farewell is also addressed to you. Having first come here as a newly-wed 18-year-old, I learned little by little to love and appreciate you. Your beauty lies in your art, in the excellence of your craftsmanship, in your hills, in your unexampled traditions of humanism and civilization. You have touched and enriched my spirit, you have given me a sense of inner peace that I have been able to apply to the work that I and my children have done in continuation of the project that my never-to-be-forgotten Salvatore left as his legacy. I would like everyone, both Florentines and visitors, to deeply sense your true values and to forgive some passing shortcomings that can be remedied in order to immerse themselves in your magnificent beauty, drawing from it love, pride, and serenity for their spirit. From my terrace, where I have admired you for seventy years, I embrace you in your entirety, and I hope that you will forever remain the jewel in the crown of our beloved Italy. Farewell all. Wanda."

A memory that always moved Tà whenever she spoke of it was of the day Grandfather took her to Palazzo Spini Feroni for the very first time. She remembered him bringing her to the corner of Via Tornabuoni and Piazza Santa Trinita to see the store with his name written in big letters on the front, and she remembered him, proud as Punch, showing off the shoes in stock.

"I looked around at all those shoes. Never had I seen such an array of materials, colors, and styles. Nor had I ever seen shoes that looked like that. I thought they were the most beautiful objects I had ever seen or could even ever have imagined. Many of the materials were genuinely unusual, but such was Salvatore's handicraft that they looked like they had always been made to be worn. Salvatore never talked about himself. The only compliments I heard paid to him were from his sister and mother—they were proud of him, just as I became prouder and prouder of him with each passing day at his side. One day, we were gift hunting in Florence for a friend. I paused to look in the window display of a shoe store, and there, on full blatant display, was an imitation of one of Salvatore's models. Angry and upset, I pointed the pair out to him, but he only laughed and, showing the enviable restraint that was so much a part of his even-tempered character, told me to put my mind at ease, not to worry, and certainly not to get angry. I remember his exact words: 'As long as they're copying me, it means I'm on the right track. You need to worry only when you no longer see imitations of my models. It doesn't bother me, because by the time they have copied my models, I will already have thought up and designed new ones.'"

Tà was thankful for all that she learned from Salvatore. She used to say that one of the most important things she learned from him, things applicable in life and later in the running of the company, was that you need always to stay on top of what others are doing, without ever losing focus on your own work. "By abiding by this rule, Grandfather created 20,000 models of shoe. So, important though it is to keep an eye on your competitors, remember that it is even more important to do your own job well."

Always faithful to this teaching, Tà kept herself abreast of what was going on around her, but never let it alter her way of being and living.

"Salvatore had a positive attitude: he looked at what could be done and at what needed to be done, not at what was not possible. I think one of the reasons we were able to overcome the horrors of the war was that he was always ready to see the light in the darkness and the opportunities behind the problems."

I'm sure that of all that we learned from him, this was the greatest of lessons.

War Is Never Glorious

One morning, I was surprised to find in my mail a speech by the President of the United States, Barack Obama. Titled "War Is Never a Glorious Thing," he delivered it on December 10, 2009 at the ceremony when he received the Nobel Peace Prize. I knew well why Tà had been so seduced by those words. War had left deep scars on her life: her father had had direct experience of conflict in World War I, and she herself in World War II.

"President Obama pays tribute to important historical peacemakers and convincingly explains why we need to defend democracy and prevent abuses. Some of you are perhaps still too young to comprehend the full extent of this, but I am sure that the Red Books will be well looked after, and that they will serve you in the future not only as memorials of me but also as sources of essential and perennial truths."

A little while later, she sent us a very interesting historical document. It was her father's war diary, a collection of his wartime entries that she collated and published as a book: *La Grande Guerra 1915–1918. Diario del tenente medico Fulvio*

Miletti (The Great War 1915–1918. Diary of medical officer lieutenant Fulvio Miletti).

"We will have occasion later to talk about this directly experienced piece of history. In the meantime, it is with filial pride that I pass on to the third and fourth generations of our family the testimony of my father, which thus lives on, just as he desired."

Thanks to his grandson Fulvio, who kept the archives of the Miletti family in Bonito, all Great-grandfather's diaries were recovered. One of them, a time-worn notebook, contains his rigorously scientific and chronological notes on the events of the war, along with his reflections as a doctor and humanist on the tragedy unfolding before his eyes. With the help of Zeffiro Ciuffoletti, professor of Contemporary History at the University of Florence, Tà had managed to put together not only a memoir, but an authentic historical record.

"I was born after my father's return from the front. Only later, through the discovery of his diary entries and photographs, did I understand what he had had to endure. His diaries gave me some idea of the awful experiences of this young officer who, motivated by a spirit of comradeship, looked after soldiers with appalling injuries from the front in a small makeshift field hospital. His memories touched me deeply and made me extremely proud of him."

Before publishing the book, Tà often used to repeat the line from it that had impressed itself most deeply on her mind. Fixing her eyes on an empty space and moving her hand in the air to set the solemn rhythm of her father's words that she had learned by heart, she would pronounce: "With my mind serene, I go now to offer my whole self to my free and great Fatherland; and if it falls to me to make the ultimate sacrifice, let there not be weakness and tears, but the lasting memory and pride of the strong." To us, now, the words come across as rhetorically overwrought, but they thrilled Tà every time.

"How many young people today have the same love of country and cherish ideals and principles such as those? Few! Very few! Of course, it is hardly their fault. Those who are supposed to be preparing today's young people for life are completely failing to provide them with edifying or uplifting precepts, such as respect for a history that, through good times and through bad, through calamities and recovery, has enabled ours to become a wealthy and modern nation. Sometimes what we are looking for is not in front of us, but behind us."

Tà had been very struck by how during the war women took on responsibilities, and by the great courage and purposeful-ness they showed as their husbands left for the front leaving them alone with their families. For some of those who left, a he-roic destiny was in store—something that would later touch her, albeit differently, when she lost her beloved husband.

She did not like to talk about the war because, as she used to say, it was the most terrible thing a human being could witness; but when she did talk of it, her memories were very clear.

"We weren't prepared for it—well, no-one ever is. As for Flor-ence, the war descended like a baleful black cloud that slowly spread its insidious misery over the city. One day during the fi-nal disastrous stages of the battle, I was resting in my upstairs bedroom when I heard a loud noise from below. A troop of Ger-man soldiers had entered the house. We never used to close the gates, so they drove their trucks up through the front garden and pulled up right at the front door. I couldn't believe my eyes when I saw them there. It was an absurd scene. The soldiers were shouting in German and our maidservants were shouting back at them in Italian. They rifled through the closets and drawers, and moved all the cushions off the sofas. The troop leader told me they were going to use the house as a German army command post. After all, Il Palagio was perfect for that: it was built as a fortress on top of the hill and commanded a stra-tegic view of the city. I was desperate. The last thing I wanted to do was leave my home. I immediately called Salvatore in the office. He rushed home and argued back and forth with a Ger-man general in search of a solution. The Germans eventually left, but they placed three families in the house, as they had also done with the Corsini princes, who were our neighbors."

It is hard to picture Tà in the house after it had been seized and occupied. When she was talking about those days, I could feel all her anguish and fear, especially of the bombings, seep-ing through. Grandfather, practical and providential as ever, had had a small tunnel dug next to the villa to serve as an air-raid shelter.

"We lived day to day. There is nothing else like the sound of an air-raid siren. We sheltered in the cellars or in the tunnel to protect ourselves from the bombs, which luckily never hit anyone. It was almost impossible to find food because the Germans had commandeered everything. Our farmer continued to till the land, so we always had olive oil, vegetables, fruit, wine grapes and wheat grain with which to make flour. Meat was a rarity, and we had to make do instead with a nice bowl of minestrone, being careful not to waste any as there were many mouths to feed. If the Germans had discovered the food, not only would they have confiscated it, but they would also have arrested us."

Tà recalled how Grandfather had hidden an entire wheel of Parmesan on behalf of a neighbor, and lived in dread of its discovery. "I don't think I've ever been as afraid of anything as of that stupid cheese. We put the wheel of cheese in the cellar, then took it into the quarries in the woods. I wished for a wonderful family of mice to come along, eat up all the cheese, and make it disappear. I was in a state of high anxiety. The Germans, thank goodness, never found it, and Salvatore was very gratified to be able to return it to its owner."

In the early days of the war, Grandfather used to go into work every day. But as the war wore on, things became ever more complicated until, finally, Florence was occupied, the roads were sealed off, and he was no longer allowed to pass.

Tà's life in those years was utterly dedicated to raising her family. Fiamma was born in 1941, and Giovanna in 1943.

"It was an immense joy, despite the sorrows and horrors of war. Bringing children into the world is wonderful, even in the face of an uncertain future. I have always cherished the thought that God does not make miracles of creation only to give them a squalid existence."

I shall always be completely mystified by Tà's faith. Not even in the face of her life's several misfortunes did her faith ever waver. For her, faith was something that went beyond the ordinary; it was the instrument of her inner strength that saw her through all adversity. Through prayer, she found the energy to go on. It also came to her aid when Grandfather Salvatore found himself in a trickily paradoxical situation.

Owing to Salvatore's international success, the Germans were convinced he was a spy for the Americans, while the Americans thought he was a spy for the Germans because he had opened a store in Berlin. And the partisans, too, regarded him with a certain suspicion.

"Hard though it is to credit in these days of access to information in real time, during the war we were too far removed for much information on the political situation to reach us. So, even though we heard of war atrocities, we were mostly in the dark about what was going on. Only several years later did we learn the truth about the Nazi and Fascist barbarism. The devastation visited upon us in Florence, although it was less violent than elsewhere, still gave us some idea of the depths of brutality and horror to which man can sink."

August 3, 1944 was one of the worst days. Florence had been declared an open city, which meant it would be spared from the bombings that had destroyed so many other places. Hitler called it "the jewel of Europe." Even so, for fear of what he might do, the city had all the works of art that could be moved from museums, churches, and palaces brought to Palazzo Pitti. Protective sandbags were piled up around large statues and great architectural works. Tà knew that the city was prepared for the eventuality of a bombing, but unfortunately not for what happened.

On July 29, 1944, the inhabitants of Borgo San Jacopo were forced to find refuge in Palazzo Pitti because the Germans, breaking their word that Florence would be treated as an open city, had mined the bridges. The people were given a couple of hours to move out and were not allowed to take anything with them. They came to Palazzo Pitti for safety and slept where they could on the floors. On the afternoon of August 3, an order was issued prohibiting anyone from leaving the house or looking out the windows.

"Just before nine on that same evening, the city was rocked by a series of explosions so strong that we heard them from the cellars of Il Palagio. I can still hear the terrifying, monstrous sound the bombs made. The children were frightened and crying. When the explosions stopped, we ventured out of the cellars and went outside to see. A great pall of smoke and dust lay over Florence, and bits of detritus were swirling back and forth between the riverbanks. We felt chilled to the bone at the realization that the Germans had blown up all the bridges. The next morning, we heard on the radio that Ponte Vecchio had been spared, but the destruction of the Ponte Santa Trinita, one of the most beautiful bridges in the world, was an absolute sacrilege. When I eventually got to see the bridge, it was a sorry sight indeed. The span was gone forever, and the bridge had been reduced to two lumps of rock in the middle of the river."

Tà loved that bridge. Many times she had gazed enchanted by its beauty from the windows of Palazzo Spini Feroni, which, thank goodness, was not irreparably damaged. All its windows had been blown out, but that was nothing compared to what lay around. Tons and tons of buildings, entire streets that had remained intact over the centuries, had deliberately been demolished just to create mountains of rubble to impede the entrance of the Allies, who, having crossed Ponte Vecchio, were trying to bypass the Germans by making their way through the northern part of the city. A week later, the Allies occupied Florence passing right down the street in front of Il Palagio.

"For us, this was the worst part of the war. The Americans were shooting at the Germans up in Fiesole. As for us, we bunkered down in the cellars with all our neighbors. We sang songs to keep up morale. The Germans wanted to dynamite the villa and turn it into a rubble barricade against the Americans. After a long night of negotiations during which various bottles of wine were opened, Salvatore managed to persuade the German commander to spare Il Palagio. The commander, however, said that they would dynamite our neighbors' villa instead. So Salvatore opened a new round of negotiations and another bottle of wine. He could not allow our home to be spared at the cost of theirs."

They reached agreement to demolish only the outer walls of the villa to hinder the passage of the Americans, whereupon a small miracle happened. Incredibly, the eleventh-century chapel, built under the precinct walls of Il Palagio, somehow or other survived the dynamiting. "Ever afterwards we called it the chapel of Saints Crispino and Crispiniano, who are the patron saints of shoemakers," said Tà smiling.

The retreating Germans marched up to within a few meters of the front door, whereupon Tà heard the biggest explosion of her life. "Everything shook, the windows were blown in, but again, the chapel would not collapse."

The Germans continued to move north, up the road to Fiesole, from where they were swept away.

"With the Germans gone, we were free to walk around again with our children in our arms. I could hardly believe it. The American soldiers were fantastic. I will never forget how kind, smiling, cheerful, and friendly they were. They came with candy, chocolate, and white bread for all the families. Their mission now was to lift our spirits out of the doldrums of war. We will always be grateful for that memorable time. When we were able to get back to Florence, we saw the terrible damage that had been inflicted on the city. Before the ruins of Ponte Santa Trinita, I wept for the sheer wantonness of the destruction. The Florentines showed great courage and skill in putting the bridge back together. People dove into the River Arno to look for the original pieces from the four statues of the seasons that had stood on the bridge. An arm might be found here, and another one there. One of the statue heads was not found until 1961. The reconstruction of Ponte Santa Trinita was not only an enormous endeavor, but also a fine example of civic pride in action. Salvatore looked out of the windows of Palazzo Spini Feroni to watch the work progress day by day. It took ten years, but the bridge today is almost as beautiful as the old one." Tà omitted to mention (for it was not her custom to show off) that Grandfather was among those who funded the reconstruction.

One of the worst moments in that period came in August 1945, when Grandfather was arrested. Someone had written an anonymous letter to the Tuscan Committee of National Liberation (that is, the partisans) to report old rumors that he had collaborated with the Germans.

"Sadly, my suspicions fall on someone very close to us, who acted out of envy, but I shall never know for sure. Whoever it was, he did not take into account what a great man Salvatore had always been, how honest and upstanding," Tà said with sadness. She often put us on our guard against envy, which she saw as the worst form of negativity. For this reason, she often advised us to remain discreet and humble even in the face of great success.

Salvatore was arrested just as Tà was expecting her third child, my uncle Ferruccio.

"God only knows how I prayed that he would not arrive while his father was in prison. I have always enjoyed divine protection and so I had faith that the matter would soon be resolved. But I knew very few people in Florence and I did not see how I could get things moving."

Tà somehow managed to receive messages from Grandfather telling her whom to contact. One name he gave her was that of a midwife for whom he had built special shoes to help her walk after an accident. The woman dropped everything and came round to Tà's to assist her during the birth. But day followed day without his return, and she grew increasingly anxious. "It was like being in the Far West," said Tà. "There were no rules to follow and people meted their own justice." But on September 8, 1945 Grandfather Salvatore returned home, free from any false accusation.

"That date will forever be twice blessed. For on that same night, Ferruccio, our first son, was born. He seemed to have been awaiting his father's return to come into the world. Salvatore was by my side, as I had dreamed. Notwithstanding the difficulties of those years, I know they were a blessing because they fortified us as a family and enabled us to look to the future with eyes of hope."

Rebuild

The end of the war ushered in happy times for Tà and her whole family.

"There was a great feeling of freedom in the air, even though the problems that still needed solving were huge. The people of Florence were finally as one in their common desire to bring the city back to life after the long years of occupation and destruction. The streets were still full of rubble, but this didn't mean people couldn't still meet up socially. We met many people we hadn't seen for ages. Those who did not have a car got around by bicycle. And those who did not have a bicycle got around on foot; but the great thing was that, finally, we were FREE," said Tà putting the stress on that last word as if to underline the meaning of a concept that was so dear to her. "Nobody moaned about the struggles and privations, for we were all looking optimistically to the future. Florence, cut in half by the blowing-up of the bridges, was stitched back together with temporary bridges that, though not pleasing to the eye, served their purpose well. These were extraordinary times for us. We were thankful for what we had and excited by Salvatore's desire to start over. Our children could leave the nightmare of the war years behind and Salvatore could finally get back to work and bring the full weight of his creativity to bear on the task of rebuilding his severely weakened business. He was like an explosively creative volcano pumping out new design ideas for his shoes and new strategies for expanding his business. When trade restrictions were lifted, he was able to start working again with superior quality materials and products. The first step was returning to prewar elegance. Salvatore traveled up and down the country visiting one store after another without, alas, his beloved Alfa Romeo, which the Germans had commandeered. Repairing the damage to Palazzo Spini Feroni and getting the place back up and running took a while. But slowly, day by day, each piece was put back in its proper place, in the office as in the city. I set about rebuilding a normal life for our family. The birth of Ferruccio in those first days of freedom brought us immense joy. He was a chubby little thing, quite the opposite of his tall and slender self now. Indeed, he was so rotund that he found it hard to stay upright. Salvatore made him a pair of brown suede shoes with special soles perforated with little holes that worked like suction cups, which helped him stay on his feet. It was an invention of his that he then patented in November 1946," said Tà. She always kept those little shoes, which stirred tender emotions every time she looked at them, for they reminded her of their maker.

In Tà's studio in Il Palagio is a showcase displaying a collection of shoes of all kinds. When we were children, being allowed into this room was an event in itself. The few times I managed to sneak in, I was quickly chased out. There were always packages and parcels lying around the room, and I fondly imagined that they might be gifts for us. But the showcase with the collectible shoes was really the main attraction. I would stick my nose up against the pane and admire the display for as long as I was allowed. Whenever I saw Tà go into her studio, I would hold my breath in anticipation as if it were Christmas Day, because she never emerged from it empty-handed, but always bringing a "little surprise" with her. Not all her gifts were for children; there were often gifts for the grown-ups that she had put aside pending our next visit. Quite often, they turned out to be silk items of various sorts. Only later did I discover that Tà had been taking the company's offcuts of printed silk and having them made into the most disparate objects: tablecloths, quilts, placemats, and handbags. Those silk prints meant a great deal to me. They were the product of my mother's creative genius and they made me very proud of her. Before the Salvatore Ferragamo company had opened its first offices in Milan, she used to work from home, so it was not unusual to find her print designs scattered around the living room. My sister Angelica and I used to play jungle adventures with the fabric animals she made for us, and we would walk all over mother's precious drawings as she exasperatedly tried to work.

Tà's studio was accessed from the library, which doubled up as the television lounge. It was here that she would sit down punctually at 8 o'clock in the evening to watch the news on the main national TV channel. Below the boiseries full of books and photographs was an elegant sofa of blue satin on which any guests would be expected to sit under strict instructions to keep quiet. For herself, she preferred a large leather chair next to the round table, where she spread out a white cashmere plaid and placed her thick A4-size notepad on top. It may well be that the TV news inspired some of the thoughtful observations that she wrote down. She was disconcerted by stories of violent crime and human tragedies. Many letters for the Red Book would contain some commentary on events that had stood out in her mind. Tà felt true compassion for people in trouble and was most affected and moved to sad comment when the victims were young. While watching the news, she would never speak a word, as if her listening silence were a sign of respect for the world happening outside her own daily life. Anyone who dared break the rule of silence would be met with a reproachful shushing sound: *"Zitta, zitta, stai un po' zitta!"* (Shhh-shhh! Just shut up for a moment!), which would be followed by a peculiar sigh that brooked no response. Perhaps that is the phrase she is most associated with: she could silence anyone.

The hushed library with its boiserie walls and carpeted floor communicated with her mysterious, object-filled studio. In actual fact, Tà did not spend much time in that room, but she kept it strictly locked and added the key to her already substantial bunch. Every door had its own key in that huge house whose every nook and cranny and every detail she knew intimately, where everything had and was in its proper place. Her aesthete's eye took in every detail. As she passed from room to room, she would pause to straighten a cushion here, snip off a dead leaf from a plant there, take note of a thread bunching in the carpet, or of a stain on a piece of furniture. She would then take up her pad and note down everything that needed to be seen to as soon as possible. In order of importance, naturally.

I am reminded of a letter for the Red Book, addressed exclusively to us granddaughters, in which Tà offers some housekeeping tips.

"Even as an inexperienced newly-wed who was no expert on how to wash wool, cotton, silk, or linen, I realized that the washerwomen knew even less than me, so a lot of stuff was getting ruined. I tried to get to the root of the problem by examining the soap used and the temperature of the water. I found that the different fabrics were not being treated properly. So here are some tips, even though I am still not much of an expert. Never, on any fabric, use water that is too hot or soap that is too strong or of poor quality. If in doubt, ask a laundry service that you trust. Some top-quality things are ruined at once if washed the wrong way, but will stay beautiful and intact for years if treated right. I was just 18 when I got married, as you know. My mother died when I was in boarding school, so no-one was around to offer me advice such as I have given you above. You probably already know these things, but just in case you don't, pay attention to what I have told you because it is a real crime to waste stuff, especially nowadays. Sorry if I have bored you a little. A big hug and all my best wishes, your Tà."

I loved this letter. It moved me to tenderness but it also reconfirmed how attentive she was to every detail, including in the home, and how she wanted us to do the same. She found wastefulness and carelessness to be inadmissible flaws.

The entire household of Il Palagio spoke of Tà's love of beautiful things, of her energy and meticulousness. Everything came under her watchful, perfectionist eye. She ran the household a bit like she would later run the company. Everyone had a well-defined and appreciated role under her supervision.

None of her children attended preschool. With its cooks, serving staff, farmers, gardeners, and drivers, Il Palagio was very well equipped to teach them plenty of skills in diverse fields.

"Despite the help, I was always busy with things to do," said Tà in a tone of wonderment. Knowing her, it does not surprise me in the least. It makes me smile when I think of how she looked after children. From when I was born, I never saw Tà not working, so it is hard for me to picture her as a patient mother. "I breastfed all four of them, including your mother, with the help of a wet nurse," she told me one day when I was visiting her in Florence with Ottavia and Leo. The children, seeing her in authoritarian pose behind her office desk, had asked if she had had any children. Fulvia, my mother, born in 1950, was the fourth of six children. I would have thought that the use of a wet nurse was an outdated custom by then. And yet Grandfather Salvatore and Great-grandfather Fulvio went specifically to the town of Frosinone to find one who would be suitable. In choosing a wet nurse, the things to consider were the size of the breast, the condition of the nipples, and the baby's mouth. When Uncle Leonardo was born a few years after my mother, Grandfather Salvatore went alone to choose the nurse. "He got so embarrassed! He tried but failed to copy my father's clinical attitude, and gave up. Fortunately, there are no wet nurses anymore and, in particular, ones chosen by these methods," she said laughing at the look of amazement on the faces of my children.

English nannies also play a part in our family history. Grandfather wanted his children to be able to work with him and he foresaw that the United States would continue to be the strongest market for the company. Being able to speak and write correct English was therefore indispensable. So Tà chose to hire only English babysitters, a policy that has come to be known in our house as "the sad story of the English nannies." She went through one after the other: "Either they were unprofessional, or they could not accustom themselves to life in Italy. But some stayed with us for several years, which allowed me the satisfaction of accomplishing my goal of having children who speak perfect English. In later years, I got given the job of picking the babysitters for you grandchildren. I once helped Ferruccio find one for his kids. We made our selections at Palazzo Spini Feroni; this was the 1970s, and the 20 or so girls who turned up had very long hair and were wearing miniskirts. I lined them all up. Not one of them inspired any confidence in me. No, no, no, no... Then I saw a respectable-looking middle-aged lady seated at the back of the room. I made a beeline for her and informed her that she was hired. But alas, she was the mother of one of the girls I had just turned down."

The person we grandchildren really wanted to look after us was the wonderful Tata Bea, Tà's lady-in-waiting and housekeeper, as well as the world's most patient and good-natured woman, and not just because she put up with her employer's impulsive character. Tata Bea was sweetness incarnate, always so gentle with each of us. Another reason I liked going to stay at Tà's was that I knew Tata Bea would end up looking after me. She bathed us in the evening and told us bedtime stories. She never got angry with us, she was our ally, and we reciprocated by behaving well. If she was upbraided by Tà, we would rush to console her. I once saw her crying, and took her hand. Yet she immediately told me that Tà's fits of bad temper were because she was tired as a result of her responsibilities. It took me years to understand this.

As a child I feared Tà's bad moods, nor was I alone. Despite always being terribly busy, she could always find time to give someone a dressing-down.

"No number of nannies and domestic staff can replace the mother's watchful eye or her central role in the life of the child. This, I am sure, is the only way to set your conscience at ease. To raise a child is like running a railway. Parents are supposed to look after the station, the platforms, and engine maintenance so that the trains can depart for their different destinations. Children must be left free to express themselves but," she would add emphatically, "they must not go off the rails."

I am pretty sure the station and the maintenance work in the Ferragamo household were run impeccably well: so much so that all the trains left by the same track, the one laid down by Grandfather Salvatore.

"The self-discipline that my father taught me kept me on the straight and narrow path through life," was one of Tà's sayings. "From Salvatore I then learned the rules of life."

She once saved and sent us an article describing in effective detail how consumerism and excessive wealth may cause untold damage to children.

"The child's mind is highly susceptible to wrong-headed attitudes. As we all know, life itself and this world of ours demand a great deal of work and self-abnegation. It is not good for a child to have the wrong expectations. The article is self-explanatory, so I don't need to go into details here. I know you are wonderful mothers and fathers, but today's consumerist lifestyle distorts our view of many things. It is important to inculcate in our children a sense of respect for others, and I am thankful once again to Salvatore for teaching this principle to our children from an early age. It is one of the virtues for which they are acknowledged. I apologize for taking the liberty of sending you this article, but I'm sure you will appreciate the intention behind it. A big hug to all of you and to all your children, Tà."

At the time of their marriage, Grandfather was regarded as one of the most successful men in Italy. He had achieved this through hard work, without any inheritance or family help. From personal experience, he knew that there was nothing better than making the best and most constructive use of one's special talents and interests. But he also knew how to value money. Each child received a monthly allowance, but it came with stringent conditions. The sum, never very much anyway, was correlated to school performance. Tà and Grandfather kept a blackboard chart into which they would enter the highest grades received by the children in their various school subjects. The aim was not to frustrate them—quite the contrary, it was intended to spur them onwards and upwards. They could do what they wanted with the money, but those who saved up got a bonus at the end of the year of double their savings. In the summertime, too, when they were at the house in Forte dei Marmi, the arrangement stayed in place. The children earned an allowance for doing small jobs: the boys for making wooden objects, the girls for embroidering napkins and handkerchiefs. Free to choose, they usually chose to spend it all at a toy store in Pietrasanta. But when Grandfather arrived at the weekend, those who had saved up were rewarded.

"Dire consequences, alas, attend the lust for money. I see evidence of this everywhere today. Many young people have so much that they don't appreciate the value of anything. It's a terrible thing to see. After the privations of the war years, it was very tempting to spoil children by giving them anything they asked for. Salvatore and I, however, could see that in the long run, to spoil them would be to make a fatal error. Life doesn't give you everything you want when you want it, so why should parents?"

My mother used to tell me that she had few toys as a child. The rule was that at Christmas and on their birthday, each child would receive a single, special gift. "And how they appreciated it!" said Tà. This sage custom was passed on to us grandchildren, albeit with a tweak to the rule. I never returned from Christmas at the Ferragamo house with more than one gift; nor did I ever receive a gift twice from the same person. A month before Christmas, so that everyone would have time to choose carefully, each of us would draw by lot the name of our gift recipient. The only exception was Tà's "envelope," a sum of money that she apportioned according to age and sex, which meant that my male cousins usually got more. The females, however, would be rewarded their due in other circumstances.

Tà always told us not to be discriminatory and to treat the humblest as we would treat royalty. Grandfather was exemplary in this respect. For him, good manners were not an accessory but a necessity. He made sure our parents knew that they always had to acknowledge people with a greeting, look everyone straight in the eye, and always say thank you.

"Around the dinner table, we talked about everything in the presence of our children, and they absorbed our way of acting, behaving, and thinking. We did not have particularly strict rules, but those we did have, including table manners, had to be respected. Anyone who dropped anything had to pick it up at once. Anyone who dirtied had to clean. Anyone at fault for their behavior had to apologize immediately. The girls had to make their own beds, the boys had to help with the heavier jobs. The house had plenty of staff, who could be very helpful but were also very busy people who warranted respect. Salvatore used to talk easily and naturally about his work to me in front of the children. The whole family was therefore always fully abreast with what was going on, and Salvatore could give free rein to his zest, enthusiasm, and creativity. He associated work with self-realization and the happiness of a dream come true. Work was never the source of fatigue, tedium, or grievance, even when it demanded effort. Everyone told everyone else about how their day had gone. Once Fiamma announced that she felt exasperated by how one of her teachers was treating her. She was convinced he hated her because he never addressed a word to her. Salvatore advised her to leave a flower on his desk. The experiment proved successful, and the teacher in question changed his attitude toward her. Fiamma was content, while everyone learned the lesson that a small gesture of kindness can sometimes make all the difference."

Tà was the doyen of acts of practical kindness. Sensitive and attentive to others, she always had the right word and the right gesture ready. No matter the environment or situation, she could always establish a feeling of affinity with her interlocutor, whether prince or laborer. I remember once how before stepping into her office, she paused to take in the sight of the girls in reception. "You all look totally fabulous today!" she told them. Then she turned to me: "Sometimes a single compliment is worth more than a book of instructions."

Tà used to tell us many stories that demonstrated the importance of elegance and aesthetic sensibility.

In 1947, Grandfather was invited to Dallas to receive the Neiman Marcus Fashion Award for his hugely successful "invisible sandal" made from transparent nylon fishing line. It was his first return to the United States after almost twenty years. For Tà, it was her first visit to the land that Salvatore loved so much, so she was filled with excitement and curiosity.

"We boarded the *Queen Elizabeth*, a magnificent cruise ship, and crossed the ocean to New York. Back then, people did not hop on and off airplanes like they do today. A transatlantic trip was seen as an unbridled luxury; it was really the height of glamour. The service was amazing—each passenger had a personal attendant. Dinner was an event every night: ladies wore evening dresses, and Salvatore looked great in his tuxedo."

When speaking of aesthetic matters, Tà adopted an irresistibly charming tone. For her, elegance was everything. She dressed with discreet refinement and always wore a necklace of pearls around her neck, even at the seaside during the summer. Being well dressed and neat was part of her self-discipline, but was also intrinsic to her character.

"On the ship there was a small staircase that led into the dining hall, like a stage on which everyone made an entrance, pausing for a moment to be seen. All the passengers were very elegant, but every evening all eyes would invariably turn toward the most beautiful and famous of them, Rita Hayworth. She had such a polite, delicate, exquisite manner..."

On that same voyage, Tà met Christian Dior, who was also headed to Dallas, also to receive an award from the Neiman Marcus company. Dior told Tà that short skirts were the result of wartime restrictions, and that it was time to put that period behind them by creating longer, more feminine skirts. He was convinced this longer style would be a hit, and he was right—for a while.

"They got on fabulously with Grandfather. The Neiman Marcus event included a fashion show with models dressed in Dior's clothes and shod in Salvatore's shoes. To their enormous surprise, they saw that their creations seemed to have been made to match. Though neither had planned it, their aesthetic styles were perfectly complementary."

At the time, Dior was developing his first perfume and promised to send grandmother an early sample. A few weeks after her return to Italy, Tà received the first bottle of *Miss Dior*, which remained her favorite perfume for years. Even now, I would be able to identify that scent from a range of thousands.

"As we arrived in New York on September 2, 1947, I was breathless with anticipation. I had woken up at 5 o'clock in the morning and gone up on deck with Salvatore to watch as we approached our destination. The city was silent at first, but as the ship drew slowly near, it began to come to life. We passed under the Statue of Liberty, just as Salvatore had done on his first voyage. We took a taxi from the port to the hotel, and I had my nose glued to the window looking out all the way. I couldn't believe what I saw before my eyes. I had never seen so many automobiles, so many buildings, stores, and people in my life... We stayed in New York for a week. There were some business meetings, but I never missed an opportunity to visit the city and go shopping. What surprised me the most was the positive attitude of the people, their incredible optimism. I had the feeling that nobody was bothered about who you were or where you came from. It seemed to me that everything was possible in that country. You simply had to be willing and prepared to work, and you would make your life a success."

I recall how on all the several occasions I met Tà in New York, the city was still able to inspire her with this sense of euphoria. She would receive us in her apartment at the Olympic Tower, where we would be told about the fascinating people she had met at work and about her latest ideas and plans for the future. Tà always returned from New York both pleased and bursting with almost volcanic energy and enthusiasm.

"The award ceremony in Dallas was beautiful. After the show, there was a gala dinner, with speeches from each of the award-winning designers. Salvatore had not prepared a speech, and was so flustered that he was barely able to whisper out a few thank yous, which were met by the applause of the hall anyway. I lived that evening like a fairy tale. It was a welcome from a country that means a great deal to our whole family."

The United States had not only nurtured the shoemaker of dreams, but had also enabled him to build a special relationship with the world of cinema that became part of the company's cultural tradition and endures to this day. When Grandfather got his business back up and running after the war, the new generation of actresses and actors came knocking on his door. And never left him thereafter. No other designer has dressed so many stars of cinema: Mary Pickford and Joan Crawford in the 1920s; Greta Garbo and Katharine Hepburn in the 1930s; Ava

Gardner and Lana Turner in the 1940s; Audrey Hepburn and Sophia Loren in the 1950s; Brigitte Bardot in the 1960s; Madonna, Drew Barrymore, and Nicole Kidman today.

To act the part of Evita Perón in the famous Alan Parker film, Madonna asked specifically for a reproduction of the shoes that Grandfather had made for the real Evita when she visited Italy in 1947. Evita was one of Salvatore's most loyal customers, and ordered dozens upon dozens of pairs of shoes from him. A museum in Buenos Aires, which was inaugurated in her honor in 2002 in a magnificent historic building a few short steps from my old apartment, displays some of the shoes that he made especially for her, using extremely rare and costly materials.

"Salvatore told me that Evita was one of the most astute women he had ever met. Madonna played the part very well. In *Ever After: A Cinderella Story*, Drew Barrymore wore sabots that, though not made of glass, entered the history of cinema nonetheless. Then there were the 20 pairs of shoes worn by Nicole Kidman in *Australia*, the shoes worn by Jack Nicholson in *The Departed*, by Catherine Zeta-Jones in *Traffic*, by Tom Cruise in *Mission Impossible*, as well as the many others that I either can't call to mind or don't even know about, but all of which continue a tradition that redounds to the honor of Salvatore, whose name is still, after almost a century, acclaimed as a symbol of style in the world of cinema."

Tà told me this proudly after I had gifted her the catalog of the Evita Museum of Buenos Aires and we were leafing through it together on a cold Sunday just before Christmas, in front of her splendid Neapolitan-style Christmas crib, which she unfailingly put up every holiday season. She recognized a pair of Salvatore-made shoes in the catalog and commented emotionally how he had managed to stamp his presence on every country of the world and to always build good relations with important people.

"Shortly after we got married, Salvatore told me about his first experiences in Hollywood in the 1920s. I listened in fascination to his stories, though I knew absolutely nothing about cinema. There were no cinemas in Bonito and the only time I went to the movies was on special occasions in Naples. Movie stars were rare in those days. I could never have imagined that one day I would meet and, in some cases, even make friends with people who had seemed like fantastical beings for me back then. Some even visited me at home. When things became easier after the war, many actresses traveled to Florence to visit the boutique. When Salvatore came home for dinner, he would tell us about who had been in the store. One fine summer morning in 1949, the person who came into the store was the divine Greta Garbo. She told Salvatore that she had no shoes and wanted to spend a long time walking around the city."

She had been his loyal customer ever since the days of the Hollywood Boot Shop. Grandfather created some special models for her that later became very popular: the *Greta*, the *Zita*, and another model with a closed toe and small heel, also made for long walks.

"Garbo loved Salvatore's shoes and was the only one of his clients who could argue with him. She was enamored of flat shoes and absolutely refused any kind of heel. Salvatore, however, managed to convince her for the health of her feet to wear the heel he had designed for her, the sole purpose of which was to raise the arch of her foot. She was a very private person and extremely jealous of her privacy, but she had a close relationship with Grandfather. She arrived in Palazzo Spini Feroni dressed completely informally in a blouse and pants. When she left, a crowd of people was waiting for her outside the shop. She got into a waiting car and, without giving anyone a smile or an autograph, was whisked away. Salvatore was so respectful of her privacy that I never had the pleasure of meeting her either. Which is a pity because I was keen to make her acquaintance. In Florence she was famous for her walks alone around the city, and Salvatore's shoes were part of her daily routine."

As she told me this, on the living room table was the catalog of an exhibition of Greta Garbo's wardrobe organized jointly by the Museo Salvatore Ferragamo and the actress's grandchildren. After her death, many pairs of shoes that Salvatore had made for her were discovered in her New York apartment. Garbo's grandson came all the way to Florence to meet the matchless Stefania Ricci, director of the Museum and head of the company historical archive, who deserves recognition for the fine work she has done in tracking down most of the shoe design patents registered by Grandfather over the years. The grandson was storing Garbo's entire wardrobe at his home on Rhode Island. Thanks to this happy meeting, in 2010 an exhibition dedicated to the outfits of the curious and mysterious character who was Greta Garbo was organized at the Triennale di Milano in celebration of her highly distinctive, completely personal, simple, yet extremely elegant style. I marveled at the number of accessories she had, hats as well as shoes. They added a finishing and defining touch to her understated style.

"In addition to Greta Garbo and Jean Harlow, whom Grandfather greatly admired, another Hollywood star, Claudette Colbert, was an important person in our life. She was an excellent actress as well as a very dear and affectionate friend. We became friends in the 1950s when she was in hospital in Montecatini Terme for treatment of Hailey's syndrome, a disease similar to herpes, and Salvatore was looking after her. She had been in desperation over her condition and didn't know where to turn. Salvatore managed to find a doctor in Switzerland who cured her in a month. Claudette was extremely grateful to him for that kindness, which marked the beginning of our enduring friendship. After Salvatore's death, she visited me in Capri many times. One evening after dinner, we were having fun dancing with Costanzo Paturzo, the local "King of the Tarantella." It was so funny to see Claudette, so sophisticated and delicate, cavorting about with this most unabashed Neapolitan showman."

Though I was only five or six years old at the time, I still have joyful memories of Tà's parties on the terrace of Villa Tirrena, with the views of the moonlit Faraglioni sea stacks and Paturzo entertaining the guests and the family with songs and dances. When Tà did join in with the dancing and singing, which was not often, she did so with gusto and laughter, carefree at last. Dancing was one of Tà's favorite things, not that she treated herself to this pleasure as much as she deserved, though my aunts and uncles do have some memories of her indulging in the occasional covert morning dancing to music before going to the office.

She was especially fond of Claudette Colbert, with whom she shared vacation time.

"Claudette once invited me to stay at her beautiful home in Barbados just a few days after Ronald Reagan and his wife had left. I felt honored to receive the same treatment as the President of the United States. Claudette was a wonderful hostess. We breakfasted together every morning under a fabulous gazebo in the garden, surrounded by monkeys that ran up and down the trees trying to steal our bread. Then we went for a swim in the ocean; she was elegance incarnate even in a bathing suit. She always wore a hat and sunglasses. She was perfect. Like me, she had been widowed: her husband, a soldier, died shortly after the Barbados house was built. We had this great sorrow in common."

One evening in Capri, as we were on the terrace admiring a gigantic moon that lit up the Faraglioni like daylight, Tà turned to me with glistening eyes and said, "Do you know what I miss most, Ginevra? Your Grandfather's hand holding mine. When he held my hand I felt a powerful surge of energy, and I felt happy and at peace. I miss the feeling of that hand so much."

Her confession touched me. How often we take a gesture of affection for granted!

One summer, between one trip and another, I dropped in on her in Capri to say hello. Tà often had guests, not all of whom were bundles of fun, but this time I caught her on her own, so I had the luxury of just her and me spending a few days together. Every day we took breakfast together on the terrace before going down to the little piazza for some errands. In reality, Tà liked to check out the window display of the Ferragamo store and compare it with the window displays of other brands, and take mental notes that she would then make known to the office. The other shopping activities were essentially for fun. We stopped to order caprese cakes to be picked up in the afternoon on the way back. Now and then we would visit Alberto and Lina, who ran a jewelry shop near the piazza, where Tà delighted in looking at and commenting on the fabulous jewels. From there, in one of those open taxis that go whizzing up and down from Marina Piccola almost touching one another as they round the curves of the narrow roads awash with bougainvillea, we arrived mid-morning at La Canzone del Mare, a historic bathing resort frequented by the Neapolitan aristocracy and the intelligentsia. Here Tà took her daily swim in the saltwater pool, then went to take her place at the table with her friend, the unforgettable Dorotea Liguori. Of Japanese origin but with Italian blood, Dorotea was a very wealthy and worldly woman of business who worked in the jewelry trade. She was a petite lady, simply bursting with intelligence from every pore of her being, with a face that was both comical and wise, albeit mostly hidden behind enormous dark glasses. She went around bejeweled from head to toe at all times of the day and night. Dorotea inherited the empire of her father, Don Gennaro Liguori, who had started out importing pearl and coral from Japan before expanding its activities across the entire jewelry sector. She was a brilliant, international, and cultured woman who managed to further increase the economic wealth and cultural worth of her company. In the 1970s, she had a luxurious five-star hotel, the Sakura, built around her house in Torre del Greco. She had a different story to tell every day, with which she generously regaled us as she sat before a table spread with the finest delicacies the island has to offer. Tà had a great time with Dorotea, whom she held in genuinely high esteem. They were two single women, and they were both deeply devoted to work. A few days in their company was like attending a course on business enterprise, spiced with very sophisticated touches of femininity.

In the afternoon we returned home, always giving ourselves plenty of time to do things without any rush. I do not think that in all my life I ever saw Tà stressed out from being in a rush. Yet she always had an infinite number of things to do. She always managed to plan out her day just right, devoting the right time to everything and allowing herself time to pause for reflection on important matters. After giving orders for dinner, she would take out her notebook, which she never abandoned (not even for her holiday in Capri) and would sit on the beautiful terrace at sunset and busy herself with her notes. Those were days I will never forget. Tà managed to furnish me with endless advice while generously showering me with affection, which sometimes landed with a rather imperious or even harsh tone. Whatever else she was, she was not cold-hearted.

One evening I broached upon a delicate subject: jealousy in the couple. She replied with her natural good humor:

"Think what it was like for me with all those actresses who came to Salvatore for their shoes: Rita Hayworth, Bette Davis, Ingrid Bergman, Gloria Swanson, Lana Turner, Ginger Rogers, Anna Magnani, Sophia Loren and Marlene Dietrich, whose size-5 foot was one of the most beautiful Salvatore ever cradled in his hands. Dietrich was obsessed with Salvatore's shoes. She worked with him on the design and on the choice of materials, and didn't miss a trick. She would order an incredible number of shoes, wear them once or twice, and then get rid of them because she already wanted a new design. Some actresses were, well, very capricious..." she said, giving me a knowing wink.

"But it is thanks to the caprice of these actresses that Salvatore unquestionably qualifies as the very first exporter of Italian luxury products—he started selling his shoes in America as far back as the 1920s. He was far-sighted enough to see how the label with the simple phrase "Made in Italy" attached to products imported into the United States could serve not just as a mere indicator of origin, but effectively also as a brand guaranteeing world-beating Italian craftsmanship and design. He was sure that his demanding American customers would want to buy other products of comparable quality, but first they had to know that such products existed.

The end of the 1940s was an effervescent time for Italy. The country was rebuilding itself and optimism was in the air. For Salvatore, whose self-belief never wavered, it was the ideal time to push ahead with his plans. To give concrete form to his ideas, he joined forces with many who shared his vision. Together with Giovanni Battista Giorgini, a very capable businessman who was a great connoisseur of Italian craftsmanship and high fashion, he organized public events in Italy as well as major fashion shows in Florence attended by designers such as Schuberth, Fabiani, Marucelli, Capucci, Carosa. Unfortunately, some of these names failed to achieve the sort of wide distribution they were looking for. Creativity alone is no guarantee of success. A company must also follow all the right steps to get its products into the hands of customers. "Think of all those talented artists whose names have remained unknown," said Tà with yet another of those apparently throw-away remarks through which she instructed me in the basic principles of business economics.

She frequently returned to the question of sales distribution, including in a letter for the Red Book.

"We should treat Ferragamo's vast, international retail distribution network as our proudest achievement and as our message to the world. The message speaks for itself and redounds to the credit of us and whoever runs our company and manages our brand. Distribution is everything. It requites and repays all the efforts of those who pour their energy and passion into creating and manufacturing, day after day, to the absolute best of their ability. Work is a type of mission, in that it sustains a system that benefits the country as whole and all of us, contributing to progress. We must be tireless, devoted, constant and assiduously attentive to keeping the shining light of our business alive in the world. The fruits of success will follow. What better reward can there be for our efforts?"

When Tà returned to the United States in 1961, she was amazed to see the Made in Italy label everywhere.

"Salvatore's dream had come more than true. Florence, his adopted city, was again supplying the world with luxury goods many centuries after the Renaissance. Italian style became renowned not only in the world of fashion but also in the sectors of design and automobile manufacture. Fashion shows burgeoned also in Milan, which boosted not only industry and the economy but also tourism and culture. Exports became a major driver of the Italian economy and provided a propitious context for postwar reconstruction. Your Grandfather was the leading light in all of this. Today, the Made in Italy label still works like a powerful brand, but the economic situation has become more complicated, especially since the adoption of the euro. Production costs have become so high that many companies have had to move their manufacturing out of Italy. I am fortunate to be able to say that our products are still made in Italy. This is what true luxury means."

Wanda Ferragamo
photographed in her
garden, 1960s

Wanda Ferragamo with
her daughter Fulvia,
her granddaughter
Ginevra Visconti, and
her great-granddaughter
Ottavia

Wanda's parents,
Giovanna Pellegrino   The courtyard of the
and Fulvio Miletti   Miletti house in Bonito

The Ferragamo family at
Palazzo Spini Feroni, 2016

The Ferragamo family trip
to Bonito, May 1994

The Red Books that Wanda
Ferragamo gave her
grandchildren to collect
and keep her letters

Wanda's brother Silvio with their
mother Giovanna, 1930s

The round-bottomed doll that always
returns to an upright position after
Wanda and her father, 1940s   being pushed over

Wanda as a girl in Bonito,
late 1930s

Wanda and Salvatore
at the time of their
engagement, 1940

The wedding of Wanda and
Salvatore Ferragamo in the
church of Santa Lucia in
Naples, November 9, 1940

Wanda and Salvatore
Ferragamo on their
honeymoon on the Amalfi
Coast and Sorrento

The Red Book open to the pages displaying the "1957 Magic Wanda!" letter with the dedication that Salvatore Ferragamo inscribed to his wife on the first page of his autobiography

The letter that Wanda Ferragamo wrote Ginevra shortly after the latter's wedding

The Flag of the United States of America
honoring Salvatore Ferragamo. The flag was
hoisted on the United States' Capitol on
June 5, 2009 to commemorate the 111th
anniversary of his birth. Then on December
18, 2010, the same ceremony was carried
out to celebrate Wanda's birthday

Wanda in the garden of
Villa Il Palagio in Fiesole
(Florence) in the early days
of marriage

Salvatore Ferragamo in the garden of his
house, Villa Il Palagio in Fiesole (Florence),
looking at the sky through a telescope
with his children Fiamma, Giovanna,
and Ferruccio, 1949

The Ferragamo family on the
steps of Villa Il Palagio in
Fiesole (Florence), 1980s

Wanda Ferragamo pictured
on the cover of a Japanese
magazine

Wanda with her daughter
Fiamma, 1942

Ferruccio, Leonardo,
Fiamma, Fulvia and
Giovanna in 1953

Wanda and Salvatore with
their son Massimo, 1959

Wanda with her daughter
Giovanna, 1944

Ferruccio and Fulvia
Ferragamo, 1953

Salvatore and Wanda Ferragamo with their six children in 1959: Giovanna, Fiamma, Ferruccio (standing), Massimo, Leonardo, Fulvia (sitting)

Mr. and Mrs. Ferragamo on board the ocean liner *Queen Elizabeth* headed to the United States, where Salvatore would receive the Neiman Marcus Award, 1947

Mr. and Mrs. Ferragamo on board
the ocean liner *Queen Elizabeth*
headed to the United States, where
Salvatore would receive the Neiman
Marcus Award, 1947

Wanda Ferragamo with
Costanzo Paturzo, the "King
of the Tarantella" of Capri

Wanda and Salvatore
Ferragamo with their family in
Forte dei Marmi, early 1950s

Family Life

The Viesca estate, my grandparents' country home 30 kilometers from Florence, was one of Tà's favorite places. In a photo that my mother hung in her Milan office, Tà is sitting on the steps of the beautiful house with that typically proud look in her eyes. Tà had built her family nest in the main villa, which dates back to the sixteenth century, and converted the surrounding farms into a high-end tourism business project. The property was rounded off by a small chapel, of which Tà was especially fond.

"The day we bought Viesca marked the start of ten years of immense joy for me. After your mother was born, your uncles Leonardo and Massimo completed our family. Only then did we start looking for a house to spend our weekends. We already had the place at Forte dei Marmi, but Salvatore wanted somewhere he could farm, somewhere to raise our children amid the beauty of the Tuscan countryside. He worked so hard and traveled so much that it was important for us to have a place to relax. Days spent in nature, with their rhythm of simplicity and authenticity, were of great comfort to him. Spending time with his children, farming and working in the country gave him rest. Viesca was consequently a true panacea."

They purchased the estate in 1955 from the Scatena family. When the former owners closed the gate behind them for the final time, they left everything behind as it was, including some 20 farmhouses where farmers lived with their families and stables for the Chianina cattle. Tà and Grandfather had the antique objects and furniture they discovered in the manor house's attic restored by local craftsmen.

"It was a comfort to be surrounded by that small community of people," Tà recalled with gratitude. "But life in the countryside was beginning to change radically: farmers were quitting the land for jobs at manufacturing companies in cities and an entire agriculture-based civilization, which had lasted for centuries, was gradually disappearing."

Tà was so fond of Viesca because it was the only property she was able to "build" entirely with Grandfather, furnishing it to her liking.

"We would leave on Friday afternoon. As soon as we arrived, the farmers came by to talk to Salvatore about the week's work. I threw myself totally and passionately into making everything neat and tidy. A house is like a person. If you don't show discipline and love, everything falls apart."

The farmhouses on the property had sound foundations, but needed a vigorous restoration. Some of them, such as the main residence and chapel, were restored as per their original design. As time went by, many buildings were abandoned and left derelict. Tà took it upon herself to restore them and put them to new use. Today, those houses are villas nestling among green hills and gardens. She also created a small museum of agriculture, a tribute she happily made to when tilling the fields was an integral part of local history. The museum houses artifacts and agricultural implements, memories of country life from days gone by, which were recovered and collected after Tà and Grandfather purchased the property: a sign of the love they both had for the Tuscan countryside.

"Although each one is a tool with its own distinct function, handmade by simple farmers, they look like works of art, like

Giacometti sculptures!" said Tà with delight and satisfaction as she showed them to us.

Activities that were once a normal part of country life, such as cultivating a vegetable garden, rearing animals and living a sustainable life, form the core of the Viesca farm holiday business today, appreciated for the most part by non-Italians who rent out the old farmhouses for weeks on end. Every so often, Tà would forward thank you letters she'd received from people who stayed at Viesca to be kept in the Red Book. One was from her friend Frederick J. Ryan, a senior White House official who complimented her on her magnificent work, kindness, and hospitality. These comments repaid Tà for all the effort and energy she had put into the place.

Grandfather was keenly interested in botany and the natural world, and wanted to pass on this curiosity to his children by personal example.

"He put up photographs of the world's main varieties of hens (Plymouth, Rhode Island Reds, etc.) in the Viesca dinette. There was one of each variety in the chicken coop, beautifully separated into special little hutches. In the mornings, Fiamma and Giovanna went to collect the eggs, writing on each one the breed they came from. This helped them learn the mysteries of nature while having fun. Delightful little girls, they were also somewhat mischievous, and not always respectful of the farm supervisor's wife who, truth be told, was by no means easy to get along with. Once the girls went into the chicken coop and deliberately mixed the chicks of one breed up with another. Since the chicks all looked the same, their shenanigans weren't at first apparent, but as the chickens grew, people began to notice. The farm supervisor's wife went crazy, running about trying to catch chickens and put them back into the right cages."

Tà was never so endearingly human as when she was delightedly and laughingly recounting these anecdotes of family life. These memories clearly took her back to happy times.

"I've already mentioned how your Grandfather managed your parents' allowances to encourage them to save. One year, he suggested the kids invest their savings in something big. Alongside teaching them the prudence of saving, he wanted to show them the satisfaction of investing their money and seeing it pay off. He suggested that they all club together and buy a calf. The children were thrilled. He took their savings, but because he was, as ever, busy with work, he forgot to purchase the calf. The following week, when we returned to Viesca, the kids were thrilled at the prospect of seeing their beautiful calf. To make up for his failure, Salvatore raced off to buy a calf from one of the farm laborers, and ended up paying far more than the savings amounted to. The children, however, never found out about any of this. When they saw that little calf, it was love at first sight. Every Friday, as soon as we arrived at Viesca, they jumped out of the car, rushed over to it, pampered it and checked that the farmers were taking good care of their calf. They were also keen to see if their investment was paying off. Two years later, it was time to sell the calf, which by then had reached a goodly size. The sale yielded about two hundred thousand liras, and although the kids were sorry to see the calf go, they were duly impressed. It was a great lesson."

Tà remembered those times as a true family idyll. They could all be together on weekends at Viesca. "Being together" was Tà's favorite thing, of supreme value to her. Day in, day out throughout her entire life she worked to secure her great wish: a united family. We are a big family, and in spite of character differences, curiously we get along very well. Perhaps Tà was right when she said there is no way to keep a family together other than making occasions to get together, get to know one another, try to understand each other.

That's why, at least twice a year, she invited us all to Viesca. It was a joy for her, and also a kind of mission. Unfortunately, I had just moved to Buenos Aires when one of these meetings took place, but I will never forget the letter and the thoughts she sent. Thanks to the Red Book, I still have it.

"My dears, it is always such a great joy to see you, especially here, all together. When we're together, I feel like I'm reinforcing the great Faith and the grand ideals that brought us this far. The Faith that nourishes our daily work cannot be extinguished, whatever the bitterness, disappointments, and ingratitude this type of work entails. And do you know why it cannot be extinguished? Because this Faith is bigger than us. Sometimes you come home discouraged, or feel like giving up because other stronger, younger people can carry the weight of work. But after a night's rest, just the vague doubt that things are not safe and sound as they should be makes that Faith show up more intense than before. And that's before I even mention dreams. Salvatore was a great dreamer and passed his dreams on to us. We remain devoted to his dreams, having made many of them come true. As he wished, his children work together in harmony; Salvatore Ferragamo is now a fashion house with a wide range of products, and distribution has expanded considerably. Salvatore would be overjoyed if he could see his grandchildren at work today, full of industry, knowing that they are honoring his memory, sacrifices, and labor. We never stop dreaming. As talented American manager Carly Fiorina (president and CEO of Hewlett Packard) liked to say, our journey is not a destination or a finishing line, it is a long and unending voyage, and this is something we hope to pass on to the upcoming generations. We have a duty to pass on our values and our Faith to them, to make them feel more involved, proud to belong to a company whose moral and cultural values they share. People who join the company know that they must show obedience, loyalty, and allegiance; they also know that they will be able to advance their careers in a secure and caring work environment. This is the climate you must create if you wish to ensure that everyone pulls together for the same cause, with enthusiasm, passion, and a shared Faith to achieve shared goals. You will get ahead in life, you will grow, and inevitably your responsibilities will grow too. My dear children, so far we've touched on questions of Faith, ideals, and dreams. I've told you how important it is to have a dream to fuel and energize your inner drive and enable you to persevere. Now I feel obligated to underscore something you must not forget: stay abreast of what is going on in your business line and be practical and hands-on in all you do. Both are essential. Do not be charmed by fancy words, see for yourself what is being done, and how it's being done, too. Arduous though it is, you'll find it is also necessary, for my many years of experience, if they have taught me anything, it is always to double-check. Details are crucial and absolutely must not be overlooked. Delegate where you have to, as you will, but check afterwards. It is your job to discreetly keep an eye on what managers are up to, both to praise them and set them right. Unfortunately, there will be some bad apples whose incompetence will spoil the barrel. That's why you need to be receptacles of ideas and knowledge about everything. Only then will you have the wherewithal to judge, select, and choose your people well. One last thing: sobriety in life and conduct, because proper self-control is the mark of a true human being. Plus, striking a balance between work and leisure will bring you peace of mind and allow you to excel both in life and work."

I can still hear Grandmother's words in my ears, so strong and close, authentic and uttered with such conviction!

Back at Viesca, one episode I found particularly moving concerns my mom as a child.

"Fulvia was extraordinarily beautiful when she was a little girl, but she was also very stubborn. When I needed to buy her a dress, I would get in a few to try at home; taking her to a store was far too complicated. When she was 5, she was more fidgety and louder than a tomboy. I had to put her up on the table in her room to try on the clothes. She looked like a little doll. With that high-pitched voice of hers, she would call out to all the staff to see how pretty she was—indeed, she was just the cutest little thing imaginable!"

I try to imagine her as I write this. I go and look for her in photos from that time. Once again, I see her black hair, big, expressive eyes, determined character, the same energy that enveloped us all and that we miss so terribly now. Having a mother is a blessing people take far too much for granted.

"I have such vivid memories of when I was learning how incredible it is to be a mother," Tà said. "It was only then that I fully realized who I am. Having a place that felt completely my own was a huge help. I was comfortable in the role of wife, mother, host and hostess. Salvatore often invited clients over for lunch and dinner, and I learned so much on those occasions. Creating a good atmosphere for your guests is the main thing. You don't need large sets of plates, silverware or centerpieces with fresh orchids. All it takes to create a wonderful environment is a few little tricks and a whole lot of love."

At Viesca, nature inspired Tà to beautify her home. Depending on the season, she used wheat, grapes, chestnuts or cabbage to add a rustic and colorful touch to all the rooms, especially the dining room. She liked to say, "Nature provides us with everything we need. Even centerpieces!" At Viesca, she felt surrounded by spirituality: "When I'm there, I'm filled with a sense of wellbeing and harmony which remind me of your grandfather."

One day, Tà confessed her amazement at discovering that Don Bosco had visited the place. She had a sandstone plaque put up over the chapel to commemorate his stay.

"You know, it was Don Bosco who said that people other than descendants can become heirs. This statement allowed me to clearly acknowledge something I had only felt deep inside: each one of us, within our own possibilities, must be aware of what we receive, and we must take responsibility to give others—especially young people—some opportunities."

Tà received confirmation from the Salesian Fathers that Don Bosco had come to Viesca from Rome to meet Marquise Nerli, a former owner of the farm, who usually hosted him for a night and then funded his initiatives. At that time, he was completing construction of a parish center (his first was in Figline Valdarno). The marchioness also promised him a farm on her land to accommodate young men according to the principles of Salesian hospitality; her heirs, however, failed to honor her promise.

"This word given and not kept sparked an idea in me: to donate to the Salesian Fathers the Grati farm, on the plateau above Viesca. That spawned a fundraising campaign called *A Brick for Grati*, in which we raised money one brick at a time. Today, the two farmhouses have been renovated and are used to give children in need and their families a vacation. It makes me so happy, and Don Bosco would have been pleased too. Few other times in my life have I felt more in God's grace. That part of the estate was underutilized, but now it is both beautiful and useful. We are, after all, but pawns in the Lord's hands, and it is absurd to deprive ourselves of the joy of doing something to help others when we have the opportunity to do so."

As one of her frequent cards of goodwill to distribute around the company, Tà decided to share the Salesian Fathers' thoughts on the family. She also sent them to us for the Red Book.

"Gentleness and firmness integrate into a harmonious and serene atmosphere... Don Bosco's brilliant idea and the unmistakable spirit of every Salesian environment... Feeling welcomed, loved and esteemed... Unconditional acceptance, stubborn Faith, friendship and cheerfulness... An ideal condition for evangelization."

Tà said that what struck her most was the concept of stubbornness in faith, which "combines optimism with the awareness that results may not always be quick or what we expect, indicating a need to persevere and be patient. This is as important for a family as it is for a business. Young people need to feel valued. However minimal, any virtue in them must not just be recognized but also amplified. Young people—and not just the young—draw strength from that."

These messages were directed not so much to us but to the entire company. Her employees were as dear to her as the family, because she knew full well how much they contributed to making Grandfather's dreams come true. For Tà, it was critical that people at the company were happy to work there, which is why she took care of the employees at all times.

Let's return to Tà's life with Grandfather. Those were years replete with business trips that Tà enjoyed immensely in his company. They often went to the United States, which they loved, but they also made frequent short trips to European capitals, because that way they would not be away from the children for too long. They loved their life at Il Palagio, which in their eyes —indeed everyone's—was one of perfect family harmony.

Artist Pietro Annigoni painted a portrait of Grandfather during this period. I have looked at it closely for many years, even if as a child I found it a bit creepy. Dressed in a black velvet jacket and red scarf, Grandfather wears a stern and inquisitive look. When I moved around the room it was as if his eyes followed me and made me feel awkward. According to Tà, Annigoni proudly understood and captured every aspect of Salvatore's soul, presenting him to the world in nineteenth-century garb in a portrait laid out in a Renaissance style. In my opinion, however, that portrait lacks the sweetness I learned about from my mother's stories, something that, on the contrary, shines through in photographs of him.

"A few months after Salvatore sat for Annigoni, an English friend of ours, representing the Worshipful Company of Fishmongers, came to lunch. He told us he was looking to commission an Italian painter for a portrait of the newly crowned Queen Elizabeth II, and asked if we might help him. Salvatore introduced him to Annigoni. So happy were the English with the portrait of the young queen that it appeared on British banknotes for years. Annigoni went on to do a second portrait of the Queen and more of other members of the royal family, including Prince Philip and Princess Margaret, which brought him the international fame he deserved as one of Florence's finest artists. When people ask me why Annigoni never painted me, I tell them the truth: I refused because his brushwork was so accurate I was afraid he'd highlight every little blemish and wrinkle. To be honest, even in photographs I think my face always ends up looking like a potato!"

With that cunning, witty expression of hers, Tà laughed with humorous self-deprecation as she recounted this story.

In one of her final letters for the Red Book, sent in September 2015, she wrote a tribute and a prayer to Grandfather, drawing inspiration from Annigoni's painting.

"Salvatore, when I look at the portrait, once more I see in your gaze the goodness you so abundantly lavished on us, which penetrated our hearts and shall remain there forever, encouraging us, supporting us, giving us strength to continue steadfastly on the path you blazed. *Grazie*! May the Lord keep you close to Himself, always."

Tà never stopped acknowledging and recognizing, in every smallest detail, the realization of the dream Grandfather so amply had illustrated to her, and to which she remained faithful her entire life: that their children would work with him and transform the company into a fashion house, a Ferragamo fashion house created by the Ferragamo family, and that the family would always remain united, all together within the company, each one in a specific role that reflected their particular interests and talents.

Fiamma, the eldest, was the first to go work with Grandfather.

"When she was 18, every day after school she went straight to her father's office to learn the trade. She never left him. She ended up not bothering to sit her high-school graduation exam: it was a great sacrifice for her, but her father's call was stronger. Growing up in a city like Florence, Fiamma would have loved to study art history at university, but she gave that up too to follow Salvatore's path. I agreed with her difficult decision. I never wanted her to regret it. She was a terrific girl with such great charisma, cheerful, with so many friends and a smile for everyone. Having her around gave an energy boost to the company as well. As if her school desk had been transported, a desk was set up for her next to Salvatore's desk. Lovingly and patiently, Salvatore began showing her every aspect of the work. Taking advantage of this close-up opportunity to see how her father worked on products, Fiamma soon became his number one apprentice. She said she learned so much at that desk! I cannot say whether it was another premonition of the future or simply instinct to persuade Salvatore that Fiamma had a definite, original talent. Either way, the time they spent together was of tremendous value to them both. Fiamma's natural gifts went hand in hand with the teachings and traditions Salvatore passed on to her, ensuring that she later become a powerful advocate of his style. Grandfather was a great teacher because he knew the value of encouragement. He would show Fiamma how to do something, set an example, and then let her get on with it herself, so she could learn it on her own. He congratulated her when she did things well; when he had to criticize something she had done, he expressed himself in a clear and balanced way, enabling her to understand where she had gone wrong without leaving her frustrated. Salvatore had complete faith in her. For all the confidence it gave her, this faith was the best and greatest of all his teachings. Fiamma began step by step. Initially, she was introduced to customers, serving ladies who came to the store to order custom shoes. When Salvatore was away from Florence, she stood in for him—a big responsibility for such a young

woman! A couple of months later, Grandfather and I went to the
United States on business. At that time, Salvatore was closing a
major deal in Italy, one that would be hugely important for the
company. In our absence, he delegated the whole thing to Fiamma. This was back when there was no such thing as email, faxes
or cell phones... and poor young Fiamma found herself alone,
most likely terrified. But in the end, to our immense satisfaction, she skillfully landed that deal. We telegrammed her from
New York. I remember Salvatore's exact words: 'You did bril-
liantly closing your first deal on your own, in the best interests
of our family and the business.'"

Giovanna joined Grandfather at work soon afterwards.

"In 1957, when she was only 14 years old, Salvatore began explaining to her how the company worked. He was so eager for
his children to work with him... Perhaps he sensed that time
was running out for him. Giovanna left high school and began
studying fashion design at the Lucrezia Tornabuoni trades institute for women. To encourage her, Salvatore gave her funding to
start-up her own business. It was a substantial loan: Salvatore
wanted Giovanna to learn what business is really like. He made
her promise to pay him back in a reasonable amount of time,
which she did. Very young and very bright, she immediately rose
to the challenge. A small office was set up for her near her father's, so that he could always keep an eye on what she was doing. Salvatore encouraged her, shadowing her through all the
little details. I did too, telling her how proud we were, how confident we were that her clothes would be a success. A year after
that, we took Giovanna with us to the United States to present
her first clothes at a fashion show at the Plaza Hotel in New
York City. We bumped into a friend on the liner, who was traveling with his two daughters. He was very impressed when we
told him the reason for our trip. He thought it was quite the
daring experience for a girl of her young age. One evening on
the cruise, we put on a small fashion show. Our friend's daughters acted as models, along with other passengers we found on
the ship who were willing to model Giovanna's clothes. It was
such great fun," Tà recalled with her trademark enthusiasm.
"The New York show attracted a huge audience, a whole host of

journalists including Eugenia Sheppard from the *New York Herald Tribune*, at the time the most influential fashion critic, who gave a rave review. Soon afterwards, Salvatore met a lady in Los Angeles who was keen to open a boutique in Beverly Hills. He showed her Giovanna's designs, and so at just 16, Giovanna Ferragamo had her own store, with her own name on it, right on the corner of Rodeo Drive. That exclusive franchise did really well for two or three years. Actresses started ordering clothes from this hot, new, young Italian designer, Doris Day, Simone Signoret and Jane Russell to name just a few. Although it was ready-to-wear, if a customer wanted a different color or a modified style, Giovanna was happy to oblige. Everything was going swimmingly, until one day the store owner simply disappeared, the doors were chained shut and the accounts frozen... But the adventure had begun."

Meanwhile, in 1957 Massimo was born, the third boy and the youngest of six.

"Massimotto was a little darling. Because he was like the family diplomat, we nicknamed him Kissinger. When he was little, he knew exactly what time his daddy came home from work at the end of the day. His favorite game was to lay in ambush for him, hidden behind a door, and then jump out with a huge 'boo!' as soon as Salvatore walked in. Salvatore pretended to be scared, then picked him up and showered him with kisses. He loved that game."

Seemingly endless possibilities opened up in the late 1950s. Tà was happy and grateful, surrounded by her beautiful family, the company's bottom line and renown were growing, and she and Grandfather were full of dreams and plans for the future. As the proverb runs, "Man proposes, God disposes." As Tà remarked, God proved this to them the hard way, leaving her scarred and in need of all of her strength and Faith.

Prayer

"I beseech Thee, oh Lord, as a son approaches a father, for I need Thy help, Thy love, Thy great goodness and mercy. Thou art my refuge above all and everything. May I find the comfort, support, and strength in You to accomplish what I have been called upon to do. Above all, may I honor the natural and super-natural principles of Your Creation, this source of life and joy, as does a good child deserving of Your Love. I thank Thee for the children Thou hast given me, for the companion I had but whom destiny prematurely took from me. And yet through his love for us all and the great strength Thou granted him during his life, he is still among us as we strive to follow his example and honor his memory. Grant my children joy in their children as I have had with mine. Above all, may they all have the gift of Faith, the one way not to feel alone, to find relief from the wickedness, in-justice and ingratitude in this world."

Tà wrote this prayer to God in 1978, seeking His help in a time of despondency. She was 57 years old, had been a widow for 18 years, had 6 children, 20 or so grandchildren, and a huge business to run. Today, asking the Universe to intercede for one's desires is called the Law of Attraction; back then, as she more simply called it, it was prayer. How many prayers she wrote and recited!

When I received this particular prayer in Buenos Aires one warm April morning, it felt like an arrow to the heart. Neatly typed on her usual letterheaded paper, those words had crossed the Atlantic Ocean to reach me and my restless soul, filling me with sudden calm and immense gratitude.

Here's this month's "circular" I thought, impatiently opening the envelope. But in fact, the letter arrived like a bolt from the blue, delivering Tà with it, helping to free me from the torpor of a tiring morning at work, sitting there staring into space, my face reflected in my computer screen on stand-by. When I read the first sentence, I wrinkled my nose at those capitalized words: Thee, Lord, Father. With a mixture of admiration and disbelief, I thought to myself, I'll never know how Tà found the time to write to God too, and then I encountered the word "help." A feeling of humility mixed with empathy forced its way into my consciousness. My curiosity was piqued. This was Tà asking for help, almost pleading for it. I had trouble reconciling this thought with my grandmother's strong, resolute figure. She wrote this letter to God in desperation, revealing uncertainty, fear, perhaps even inadequacy, the very feeling that was stealing into me on those long, hot Argentinean days... With one vital difference: I had not, even for one second, considered turning to God. I had seen her softer side over the years, yet I had never imagined Tà in the vice-like grip of resignation. Her tenacious and determined personality had always been much more in evidence. Behind that indecipherable gaze, I'd always recognized an attentive, understanding, sharp, and intelligent glare, a clear mirror of the extraordinary spirit that enabled her to live through the most demanding challenges.

I emailed Tà that very day, thanking her for assuaging my own state of mind with her prayer. As ever, I received an immediate, thoughtful, and attentive message right back.

"My dearest Ginevra, thank you for your letter and your truly sincere message, in which you open up your heart to me. There is no doubt: Faith is a great and helpful gift. It has helped me tremendously on so many occasions. We may not understand and cannot explain some things, but when you see a flower grow from a tiny seed that already encompasses the species, color, and scent, you cannot but think of a divine hand, regardless of the fact that actually understanding it is more complex. However, all we have to do is appreciate the wonderful things around us, bow our heads, and believe in them deeply, no matter how little we understand. The discomfort you feel is not surprising; it happens to us all at some point. The main thing is to draw on sure resources. You'll find that healthily letting go prompts us to better accept and endure whatever may be upsetting us at a given moment. I can assure you that if we act in a balanced manner, rays of sunshine will not fail to arrive, allowing us to continue on our path with greater hope and appreciate what life has to offer. Write to me whenever you like, ask me anything on your mind. You have great qualities. We all have so much trust and respect for you and your intelligence. Big, big hugs to you, Andrea and the kids, Tà."

I was speechless. Tears flowed down my cheeks at such words of faith, courage, and affection. I wish I could have been with and hugged her, rather than feeling surrounded and weighed down by such shallowness. Then and now, I regret not having been able to spend more time with Tà, to bask in her elegant intelligence, constructive attitude, and boundless courage. Her simple words that had flown thousands of miles on the wings of love were such a gift.

After Grandfather Salvatore died in 1960, Tà took the decision to carry on the business herself.

"There are so many things to do and I need time to accomplish them. If it is not possible for me to achieve this in this body, it'll have to be in another," wrote Grandfather in his autobiography. Tà turned those words into the lodestar of her life.

"They allow me to feel your Grandfather's honest, spiritual essence. When I reread them, I understand that he felt part of something bigger than himself. He was convinced that man's relationship with the world is not just merely speculative. Salvatore was a man at peace with himself and with his world. The irony of life is that he did not have long to live when he wrote those words. In the innermost recesses of his spirit, he was calmly convinced that his work and mission would not end with his death. He knew that they would carry on, that they would exist through others into the future. I don't like to talk much about that time; they were the hardest days of my life. Whenever I think back, even now, fifty years later, I have to hold back the tears as some new detail bubbles up."

In the fall of 1958, the Dunlop Corporation invited Grandfather to travel to Australia. The trip excited him for two reasons. First, because in those days it was unusual to travel as far as Australia: he would be one of the first fashion creators to visit it. Second, Grandfather had a kind of third eye: one eye for beauty, one eye for creativity, and a third for new business opportunities. Opening up a market for luxury shoes in a country on the far side of the globe was a dream for him, a major piece of the grand design in his head, along with famous shoes he made out of solid gold, sandals with very high heels and a gold chain around the ankle created for an American lady, the wife of a well-known businessman, which are today preserved in the Museo Salvatore Ferragamo in Florence. Inspired by the art of Benvenuto Cellini, Grandfather had had them made in 18-carat gold by artisans at the Palazzo degli Orafi, near Ponte Vecchio.

The trip lasted a month. Tà recalled how difficult it was to stay in touch.

"I missed him horribly. We had never been apart for so long. He never stopped writing to me during those long weeks, sometimes two letters a day. I would always write back immediately; the kids were a little lazier."

Tà recounted an episode several times, wishing to teach us that dropping a few lines is always welcome... More than welcome, sometimes necessary.

"A few weeks after Grandfather arrived in Australia, a letter arrived for the three eldest children in which, albeit in a lovingly fatherly tone, he said he was amazed he had not yet received a few words from any of them. This, to remind you that in life, it's not just the hours you devote to soccer or friends that are important, but the time you devote to your parents, whose love for you is eternal. Everything around you may vanish in a minute, but not your father and mother's love. That very evening the kids wrote him their little letters. Every time Salvatore was interviewed in Australia, he always talked about his six children and how much he missed them. As a result of this, many delightful people sent the kids dozens of stuffed koalas. They continued to arrive at home long after Salvatore returned. I must still have them somewhere."

Tà, of course, immediately wondered where to put them, later retrieving them as needed, using her enviable ability to recycle even the most unusual objects and turn them into well-received gifts.

That trip to Australia opened up new markets. On the way back, Grandfather wrote Tà a letter at every stopover. Tà learned her favorite, which he sent from Paris, by heart:

"My dearest, I arrived in Paris tonight, and am now so close to being home with you and the children once more. After dinner, I took a walk around the city, but I soon went back to the hotel because without you by my side, even the beauty of Paris is painful. I don't want anything if I can't share it with you. I'll be home soon."

What wife wouldn't want to receive such a letter? Tà couldn't wait for Grandfather to come home. She went to pick him up at the airport in Rome, but when he descended the stairs from the plane, she immediately noticed how tired he looked. She had never seen him like that. She put it down to the long trip, and suggested they take a couple of days off on Capri, one of their favorite places, before he returned to work. Grandfather agreed, even though he was dying to see the children. They stayed three days, Grandfather was able to get some rest, and a little color returned to his face.

"By the time we returned to Florence, I thought it was all behind us, but before long, Salvatore began feeling unwell. He never complained, in fact he kept working and attempted to conceal his discomfort from us all. Things went from bad to worse, so I insisted he get tests. After a series of tests and x-rays, the doctors diagnosed liver cancer. He had surgery, but it was too late. The shock was enormous, and the prognosis not good.

Back then, we didn't have the medicines and treatments we do today. We went home and attempted to live our lives as normal, but after that news there was nothing normal anymore. Salvatore spent time at Il Palagio, resting up in the garden or in the house. It was important for him to regain his strength. As soon as he felt a little better, friends started visiting again. Queen Helena of Romania, a loyal customer and great friend, had moved from her country to San Domenico; she came over every afternoon to have tea with Salvatore, engaging him in long, pleasant conversations. The Queen loved hearing about America, Salvatore's experiences in Hollywood with the movie stars, and the extravagance of American actresses. Her attentiveness and understanding moved us all. I would not have imagined a queen could be so democratic and sensitive to others—a true expression of style and a deep nobility of feelings, but then again, it was Salvatore who elicited gratitude and respect, both of which he fully deserved."

They didn't tell the children about their father's real condition for fear of alarming them. All they knew was that he had not been feeling well and was taking a little time off to recover. The little ones were thrilled, because they could finally enjoy their daddy. The older ones, however, began to get suspicious at all these doctors and people coming and going, and hearing so many whispered discussions. What's more, Grandfather wasn't getting any better.

"As for me, I stayed close to Salvatore at all times, and then one fine day he told me to go to the office. He began sending me there every day to check on things and bring him back the mail. He was truly amazing, so brave and such a true gentleman. He knew he didn't have much time to live, but he did his best not to think about it. He realized that playing that part would make it easier for me. I didn't think it was possible to love him any more than I already did, but during that time my love and admiration for him redoubled. I'll never know, but maybe that was his way of launching me into my future role. I became accustomed to heading into the city every day and spending a couple of hours at the office. One day, sitting at his desk, I heard a commotion outside the door. Finally, the door opened and Salvatore walked in, followed by a new doorman, hot on his heels. The doorman hadn't recognized him and was apologizing for letting him through. Overcome with emotion, I began crying. I ran over to hug Salvatore. Feeling better that day, he had decided to surprise me. Then we both burst out laughing at the poor doorman, who had tried to hold him back as if he were some outsider."

That summer, Tà took Grandfather and the whole family to Forte dei Marmi, while she and Fiamma shuttled back and forth to Florence to keep the business ticking over. Oh, how Grandfather loved that house a stone's throw from the sea.

"We would bring him his favorite sweets and desserts and try to keep up a cheerful and convivial atmosphere. It took not inconsiderable effort, but we did it for him. I like to think Salvatore felt relaxed and at peace in that desperate situation," Tà said, holding back the tears. As was her wont, she kept the hardest moments hidden away, deep in her heart.

Grandfather died on August 7, 1960, just five months after he was diagnosed.

"It's really impossible for me to describe how I felt. It was as if the world had fallen in on me. I could not believe that this fabulous man, so noble, generous, good, and kind had been taken from me at the age of just 62. I simply couldn't grasp it, not so much for me but our kids. Fiamma was 19, Giovanna 17, Ferruccio 15, your mom only 10, Leonardo 7 and Massimo 3. I found no way of explaining how God could have decided to pluck their daddy away from them."

In a packed church, the funeral was held in Florence in mid-August.

"Many people cut short their vacations to say their farewells to Salvatore. I could feel that friends and colleagues were there for us, physically and emotionally, many of them in tears, hugging me and expressing their condolences. I was moved when some of Salvatore's coworkers approached me and said: 'Don't worry, Signora Wanda, we'll get through this, we will!' My heart broke at the sight of the children. When I saw them all there together, sad and frightened, I somehow found the strength to sit them down around me and say: 'We must thank our Lord for everything your daddy has left us: the good times we shared with him, the trips, the merry evenings, the discussions, advice, our lives together... No-one can ever take that away from us. Daddy will always be in our hearts, from Heaven loving and protecting us now. Daddy will be our guardian angel!' These little words proved to be as magical and comforting to me as they were to them."

To this day, I wonder how Tà found the strength to overcome all this, to find the Good in such immense pain for her and her children. It must have been in her Faith (with a capital F), which she always said was her true buttress. The days after the funeral were, for Tà, confusing and terrifying.

"The great heat at Forte dei Marmi was simply unbearable. I couldn't conceive of life carrying on normally, among families on vacation, lifeguards on the beach, dancing every night... I felt devastated, so I decided to whisk everyone off to Viesca. I hoped that the solitude and peace of nature would raise my spirits a little. It didn't. I was assailed by terrible depression. I knew I had to find a way out as soon as possible. I left the children with the nannies and housekeepers and took refuge in a small hotel in Vallombrosa, a hamlet in the hills near Viesca, hoping the fresh air would buck up my ideas.

I felt alone, frightened, cut adrift. What was I to do? How could I raise six children without Salvatore's help? How would they grow up without their father? The pain made me numb, too sad even to cry. I was obsessed with the idea of a future without Salvatore. But then I began to realize that his spirit was with me. His love still held me. Little by little, I began coming to my senses, to see the path before me with increasing clarity. It was almost as if some external force, something that didn't belong to me, took over. One thing I am certain of is a constant flow of energy that exists within each of us and pushes us up or down, toward God or toward Hell. My energies were, I knew, raising me up at that moment. I was filled by the love I felt for Salvatore, by the desire to pursue his dream on his behalf. I made a vow to myself: to fight this battle with depression immediately. I had no choice. A few days later, the negative thoughts dissipated. My world finally seemed to be lit by the sunlight of a new day. I felt revitalized. I had a mission and a purpose for carrying on."

At 38 years of age, Tà was widowed with six children. Grandfather had built a company that was highly regarded and very solid, albeit totally identified with him, his talent, and his integrity. Tà felt blessed by the 20 years of marriage to him. Not only had he loved her with all his heart and taught her so many things, but he had also left her a legacy that was spiritual as well as material.

"Ours had been a true, wonderful love story. We shared everything, starting with our dreams, which we talked about often. Salvatore was not content to stop with the success of his shoes alone, he wanted to transform the company into an all-round fashion house. His greatest dream was to see a woman walk out of his store dressed in Ferragamo from head to toe. After starting to work with him, Fiamma and Giovanna instilled hope in him that this dream would come true."

Tà was horrified at the thought of giving up everything Salvatore had worked so hard for.

One morning, she went to a store in nearby Figline. She had known the owners for many years, and after affectionately offering their condolences, they asked her a question that became a veritable turning point for her: "What are you going to do now to save the company?"

In fact, it ended up being quite a challenge. Tà had to deal with things quickly and totally on her own. "Do I sell up the business or find a way to carry on?" was the constant, nagging, stifling question. Selling the company was emotionally too hard to countenance, even if it would have been the most straightforward thing to do. No end of companies were interested in buying them up. A few days after the funeral, an American company made her a very attractive offer that would have allowed her and the children to live comfortable lives.

"I would have devoted myself to their upbringing and lived a stress-free life. On the other hand, keeping the company would be satisfying, yet it would also be burdensome. And no-one else could lead it. I would have to sit in Salvatore's place, at his desk, and put myself in charge. Was I really capable of it? I had never worked in my life, and I didn't know where to start. I had no training whatsoever. Until then, I had looked after the children and the house, drawing on the limited academic education women of my age had at that time. I didn't even have to look after the household accounts, so I had no notions to fall back on about any form of financial or economic organization. I knew nothing about sales and distribution. I was capable of running a house with a staff of 12, but how would I manage dozens and dozens of employees at the office, in the factory and in our stores? I would need to learn so much about management and manufacturing. On the other hand, I knew I would have many trusted people to rely on within the company. Their loyalty and devotion to Salvatore warranted the decision not to sell up. Salvatore had left me a very well-organized company with excellent craftsmen who made the finest shoes in the world, and I was confident that I could count on my children too. But I was a woman, and at that time it was rare indeed to encounter a woman running a big business. To create their companies, women such as Gabrielle Chanel or Estée Lauder had, in addition to their genius and creativity, drawn on the collaboration of trusted individuals and partners. In my case, it was a matter of putting myself in charge of a company that had been created and run by its founder, my husband, a man who had been both its creative and business leader. I would receive help from Fiamma and Giovanna and, sooner or later, my other children, but basically in that very moment I was on my own. I did not know if I had what it takes, the skills to do it."

Tà was tormented by the choice she would have to make, but then something happened that helped her. After the funeral, a real-estate agent contacted her to ask if she was interested in selling Palazzo Spini Feroni, pointing out how much it would cost her to pay the inheritance taxes.

"Would you sell a son?" Tà retorted haughtily. "Of course not, and we won't be selling Palazzo Spini Feroni either!" The estate agent mumbled that he had been duty-bound to put the question to her on behalf of a Florentine client who was looking for real estate bargains. "Ah!" replied Tà. "Since you're in the research mode, if you happen upon anything interesting, anything very impressive mind you, let us know because we might be interested in buying it."

Ultimately, it was in that little Vallombrosa hotel that Tà made the decision that would change her life. After days of prayer and contemplation, she resolved to keep the business in the family and complete what Grandfather had left undone. He had made it abundantly clear in his book, "If it is not possible for me to achieve this in this body, it'll have to be in another."

Tà realized the body in question was hers.

Fifty years after Grandfather's death, a letter arrived for the Red Book. This time the recipients were not the grandchildren, but Grandfather himself.

"Dear Salvatore, I write as the spokesperson for your children, their families, your friends, your collaborators and all the people who, fifty years after your death, remember you with undiminished esteem and respect for your professional and human endeavors. We feel a desire—nay necessity—to remind the world of how intense your teaching and trail-blazing example was for us and for all the many others who have managed to project the values of Italian culture, craftsmanship, creativity, and ethics out into the world. From you, we inherited the onerous if stimulating commitment to continue tending the seeds you sowed. Having been at your side for so many years and shared in your anxieties and successes, I was the first to map out the path to be taken, a proud custodian of your cherished dreams for the future. This is a significant moment for me too: the fiftieth year of my constant, uninterrupted work at the company, where every day I renew my determination to achieve the results to which you aspired. I and our children have continued to follow your teachings with faith, tenacity, and enthusiasm, happy not just to honor your efforts and incomparable example, but determined to realize the desires you had for the company to develop in an atmosphere of full, healthy, family harmony. On this truly special occasion, when I think of how much I've missed you, I look back at these fifty years and they feel like an eternity. At the same time, they have gone by in a flash, surrounded by our children who have fully repaid me for my efforts, each in their own way making a vital contribution to

propelling your name out into the world. I write to you from
Florence, your favorite city, the place you chose to live when you
came back to Italy for its matchless combination of beauty, culture, art, and history. After living in the United States for 13
years, you did not hesitate to settle here, attracted by the tradition and skill of Florentine craftsmen who, more than anyone
else in the world, could make the extraordinary creations you
had in mind. Thousands and thousands of shoes were already
leaving this beautiful Florence of ours for destinations the
world over, messengers of Italian craftsmanship and beauty beyond all borders. Thanks to you, Florence was and is our adopted city, a place we respect, protect, and defend. A place that,
every evening as I return from the office, I admire from the
terrace of our beautiful house, as my thoughts fly to you."

To Work!

To safeguard her health, once a year Tà would allow herself some spa treatments. Her favorite destinations were Ischia, Quiberon, and Deauville. While she was away, she followed a specific diet and did Thalassotherapy, "the only treatment that really does me good, that I cannot do without," she said in a letter she sent from Deauville. She may not always have enjoyed herself, but she certainly rested and relaxed: Tà was at her best in putting her ideas in order and writing beautiful letters during these moments of creative rest.

Tà entitled a long letter to Grandfather Salvatore "My Life After You Left Us," which could have been the incipit to a beautiful autobiography. She wrote that letter in different steps over a period of time, each episode a general report on the company, the children, and the family. She began this long letter in Quiberon in 1989 and continued it for many years with only a few breaks, always returning to it on her rare time off work. Seeking to share with him all of her joys and concerns, Tà wrote to Grandfather with intimacy and humility. She would tell him about everyday life, interesting people she had met, new stores, and the general state Italy was in. Each episode provided food for thought and included suggestions for possible solutions. In short, for Tà writing was a way of expressing and enhancing her intelligence.

I was thinking about all this in front of my computer monitor, in the noisy offices of *La Nación*, a blank page before me that by evening had to be written and edited to perfection, in flawless Spanish to boot.

Then my mind flew back to Italy, to an afternoon with Tà when, during one of my last visits, she took me to Viesca to show me the work she had carried out on several houses. She was pleased with the progress, but at the same time regretted not being able to enjoy that cherished place with her family anymore. Her business sense, however, suggested to her that renting out those houses would provide the income she needed to make Viesca even more stunning and beautiful.

Yellow autumn leaves colored our conversation as we walked through the garden. She told me how happy it made her to see good results in any field. She had often felt lonely and wearied by her work commitments and the sacrifices they entailed, but she assured me that nothing gave her more satisfaction than seeing the success her efforts yielded.

It was already dark by the time we returned to Il Palagio. As usual, we sat in the TV lounge to listen to the news. At precisely 8:30 we sat down to dinner. She had asked for pumpkin risotto, my favorite dish, to be served. We laughed until we cried when she told me that the real secret for that recipe was to not over-dry the rice: it had to remain "slobbery." Tà would occasionally use rather strange terms that made her descriptions rather piquant and intense.

That was the time that she gave me a book, *A regola d'arte*, published for the exhibition inaugurated in 2010 at the Museo Salvatore Ferragamo to celebrate the company's strong ties with the artisan tradition in Florence, a tribute to the craftsmanship in which Grandfather firmly believed and of which he felt part. This time, instead of being illustrated with his creations, the catalog presented the faces of the people who had made it possible to manufacture Salvatore Ferragamo products. The exhibition coincided with Tà's fiftieth anniversary as head of the company. Her wise words vividly and lucidly introduced the catalog:

"This publication is intended as a tribute to all of the many people who devote their daily energies to the company, the broadest demonstration of the message that, through our products, we convey to the world. Everyone knows the importance of work, but far fewer people are aware of the other valuable elements that nourish a business. In addition to the basic idea, which is the initial fulcrum, a company's result is an amalgam of the moral and cultural principles that are indispensable for moving forward and progressing, achieving renown and success. This is something that my husband Salvatore taught me. One significant episode I will never forget educated me about the deep moral values dwelling in the people around us. It occurred exactly fifty years ago, when I was beset by the pain of losing Salvatore, and on the horns of the dilemma of whether or not to continue his work. At his funeral, I was surrounded by many of his loyal employees; at the end of the service they greeted me, warmly shook my hand and said: 'Don't worry, Signora, we'll help you, we'll get through this!' Well, that strong message conveyed at a time when I felt totally lost has stayed in my heart ever since. Not only did they keep their promise, but they also managed to pass it on to newcomers to the company. Consequently, we have created a solid and beautiful climate of serenity and confidence to keep the business going, along with great pride in belonging. This climate has never disappeared, and we will do everything in our power to keep it going and pass it on to our successors. Without a doubt, the business's most vital cultural energy is its people—people who have been here for many years and are still here today, projecting into the future an excellence appreciated worldwide. The unique and incomparable values expressed in their faces are the culmination of an unrepeatable story, a story that is unmistakably Italian and, above all, particularly Florentine. It is the story of a deeply held culture that has generated pride, imagination, creativity, determination, and sensitivity, the values that drive us and our craftsmen to achieve ever more ambitious results, constantly striving for perfection in our products and for our company. In our artisans' hearts, minds and of course hands, these very values have fostered an extraordinary uptick in production. A never-ending quest for innovation and new technologies enables manual work to evolve not just at our company but at many other top Italian companies. The adoption of processes that become more and more sophisticated every day enable us to create increasingly perfect and reliable products that already existed in their creators' hearts and minds, but which their hands alone could not have made. All this is, for Italy, a source of pride. It certainly is for us. Your faces convey the extraordinary spirit and constant dedication to perfection that, over time, have become a template for generations to come. May you all continue, with the greatest happiness and peace of mind. Wanda Ferragamo."

Since that first day of September 1960, when my grandmother decided to carry on the company without her beloved husband, a host of people have worked alongside her, giving her the courage she needed to continue her work. On the other hand, she had the ability to keep them close and on board.

Employees who had gone away for their summer vacations and had waved goodbye to Grandfather returned to work to find his wife sitting at his desk.

"I sat down at that desk and took a deep breath, and then another. It was the first day of my new life. In a way, it was almost a good thing that Salvatore had departed in early August. With things on temporary hiatus at the company because of the summer break, I had had time to think things through and reflect. I knew I wasn't alone. Above all, I could rely on three people, but it would not have been possible for me to get going without everyone's help, particularly Fiamma, who was always by my side, a dedicated confederate in this new adventure and an irreplaceable pillar of strength for all of us. Not only was she the message-bearer of Salvatore's teachings within the company and for her siblings, but she also became the Ferragamo company's magnetic public face."

Tà and Fiamma, two women facing a huge challenge...

Then there was Jerry Ferragamo, Grandfather Salvatore's nephew, who was in charge of production and whose contribution to the company, then as now, has been and still is fundamental. Jerry's father, Grandfather's brother Girolamo, had died when Jerry was just 3 years old. The child returned from America to Bonito at a very young age; Grandfather Salvatore followed his studies from afar, feeling an affection for him no different to his feelings for his own children. Jerry enrolled in medical school, but that was not to be his path. One day, he went to visit Grandfather in Chianciano, where he was taking the waters, and asked if he could come work with him. Grandfather was delighted: his children were still too young, but Jerry was old enough to learn about the company's technical aspects and product working methods.

"I really don't know what I would have done without him," said Tà. "He was always so faithful to Salvatore's instructions, generously passing everything on to your parents."

Tà sent us a letter Jerry wrote to her in 2009, on the occasion of his eightieth birthday, for the Red Book. I've known Jerry forever, he's part of our family. He, his wife Loretta and their two children, Stefano and Silvia, have been at all our family celebrations. I've always thought of him as an extremely sweet person. He has good eyes, something I noticed as a child because they were so bright, as if he was always about to be overcome with emotion. His reserve never allowed me to get to know him better, but in the letter below, his words paint a picture of calm and consistency.

"Dearest Aunt Wanda, I thank you from the bottom of my heart for your much-appreciated participation and the gifts you gave me for my eightieth birthday. Your demonstration of affection and esteem honors me, and I am truly grateful. As you are well aware, my strong, charismatic and beloved uncle Salvatore was an inexhaustible source of ideas and initiatives, as well as an invaluable example for the life values that have helped me to work with the utmost efficiency. I have also adopted admirable concepts of life philosophy and wide-ranging views from you, bringing great satisfaction and joys that I have been able to share with you and all of my beloved cousins. A loving hug, Jerry."

Preceding Fiamma, Jerry was the first family member to work with Grandfather. He compiled his experiences working at Ferragamo into a book, a wonderful testament to his contribution to the company.

"Jerry and Fiamma made such a great partnership, all bickering and affection," Tà recalled. "Fiamma was the creative who sketched things, while he said, 'This cannot be done, this costs too much, this is complicated.' In short, he filtered Fiamma's ideas through his prism of prudence. She would get annoyed there and then, but in reality she held him in very high esteem, and he valued her too. It was such a positive dialectic."

Jerry admired Fiamma's strong personality, her precision at work, and her ability to organize her team of workers, in whom she instilled confidence and in doing so she stimulated them to grow and improve. He appreciated her common sense and natural way of smoothing out sharp edges, always solving problems in the company's best interests. The love she had for her work and for shoes, which spurred her to become the greatest ambassador for the company, enabled Ferragamo to expand throughout the world.

From that very first day without Grandfather, Tà sought to take care of everything.

"My specialty, or rather, my primary concern, has always been financial. If the finances are in good shape, then everything else runs much more smoothly. This had been one of Salvatore's teachings and I knew how vital it was; that's why I have always been very careful on the risk of entering into imprudent business ventures. I have always taken a safety-first approach, even if I may have missed out on some profits."

Tà often conveyed her prudent approach for the Red Book. One day, she wrote the following to us:

"To save the company (when the opportunity arises), prepare for this eventuality every day, drawing on the company's culture, management, and administrative oversight. I believe that only a family member, somebody who commands others' trust, should be in control of the money. I've seen too much trouble in other families as a result of delegating this task to others. If the Ferragamo company has made progress and all our families have benefited, know that it has been thanks to wise and prudent management, first in my hands, then in Ferruccio's, who commendably conducted this specific task. We owe him the fullness of our gratitude. Similarly, I must praise Leonardo who, when the time came, managed to completely revolutionize our distribution in Asia, raising it to a very high level indeed. In their respective tasks, Fiamma, Giovanna, Fulvia, and Massimo are the pride and strength of our Brand" (with a capital B). "May you follow in their footsteps, and God bless you all! Nonna Tà."

In another letter, she warned us about the attendant risks:

"My dearly beloved, sometimes we encounter setbacks that affect our families or our business. The way to deal with them is to keep back some cash reserves. Bear this in mind!"

For as long as I knew her, Grandmother always stressed the importance of saving. I never saw her lack for anything, but I most certainly never saw her wasting or squandering anything either. Nothing bothered her more.

In another letter destined for the Red Book, she wrote:

"I wish to clarify for you the meaning of savings in life. Savings are critical for every individual, family, company, and business. Savings foster peace of mind in tough and challenging times, which may happen at any moment in your path. You should save even modest amounts of money, judging exactly how much on a case-by-case basis. The other reason why saving money is important is that the opportunity may come along to make a worthwhile purchase and you'll need the cash to seize that opportunity at that very moment. I can assure you I've often heard friends and business leaders alike say, 'It's a good thing I had the resources, otherwise I wouldn't have been able to handle this challenge or take advantage of this great opportunity.' Please remember this."

Tà was under enormous pressure when she first sat down at Grandfather's desk. Looking across the large desktop, covered as ever in objects, papers, samples, scraps of leather and other materials, she felt lost but she didn't lose heart. She had two sheets of paper before her on the desk. The first showed the company's revenues, the second its expenditures.

"I immediately realized that if the sum of the first sheet was larger than the sum of the second, things were set fair. I've always been blessed with a good dose of common sense, so when I saw that the sums added up, the first thing I did was buy property. I've always advised my children to invest in real estate, because you never know, there's always a chance that our shoes stop selling overnight."

She purchased a number of properties, one for each of her children, which could generate income if the business failed. Under Italian law, children's incomes cannot be accessed to repay their parents' debts, so this was Tà's way of protecting all six of them against potential problems in the future. Another enormous help was Marisa Balestrieri, the company administrator, who taught Grandmother everything she knew about accounting, administration, and banking. Tà used to introduce her to customers as her teacher, until the day came when Marisa acknowledged that Tà no longer needed her, since she now knew more than her mentor. Another key figure who helped Tà rise to the challenge was accountant Giuseppe Anichini, who is still with us today, whom we all respect for his wisdom and professionalism. Tà had complete faith in him.

Before he died, Grandfather left two important business deals "open." The first was an order for 12,000 pairs of shoes from Saks Fifth Avenue, one of America's largest and most elegant department stores, due for delivery after January 1, 1961 for their spring collection. The second deal emerged when David Dulberg, a Saks Fifth Avenue buyer and a close friend of Grandfather's, visited Tà.

"I told him I was still very concerned about the company's future and my chances of making it without Salvatore. He led me to the room in Palazzo Spini Feroni where he knew Salvatore had archived many of the drawings and patterns he had made throughout his life. Gesturing toward that immense quantity of work, he said, 'Wanda, look around you. These designs are nothing short of fantastic. There is no reason for you to worry. There must be twenty years of ideas in here to work on.' Those words instilled boundless confidence in me. David knew the business inside out, and he knew exactly what people were buying. He was someone I had to believe. In any case, Fiamma's talent shone through so strongly that we didn't even have to go back to Salvatore's drawings, although they continued to serve as our main source of inspiration, lighting up the way like a beacon."

Another crucial figure in the transition from Grandfather to Tà was Ned Schwartz, our United States agent who organized shoe distribution to the finest stores across the country.

Nothing in the company was outside Tà's purview. Aside from offering constructive ideas and applying sound financial principles, she had grown to be a real ace at management.

One of her "circulars" for the Red Book was entitled: "How I tidied up and oversaw Management of Ferragamo Limited in London when I took over from Salvatore at the company." That verb, "tidy up," was so typical of her.

"My dearly beloved, as you know, in order to operate successfully in England and ensure good distribution there, we had to set up a company under English law with a local administrator. After Salvatore's death, when I looked into Ferragamo Limited's performance, I noticed that expenses had gone up too much, and that the sums sent to our Headquarters in Italy for goods received from Florence arrived not just late, but curtailed by almost half. I was concerned and set out to monitor the situation more closely, clearly, and in a more verifiable manner. The first thing I did was change banks. I gave the new bank highly specific instructions. I opened two accounts for Ferragamo Limited—an "A" account on which only I could sign, from which I withdrew what was needed for the company's performance, and a "B" account, on which the agent could draw to pay salaries, taxes, etc. The agent would send me a list of what he had to pay, and I would send him these necessary, properly-justified funds, to proceed. Before long, the situation changed and improved considerably. Payments started coming in regularly and everything went smoothly. Faithful coworkers Roberto Gaggioli and Marisa Balestrieri are witnesses to all this. I trust that this episode will be as much of a learning experience for all of you as it was for me. Managing your own resources is sacrosanct; the same applies to our company."

In her letters, Tà invariably capitalized the words management (*Amministrazione*) and company (*Azienda*).

One of Tà's greatest challenges was to strike a balance between the responsibilities of bringing up her children and filling her new role at the company.

"It took a kind of sleight-of-hand at which I became rather adept. I would be trying to focus on a new product line and then two seconds later I had to handle some request from one of my children. In a way it was good, because family time and activities helped fill the void Salvatore left behind. With hindsight, my enthusiasm and commitment to work were a stratagem to keep me busy, to avoid dwelling on the sadness that had threatened to eat me alive. As Salvatore had taught me, I strove to turn problems into opportunities and productivity."

Right from the start, she realized it was essential she be in the office every day. She wanted the company's employees to witness this continuity, to trust her, to understand that she was serious and committed, not just to keeping the company going but to growing it.

"Every day, there was some decision or other to make. Big or small, it didn't matter; the main thing was that I was sitting there in the office. I worked hard to build good relationships with the people who worked with us. I enjoyed showing an interest in them all, which helped to establish a sense of trust, plus I wanted them to know that their work was respected and appreciated. As is inevitable in an environment where everyone wants to get ahead, there were tensions and competition in some areas of the company, but thankfully without destructive behaviors. Right from the outset, I decided that the office should be a family environment, reflecting the company's identity, which also helped establish the trust I believed was essential. It would be fair to say that I imposed my own style. Many years later, when I read a biography of Lee Iacocca, the Italo-American manager best known for saving Chrysler in the 1980s, I was struck by an expression he used: to be a 'pragmatic dreamer.' I recognized myself totally in that. From the very start, I instinctively knew that this was the right way to go. Fiamma and Giovanna were incredibly supportive. I loved having my daughters with me: they were like two guardian angels. Usually, it's the mom who takes care of the kids, but here it was the other way around. When they sensed—or could tell from the look on my face—that I was sad or down, they would come into the office with a smile, show me a drawing, bring me some coffee, perhaps tell me about a new idea... They always managed to cheer me up. Sometimes I would play a little game with myself and try to erase the fact that Salvatore was dead. As soon as I had a free moment and that sense of emptiness returned, I would stubbornly assume he was simply traveling, and focus back on the work. The evenings were the hardest. On occasion, I would get home late from the office, the older kids were out with friends and the little ones asleep. Thinking they were being prudent (they know I hate waste), the staff had already turned off all the lights. When I got home, everything was so silent and dark. I would take off my coat and sit down in front of the television to seek some companionship. On such evenings, the emptiness was palpable, enormous, creeping into everything."

Loneliness tormented Tà. Many times, especially after her children left home, I heard her complain about how often she was alone. But she had made her cultural and existential choice a long time ago. From the day she decided to work at the company, she abided strictly by a limited set of rules: dinner, then early to bed, every day. She pared back her social life to the bare essentials so she could be with the children when they were still young, and she adopted healthy habits that would allow her to always be clear-headed and well rested to best cope with challenges at work. She always used to refer to that period as her equivalent of getting an MBA. Although she never did study for a master's degree, she certainly warranted one in terms of experience and discipline.

"The first few months working at the office flew by, and soon the Christmas break came round. I knew it wouldn't be easy to celebrate Christmas as we'd done before. I just couldn't bear the thought of the children racing down the stairs to see what

Santa had brought them without Salvatore sharing in their happiness by my side. So I decided we would not stay in Florence that year. Instead, we spent the holidays at the San Domenico hotel in Taormina. After all, a change of scenery was a good idea."

Tà knew and respected her limits. If she was tired, she rested. If she wasn't feeling well, she took care of herself without unnecessary medication. If she was sad or worried, she asked God for help.

"The older ones left for Taormina by train, while the younger ones came with me and the English nanny by car. The hotel offered tons of activities for the children, and they all had a great time. I had my work cut out to ensure that they behaved properly, for the hotel was frequented by the high Sicilian aristocracy. Massimo and Leonardo, little terrors that they were, were the hardest to rein in. Losing their dad affected our children differently. Although they were plagued by sadness, the older ones were so good, they tried to create a cheerful atmosphere for the little ones, and I'm sure for me too. Fulvia, Leonardo and Massimo were too young to fully understand what had happened, nonetheless they suffered greatly. When Massimo started going to school, he felt uncomfortable about not having a daddy. One day, he asked our driver Enzo to pretend to be his father."

As some kind of equilibrium slowly returned to the family, Tà began her new life and acknowledged its concomitant sacrifices. She knew she would have to devote herself exclusively to the family and business, and that she would have no time or energy for anything else. Few vacations, no evenings with friends or out at the theater or opera.

At social occasions, parties, weddings, fashion shows and events, as I was happily enjoying my second or third glass of champagne, I would stop and watch her. She seemed out of place among the people surrounding her, who would be babbling away, drinking, eating and smoking, often to excess. She watched in silence, but in a matter of seconds she had taken everything in. Tà never spoke first—she asked questions and let others do the talking. And she listened in. I often wondered if she was bored. I now know for sure that at such moments, she processed only what seemed right and necessary for her to take in, eliminating the superfluous. When she chose to devote herself to her family and the business, she also decided that she would never question this choice, nor look back with regret or melancholy. She never did.

In the spring of 1961, Grandmother went on her first business trip to New York, where she met the company's U.S. distribution agent who maintained relations with the heads of major department stores Saks Fifth Avenue, Bergdorf Goodman, and Lord & Taylor. The clients greeted her enthusiastically, assuring her that their business would continue. At that time, there was a Ferragamo store at 424 Park Avenue, one of whose regular customers was Marilyn Monroe. Tà paid a lot of attention to that store, how the shoes were displayed and arranged, the furniture, and the general atmosphere. Salvatore Ferragamo was one of the first Italian brands to have a boutique in the United States, and this store gave Tà some ideas about the company's future expansion.

After that trip to the U.S., once back in Florence, the London store manager forwarded a host of requests from the press, keen to meet a family member and find out how the company would continue without Salvatore. In what was her first test as a stylist and a stand-in for Grandfather, Tà decided to send Fiamma, who would present her first collection and meet the journalists.

"Fiamma was very young and was traveling alone, so rather than a hotel, I reserved a room for her in a nunnery. Poor thing! The nuns were very strict with their schedules, and the rooms quite spartan. When one of the reporters asked how she liked London and where she was staying, Fiamma quietly replied, 'At The Sisters of the Resurrection.' The reporter asked: 'Where is that? I've never heard of that hotel.' She had to repeat it several times, causing a good deal of mirth among the massed ranks of the London press. Fiamma laughed along with them, but I'm sure she didn't like it one bit. A 19-year-old shoe designer sent by her mother to a nunnery was so odd, certainly not common practice..."

After graduating from high school, Giovanna went to work for the company full time. Because all of the children had absorbed a great deal of knowledge about the company from an early age, joining it was almost a natural progression.

During summer vacations Ferruccio began doing odd jobs at the company that were in actual fact important. In a room at Palazzo Spini Feroni, at a time before air conditioning was installed, he cataloged Grandfather's original designs in the archive one by one. Thousands of them today form the core of the Museum collection. Still at a young age, Ferruccio spent time in production working alongside a great master, Jerry Ferragamo, who had re-thought the production processes and adopted organized systems in his maniacal search for quality and cost-containment, optimizing prices, enhancing the company's market competitiveness, and marking a new turning point for the company as a whole. Ferruccio then went to work in the retail department. Back then—this was the 1970s—there were around 15 stores, in Switzerland, London, and Italy. At the time, this was quite innovative: fashion companies were more accustomed to selling to specialty stores or department stores than to having their own retail chains. Ferruccio shared Grandfather's belief in retail and integration as a way of reaching consumers.

"Technology was advancing; new machinery needed to be brought into the manufacturing processes," Tà recalled. "It was a big step. Quality and fit were the foundations on which Ferragamo's renown and the success of its shoes were based; we had to ensure that the new machines were up to it, which was quite a puzzle for Ferruccio and Jerry to solve, but in the end they succeeded. The new machinery enabled the company to raise output and provide a previously unthinkable variety of sizes, ensuring a good fit for any foot. Still, to ensure quality at all times, many parts of the process continued to be carried out by hand. We may no longer have been custom-making our shoes, but they were still genuine Ferragamos. With courage and dedication, after production and stores, Ferruccio went into management. As his responsibilities grew, he started taking charge of the company's financial operations, freeing up a little more time for me to be a mother."

In the meantime, Fiamma became the public face of the company, traveling the world to present our shoes to leading department stores.

"Back then, shopping was an activity to savor and enjoy un-hurriedly, which made Fiamma ideal for the job. She never turned down an invitation, and no-one ever knew about the sacrifices she made. Sometimes she would visit three stores at a time, flying (which she hated) from one city to another, often accompanied by our agent Ned Schwartz. The schedule was al-ways the same: presentation of designs, a handshake agree-ment, a drink with customers before lunch, a quick dinner, and then off to the next city. In addition to her creative instincts, Fiamma had great business acumen. She loved manufacturing but was also enthusiastic about sales. She enjoyed maintaining a good relationship with clients and business contacts, and had an uncanny ability to remember everything she learned."

Not surprisingly, Fiamma rose to become Vice President of the group. She won the prestigious Neiman Marcus Award in 1967, when she was just 26 years old: exactly 20 years after Grandfather Salvatore had received his.

Tà was keen for Fiamma to be the official face of Ferragamo as she was planning to expand its distribution. By then, the Fer-ragamo brand had stores in Italy, London, New York, Munich and Paris. But Tà wanted to go further. The first big decision Grandmother took as head of the company was to build a new factory. So she looked for and found a plot of land at an attrac-tive price on the outskirts of Florence, in an area that at that time was completely desolate.

"Although we only needed 5,000 square meters, my instinct suggested to buy more. I bought 15,000, three times as much, which ended up being a very good deal because over the next few years the district grew into an industrial area, and as the company expanded, we gradually used up all that extra space. Following this piece of business from start to finish finally en-abled me to understand what entrepreneurial success felt like. It gave me tremendous satisfaction, but more importantly it was another piece of Salvatore's dream coming true—a piece I added myself."

Another important turning point came in 1965, when at the age of just 22, Giovanna made her debut in an extraordinary fashion show at Palazzo Pitti. Her collection launched a very successful second set of Salvatore Ferragamo-branded ready-to-wear items.

"I was so proud. That fashion show in the Sala Bianca was such a huge accomplishment. Giovanna contributed to the company from then on, staying on board even after she got married and made me a very young grandmother. And I have Gaetano and Alessandro, my first grandchildren, to thank for giving me the name Tà!"

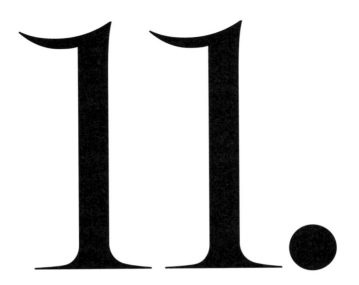

How Great It Is To Be Good

My favorite letter in the Red Book arrived when I was on summer vacation (the southern hemisphere summer) in Uruguay in December 2009. I had left Buenos Aires with the children as soon as school was out. In such isolation, the letter felt even more welcome: somebody had remembered me even though I hadn't spent Christmas with the family in Italy for a number of years. After moving to Argentina, we returned mostly in the summers, and Christmas in the snow had become a distant memory.

The letter's title, "How Great It Is To Be Good," immediately made me smile. I took myself off to my favorite place, in the secluded shade of eucalyptus trees, and began to read:

"The soul of the iniquitous is dark, their feelings tangled. They do not know how good it feels to lay one's head on the pillow, make the sign of the Cross and calmly retrace the events of the day. Truth, fairness, and honesty make our souls bright and peaceful. And so I say, do not conform to the bad in the world, allow yourself to be transformed, improving and renewing your way of thinking, acting in harmony with all that is good and pleasing to the Lord."

These counter-cultural words have stayed with me ever since, echoing inside me, helping to put everything into proportion. I talked with Tà a number of times about my work as a journalist, the responsibilities involved in doing this job in a foreign land, the sacrifices of living far away, of raising children often alone. She listened, and prompted me to think about women, work, and the role women have to play.

"Very few women ran companies in Italy when I began working. It's different now, and that makes me glad, even if I am well aware of all that it entails. Today, almost all women work. The number of things women have to do each day has multiplied and become much more complicated. Housewives must keep the books like an accountant, furnish the house like an interior designer, cook like a chef, and organize family life like a CEO. All the while keeping up the business of being a wife and mom. One thing I will say is that women who work outside the home must be very careful not to lose their femininity. When I say this, I see eyes widen everywhere, but you perfectly know what I mean... Femininity is the most noble and aristocratic thing we women possess, in the form of kindness, a calm tone of voice, a certain way of living."

These were non-negotiable staples for Tà, who despite being born in 1921, demonstrated all of her modernity and open-mindedness. Those words in particular helped me better understand her constant focus on being well turned-out, hospitable, and kindly at home as well as at work.

"There's a big advantage to being a woman behind a desk. When someone walks in, I always stand up, greet them, invite them to sit down and offer them something to drink, exactly as I'd do if I were receiving them at home, and I really like that. I believe women should always maintain a touch of femininity, no matter what the occasion, at home or out and about. I am amazed when I meet women who, as a result of their careers, lose sight of everything else. They think it makes them strong; perhaps it makes them too strong. A woman can get what she wants without having to adopt attitudes that undermine her true essence. Good manners, kind words, and a smile here and there are immeasurably powerful things!"

Tà once told me about a meeting she attended where she was surprised to see women acting aggressively, just like men. She never felt the need to change, but this didn't make her any less decisive and effective in her decision-making. Anyone who worked with her will back that up. According to Tà, being resolute and being feminine were no contradiction. In fact, they went hand in hand, as she herself demonstrated. To her, being feminine was never an impediment, nor was it so "for any woman who wants to get ahead."

Deep down inside, I sometimes suspected that Tà was either a bit naive about certain things, or very shrewd and calculating. Perhaps she was neither. Perhaps she was just a woman who had to work very hard to achieve a true balance in life, and that's why she got what she wanted.

One day, I asked her if over the years anyone had ever tried to cheat her. She replied dryly, "Not a chance! I'm sure everyone knows not to mess with me." Even with all her kind, feminine ways, my grandmother certainly didn't let anyone give her the run-around. She would set anyone straight by delivering a dry put-down at exactly the right moment.

Tà also believed women have another advantage at work that men lack: intuition.

"I thank God for giving me a good dose of intuition," she said, "and for ensuring I always listened to it." That intuition accompanied her from the day she first met Grandfather Salvatore in Bonito. Often, when faced with painful choices, I would ask her for advice. Her answer was always the same: "Trust in your intuition." Although it's not always easy, now I try and emulate her.

The imperturbable "Ten Rules of Tà" on woman's appropriate workplace behavior are perhaps the most enjoyable part of the whole Red Book. When I reread them now, they make me smile like mad. She laid the rules out in list form, and every single one provides a vivid picture of Tà.

"Rule number one: Always brush your hair well and look neat. Looking your best is a way of showing respect to the people you work for and with."

Tà compulsively brushed her hair. Before saying goodbye and giving me a kiss, she would pull her hairbrush out of her purse or some drawer to back-brush my hair. Enough to put a strain on anyone's nerves!

"Rule number two: Dress well. Do not wear clothes that are too extravagant; they should always be appropriate for the situation."

Grandmother's obsession with dressing well merits a book of its own. On one trip to Florence, I walked into her office and found her screaming and shouting. On a clothesline, she had hung up some clothes she had found somewhere in the store that were obviously not to her liking. Poor Silvano was vainly trying to calm her down. "This! It makes me sick! Not even a lunch lady at an elementary school..." she said disgustedly, rubbing a little blue cotton dress between her hands. "And what about this? What is this filth?" she asked, furiously hanging up a shirt. It took a full morning and a good lunch to restore her good mood.

The third rule was no less eloquent.

"Do not wear overly low-cut dresses. If you are going out to a dinner party after work, it is advisable to bring along a change of clothing. Sometimes you see little dresses in offices that are far too short. Simply horrible."

At this point, I imagined the funny face Tà would pull when she was horrified, remembering the time one of my cousins showed up to a dinner party in a very, very short skirt. Tà froze the second she saw her, but said nothing for the rest of the evening. Upon leaving, however, she plainly manifested all her disapproval and dislike in a snide remark she made in front of everyone. From then on, nobody dared go to Grandmother's in a short skirt.

"Rule number four: Never laugh too loudly. Far better to draw attention to yourself by doing your job well."

This dig was directed at certain cousins who had a particularly loud and infectious laugh.

"Rule number five: Always stand up when an important person walks into the room. And in general, it's important to show respect to others in any case and at every opportunity."

Actually, Tà stood up even when one of us entered.

"Rule number six: Never speak ill of the people you work with, especially your superiors. Nothing good ever comes from such chatter, it merely expresses a lack of style."

"Rule number seven: Always be kind to the people you work with, especially if they are under your supervision. The people you meet going up are the same people you'll meet going down. Better to be nice to everyone."

"Rule number eight: Always be on time. It's a form of respect not just toward your employer but a sign of the value you give your work."

"Rule number nine: Always take work seriously. That's not to say you shouldn't enjoy it; simply, respect it."

"Rule number ten: Always remember that people watch us closely because of who we are, so be careful to honor your own and your family's name."

Tà's Ten Commandments for working women ended with an imperative: "These rules apply to everyone," which was as clear as it was topical. When I passed them on to my daughter Ottavia on her first day at work, they did not seem old-fashioned to her. Indeed, she smiled and applied them to the letter.

Tà used to say how proud she was of us girls, her grandchildren. She thought we were wise, hardworking, and well aware of how hard it is to be an entrepreneur in this day and age. She suggested starting with one good idea, something very special—something she definitely found in Grandfather's dream.

At work, Tà dipped her toes into a little bit of everything, from design to materials, cutting, marketing, distribution, and corporate organization. It bothered her that fashion was considered merely as a glamorous industry. She knew as well as anyone that those 20 minutes on the runway were the culmination of millions of hours of hard, disciplined work. She was very insistent that we were well educated, both in terms of experience and academically, preferably getting a master's degree. She used to say that in order to effectively launch a product, it was necessary to position it correctly in the market, organize the manufacturing, and above all create an identity for it and then turn it into a brand. In this as in so much else, Tà was far ahead of her time.

In the 1970s, she mulled over exploiting the vineyards at
Viesca to export wine to the U.S. On a visit to New York at that
time, she was offered a pre-dinner cocktail at the Rainbow
Room above the Rockefeller Center. Although she did not usually drink alcohol, she didn't want to seem ungrateful so she asked
for the wine list. She was speechless when she saw there were
only two wines on it, one white and one red, and realized that
exporting Italian wines presented a great opportunity. However, when she looked into the costs involved, she understood it
would not be easy to undertake this business and, more importantly, that it would divert energy away from her main priority.

"Many people are doing it today. Both Massimo and Ferruccio have been exporting wine from Castiglion del Bosco and Il
Borro to the United States with great success. It probably wasn't
the right time when I thought of it, but today they have managed to make that old dream come true as well. You know, a
business needs encouragement and support, and that's not always easy to come by. We must surround ourselves with people
who share our ideals and support our efforts. But we must also
be careful not to surround ourselves with yes-men."

When Tà was invited to join the Committee of 200, a group
of American women entrepreneurs set up to support women
who wanted to start a business, she was favorably struck by
these strong, confident ladies so full of initiative. She remembered one in particular, a teacher by the name of Pleasant Rowland. Tà sent us a letter for the Red Book about her entrepreneurial story.

"Every Christmas, Pleasant desperately searched for dolls to
give to her granddaughters, but she could never find one that
was right for them. The granddaughters were too old to play
with old-fashioned dolls, and they didn't like Barbies one bit.
Pleasant was looking for a doll that would teach them good
manners, along with a little tradition. Because she couldn't find
what she was looking for, she decided to create the American
Girl dolls herself. These dolls were special because they portrayed little girls from different backgrounds, living at different
times in American history. Pleasant also confected books to tell
each doll's story. As a result, the girls could play and at the same

time learn about American history and good manners. Pleasant Rowland called her firm The Pleasant Company. She worked really hard to ensure that all of the dolls' details were accurate, their stories interesting, and that they promoted positive, educational concepts. The company was a huge success."

Tà confessed that, as a firm believer in the primary importance of education, she would have liked to be a teacher in order to pass on her experience and help young women find their footing at work. Although she thought she had not benefited greatly from the years she went to religious schools, she knew that she had received a very good education from her parents and, later, from Grandfather Salvatore.

"Everything I've learned in life is from observing people, their behavior, how they reach decisions, and how they treat the people around them."

This explains why Tà decided to become our *maestra*, using her letters to convey her positive experiences and pass on teachings she considered useful.

"One of the finest examples of education I ever saw was at the New York Fashion Institute of Technology (FIT) a few years after I started working. I was invited to lunch by the president, and then taken on a tour of the school. I was so impressed with the lessons, the commitment and how well prepared the teachers were... For one class, they'd brought in a Balenciaga dress to study how it was put together, down to the smallest detail. They had taken the dress apart on a table and were studying its intricate sleeve seams with the same level of attention medical students pay to dissecting a body."

Tà also sent us a copy of the invitation she received to accept an Honorary Degree from the FIT. The ceremony took place at Radio City Music Hall on May 22, 2007. Thousands of young people filled the auditorium. Tà proudly remembered the energy, enthusiasm, and applause when she was called to the stage to give a speech.

"Good morning everyone, and congratulations on your incredible accomplishments. I know you are familiar with the story of the lady who lived in a shoe... But I would like to tell you that it took this lady a long journey, like the one Salvatore made from the small village of Bonito to New York. We are here today because, just like each of you, Salvatore had a dream. Allow me to encourage you to follow your own dream with the same passion, integrity, and determination that inspired him. My great hope is that young people like you will fully understand, experience, and maintain success. Despite all the effort, it's a worthwhile endeavor that takes dedication, discipline, passion, and endless time in the office. To this day, I still go to the office even on Saturdays if the need arises. Saturdays, yes, because that's the day when things are quiet, allowing me to calmly draw up a list for my employees of things to do when Monday morning comes around. Then my Monday mornings are more relaxed, because everyone is busy, giving me space to devote to the most important matters. Obviously, I can do this because I am 'the boss,' as many of you will one day be. As you progress in your career, always remember that craftsmanship, creativity, innovation, and respect for tradition are the principles on which each of you will build your future in the design world. Today, this is your job; tomorrow, it will be your career. As I look at all you ambitious, hopeful, and talented young people, eager to take advantage of the opportunities that await, my wish is that in the future you reach the place I am now. To each and every one of you graduating today, my best wishes for happiness and success."

Terracotta Pots

Unexpectedly, I received a photograph in the post of ten huge terracotta pots. I immediately knew it was from Tà. The vases were like ones I had seen at Il Palagio and in Viesca, instantly taking my thoughts back to Tuscany. I was surprised to learn from the letter that the vases were now in France, after Tà had donated them to the Leonardo da Vinci Park in Amboise.

Tà had gone to visit her dear friend Baroness de Laitre at the seven-hectare park around the Château du Clos Lucé, owned by the Counts of Saint Bris. Over lunch, Tà learned that Leonardo had lived there at the castle for three years, up to his death in 1519. She found this so fascinating that she decided to make this donation. In her letter, she warmly invited us to visit the place, saying how much she loved every plant there. To some extent, we have all inherited Tà's love of gardens, flowers, and nature, something she shared with Grandfather Salvatore. "It's an amateur interest. For me, flowers are one of the proofs of God's existence. I've gotten pretty good at them, and I try to help out the farmers too." A few times Tà participated in exhibitions at the

Museo Stibbert in Florence, with its magnificent English-style park, bringing along her camellias. One of her favorites was the white camellia. "Its petals look like they're made of chiffon, and I enjoy them all through winter because they bloom until April," she told me one sunny day as we ate lunch in the garden surrounded by her countless plants. Every corner of Il Palagio was adorned with them.

She told me her sister had had a flower garden of red and white camellias, and she had fallen in love with them when she was a little girl. In Florence, when she first arrived at Il Palagio, she planted them everywhere, only to sadly watch them die one by one. On one trip to London, she came across some particularly large specimens and consulted a floriculturist, who told her that camellias must be kept apart from other plants because they dislike root interference. On her return, Tà had some holes dug, put cement around the insides and filled them with earth and chestnut peat. Camellias of all colors have never stopped blooming in her garden ever since.

The only hue she did not have was a yellow one.

"They are extremely rare, although they do flourish in Japan. On a trip to Tokyo for the Ferragamo retrospective, I met Imperial Princess Takamado, who shares my passion for orchids. I told her I had been looking for a yellow camellia for years. The very next day, two beautiful specimens were delivered to me at the hotel. Taking them into Italy proved to be very complicated. They had to undergo quarantine and, by law, be pruned and cut back. Although I cared for them lovingly, they didn't grow a single bud, and in the end they died. They should never be pruned and should be fertilized only with the right fertilizers," she told me, sure that I knew all about pruning and everything. "Once a year we hold an exhibition at Palazzo Budini Gattai and give an award to the most beautiful specimen through the Garden Club, of which I am a member."

Azaleas, which Grandfather loved dearly, and peonies were also among her favorites, but Tà had a special soft spot for roses. A small road leads down from Il Palagio through the garden toward the Maiano road. Tà would walk along it every Sunday to go to mass and as she went, she would meticulously inspect all of her roses. They too had to be in pristine condition. She noted down any shortcomings promptly in her notepad and reported them to the gardener on the Monday morning.

There is now a type of rose that bears her name. The "Wanda Ferragamo" has fleshy, pinkish flowers with shades of violet, and is particularly fragrant. It was created in 2008 by Rose Barni, a renowned grower from Pistoia, as a present Giovanna gave Tà for her birthday.

On the topic of flowers, bees and honey were another "natural" attraction Tà was passionate about that I share with her. We would talk about them for hours. Every now and then, I would bring her a few jars of my favorite honey from Uruguay or Argentina, which she would immediately taste to give me her opinion. I used to tell her how the bees there work over vast distances, sometimes near the sea and in high winds, and she was fascinated. She was thrilled when I told her about a social project related to honey and women farmers some friends of mine were running in Argentina, promoting beekeeping among young rural women to provide them with an income and, in turn, the chance to train more future beekeepers. The project, Miel de Reinas de Corazones, is up and running in Argentina and will soon be operative in Uruguay as well, making these women true "queens of the bees." Grandmother recommended eating a lot of honey in the mornings, blended with pollen and royal jelly, claiming this is a very effective remedy for every ailment.

Tà's passion for bees was another family legacy. Great-grandfather Fulvio used to treat his patients with honey. Not only did he love bees for their beneficial properties, but he was also fascinated by how they worked. His memoir contains a lovely passage dedicated to bees, including some typical nineteenth-century flights of fancy.

"Since time immemorial, bees have solved the problem of collective life, one that continues to afflict the minds of men and bloody our civilization. Man creates kingdoms, republics, and empires that turn to ruin through disorder and bloodshed, painstakingly conquering freedoms and then trading them for tyranny, making and unmaking laws that bring neither stability nor peace. For thousands of years, on the contrary, bees have been living in communities based on love, order, and work: boundless attachment to a common mother, widow of a single love, to the home and to their sisters, prepared even to sacrifice their lives; organization and discipline in all activities; passion and tenacity through work, ideally distributed among builders, foragers, feeders, guards, attendants, sweepers, ventilators, and undertakers, with nowhere to hid for the idle and parasitic, bar complete destruction. Such an ideal society has no need for either codes or punishment. Everyone is at his post for the good of all, without sloth, strife, dangerous new developments or deviance into error and evil. Such is the secret of your wellbeing, O winged bearers of sweetness and perfume, pollinating and fruitful virgins. Is it only human society then that must impose laws by force and defend itself against prevaricators and the violent? Do men live in an inferior condition to brutes? No. Unreasoning animals are guided by the infallible that is within them yet does not belong to them, and hence deserve neither blame nor praise. Man has a conscience, intellect, and will capable of sublimating him, for better or worse. Such freedom of thought and free action bring dignity as a man and responsibility as a citizen. The human collectivity is not a meeting of equal elements acting in instinctive conformity to achieve some immutable end, it is the confluence of free, intellectually, and morally different elements, direct creators of their own destiny. The problem in ordering human society is not a matter of form but of substance, the solution to which, ever topical, depends on the moral and intellectual constitution of its components; free will may direct us toward good or evil. Order, wellbeing, and peace among mankind, anchored through the worship of spiritual values and the unstinting pursuit of individual education, may only be based on the numerical and qualitative prevalence of the finest elements. On the contrary, the absolute domination of a few individuals, even if endowed with superior qualities and good will, is short-lived and scarcely effective, because—when not overwhelmed by popular rebellion—the inert weight of the masses alienated from public life and unaccustomed to a sense of political responsibility exhausts and wears them down."

With the exception of flowers and nature, no passion surpassed Tà's passion for the company. Apart from a few "natural" digressions, any conversation with her always returned to the company, at the heart of which Tà sat like a queen bee.

"One of the most beautiful things in the world for me are the three letters, S.p.A. that come after Salvatore Ferragamo on our official documents, in correspondence, and on the plaque affixed to the wall outside Palazzo Spini Feroni. Illogical as it may sound, to me they have always represented implementation of Salvatore's dream through the efforts and determination I and your parents made in the years after his death. I am unable to see them as three simple letters! From the very beginning, my strategy has been to keep the company's various divisions strong by paying attention to every office and department. I was constantly making sure that the factory, the new machinery, everything was working in harmony to maintain our products' high quality level, which has always been our brand's core value. I devoted all my efforts to quality before any ideas of expansion. Initially, our growth was rather modest, albeit positive, but my long-range goal was to grow slowly, from a solid base. A rapidly turned profit didn't seem that important to me as I was mulling over how to take things forward as well as I could. In the 1960s and 1970s, it would have been easier for me to grow the company quickly by licensing products we didn't create in-house. That was a widespread practice, and very lucrative back in the day. Licensing is based on the 'one size fits all' philosophy, even if it's clear that what works for some doesn't work for others. In our specific case, it would have been a huge mistake. We would have risked jettisoning both the Ferragamo brand's identity and quality. I certainly didn't want to take that risk, even if it meant renouncing a more rapid rise in profits. Money is money, it comes and goes, but a good reputation is hard to maintain: once it's gone, it's gone forever. Our growth has been organic, a natural unfolding of things. Every time we had an idea, we worked on it. One day, for example, I talked to Fiamma about the possibility of creating bags. Without a moment's hesitation, Fiamma said: 'Let's try it, let's make them.' And so we did, even if following through was neither simple nor immediate. Although we had a strong label and experience, the competition was stronger. It was a long and arduous task to enter a new segment of the market. We entrusted that task to an external designer, under Fiamma's direct supervision. She always responded positively to all stimuli and promptings, as did each of my children, and all of you too. We would see a product and immediately wonder if we could make it, improve it, reinterpret it in our own style."

Nowadays, like Ferragamo's wide range of leather goods, handbags are a fundamental component of the company's product line. It seems almost impossible to think that they were not part of the range from the beginning. This is true of other areas as well, such as prints and silks, of which my mom was the true champion.

One day, as part of our regular email exchange, Tà wrote to me: "Your mother's work is an example of how the company has grown naturally and organically. The silks division was created because of her. As you know, she joined the company at 18. She designed bijoux, because she loved jewelry so much. Then fate intervened. In 1970, she married your dad and they moved to Milan. Having grown up with so many siblings around, she initially felt lonely. On the phone, she used to say: 'I miss you... I miss my sisters, my brothers,' a bit like you do from Buenos Aires. I wanted to help her find a role in the company that suited her situation and respected her interests and talents, but if it had been a permanent role, she would have had to stay in Florence rather than moving to Milan. The solution popped up almost automatically thanks to your mom's intuition. Milan was very close to Como, then a crucial region for silk production, where we bought our scarves from a trusted supplier. One day, Fulvia asked me whether it might be a good idea to produce our silk products ourselves. My answer was a resounding yes. With Fulvia in Milan, we would be able to follow that line. She was well placed to take care of it."

Ferragamo began manufacturing scarves in 1972, to designs based on my mother's ideas. She started reproducing wild animals, her great passion, on silk, against backgrounds of petals and flower blossoms.

"They were not just beautiful but decorative too. I still remember the first one, in which the design featured an elephant. It was amazing. When you wore the scarf around your neck, roses and orchids popped out; when you opened it up, it was like a work of art. Imagine, years later a fellow collected many of her scarves and had them framed to hang in his home in lieu of paintings."

And so, through Tà's story, I discovered this anecdote about my mom, about which I knew nothing. She didn't like to talk about herself, and was even more loath to boast about her accomplishments, which were remarkable, not least branching out into ties. She was understated yet elegant, energetic but extremely reserved. When she finally had time to spend with us, she didn't talk about hassles at work. There were four of us kids at home: my sister Angelica, the eldest, Consolata, three years younger than me, and my brother Emanuele, the youngest of all. We were by no means calm and quiet, but Mom taught us that a woman can work at a high level even with an active family life, providing an example of a working woman that was decisive for me.

She was often on the road, shuttling back and forth to Florence, but when she was in the office in Milan she would go in early so she could be back home to eat lunch with us, to be "all together" as a family. In the afternoons she would go back to the office, where I occasionally went to visit her. Despite being very busy, she always had time for a chat, just as she always picked up the phone if my siblings and I were looking for her, even for the most trivial of reasons. I cannot remember a day when she wasn't there for us.

Through Mom's work, the silk division became a leading part of the Salvatore Ferragamo business, as it still is today. New products added alongside the scarves and ties include pillows, ponchos, shawls, and umbrellas. Mom had a truly magical eye for colors and fabrics. Like Grandfather, she followed her creative instincts rather than market trends. Her creations associated with animals like the jaguar or the tiger became Ferragamo icons. Many of her designs have been copied by other designers, famous ones included; but as she once reminded me, "my father Salvatore used to say, you only need to start worrying when they're not copying you."

When my mother married and went to live in Milan, Tà remained alone at Il Palagio with Leonardo and Massimo, who were still teenagers. In 1971, Tà took them with her on a business trip to the United States, hoping they would remember it for the rest of their lives.

"We went by ship, crossing the Atlantic as their father had done sixty years earlier, though under somewhat different conditions. We set sail from Genoa. The trip was wonderful in every respect. The boys had a great time, although for a few days they ended up being punished with enforced cabin time for being out of control. And they were so funny! They listened attentively as I explained the significance of landing in New York Harbor, for everything it had meant to their father, his family, and so many other Italians. Massimo was almost the same age as Salvatore had been when he embarked in 1915. I was happy to be able to repeat that trip with them."

This journey to the United States proved to be a turning point. Tà had a clear idea in her head: to expand the company's presence in New York beyond a handful of department stores and the one store on Park Avenue.

"I thought, if we had a larger space, we could present the entire collection in a way that emphasized the harmony among the various products, the colors, fabrics, and style. Rather than being dispersed in department stores, our products could create such a powerful effect in a boutique dedicated solely to the Salvatore Ferragamo brand."

Tà used that New York trip to find a store. She was keen for it to be on Fifth Avenue, because she saw there was more footfall than on Park Avenue. In no time at all, she spotted the perfect location in the Steuben Glass Building, which had stunning windows along the street where products could be displayed to best advantage. That was the company's first mono-brand store abroad, marking the start of an expansion of Ferragamo shops all over the world.

"When it came to choosing cities and locations, once again I let myself be guided by instinct and intuition. I used reasoning too, wondering where we would find ladies who appreciated our craftsmanship and quality, where the most elegant shopping districts were located... Everyone is surprised when I tell them I personally used to choose store locations; today, it is a much more complicated process, analyzed and researched using numbers and charts."

Tà was highly focused on stores. Wherever she traveled, the first thing she did was visit the local Ferragamo store and check that the products were correctly displayed, the salespeople tidy and efficient, and harmony reigned over all aspects. If things weren't as they should be, if the situation didn't "honor the product," as she liked to say, she had no qualms about passing comment or making constructive criticisms. To Tà's mind, the product had to be an investment for the customer. As she wrote in a "circular," "when the customer buys a product, she subconsciously feels that it must be a vehicle for values such as quality, modernity, beauty, and sobriety. Such content builds customer loyalty, making the buyer proud to own that product. Creatives, merchandising, buyers, and planners must strongly embrace the concept that the product is primarily an investment. I cannot emphasize this concept enough."

When Leonardo turned 20 in 1973, he too joined the company.

"To begin with, he was very unsure about his future. 'Everyone has their place here, Mom, but where do I fit in?' he would ask. I reassured him, telling him that he too would find his place. All he had to do was follow his passions. I advised him to talk to Jerry. I wanted him to start with the basics, the essentials. This he did, soon enough achieving excellent results. He proved to be very resourceful, taking full advantage of his time with Jerry to learn the basics of our core business. He made his first contribution by dedicating himself to a sector we had little interest in: men's shoes. We made so few of them that they weren't even included in our bottom line. Leonardo glimpsed an opportunity and decided to do things the right way, beginning with market research, product research and, being his father's son, research into the male foot."

Men's shoes joined the production line in the 1970s and immediately performed excellently, first in the U.S. then in Europe and finally in Asia. Not long afterwards, the company launched its first ready-to-wear men's line, developed in parallel with the shoes.

As a token of their gratitude to their parents, after joining the company, Ferruccio, Leonardo, and Massimo each made a pair of shoes for Tà with their own hands. "I must admit, I have no lovelier shoes than those three pairs. I still remember the looks on their faces, their gaze planted firmly on my feet as I slipped them on. They wanted me to wear their shoes alone. Which of course I did," Tà said with a smile.

Bit by bit, the product range was expanding and the company growing. Tà now had five of her six children working at the company.

"I was constantly concerned that we shouldn't lose sight of our core principles: quality without compromise and consistency in our designs, materials, and style. At the same time, I kept process innovation going while respecting our tradition, history, and the integrity of what we were doing. As I shall never tire of repeating, these principles are our Bible and our guide. I knew healthy growth would follow if I succeeded in instilling these principles company-wide, to manufacturing, management, distribution and retail, ensuring that our employees felt them too."

Tà may have felt bound by tradition, but she was also a relentless researcher. She knew that without ongoing research, work remains static and fails to evolve. In every job and every field, there must be a desire to do better, to make something new, just as, ahead of his time, Grandfather Salvatore had taught her, and as numerous still-applicable patents in our archives show.

"Culture strengthens research!" Tà wrote in a letter for the Red Book, also reminding us that effective communication is the best way to achieve goals.

"It is essential for relationships between managers and employees to always be cordial. They must communicate with one another and listen to one another. Listening is key because it helps foster a feeling of trust that makes it possible to engage in constructive criticism, something many people find very difficult. You should always criticize work that has not been done properly, but you should also make it clear that you are criticizing something specific, something that has nothing to do with the relationship with the person and the trust placed in them. At work, I learned to criticize when the time was right, often putting my thoughts in writing to make things as clear as possible. Through experience, I have learned that most mistakes employees make are the result of flawed management or insufficient information. Mistakes made in good faith are very much the norm. You must convey enthusiasm for work done, for the contributions people make to end results, because that is what creates identity and credibility. The same thing applies within a family. Ferruccio, who with prudence, application, and seriousness took over the financial side of the business in 1975, kept all of the notes I sent him over the years and filed them in the archives. He says they are highly critical, with no room for any kind of compliment. You know me, you know that's how I am."

Without giving too much away, in that letter Tà gave me and all my cousins a crash course in true business management.

Notepads

One of Tà's most endearing qualities was undoubtedly the gift of communication. When she wanted to convey something, she knew how to go about it, in words or on paper. Throughout her life, she used a large notepad to jot everything down, from her grocery list to phone calls and thoughts she wished to share, things that were missing and things that required fixing. By the end of the day, she wanted her to-do list to be as close to fully complete as possible. She would also jot down concepts she wished to recall in order to circulate them within the company, to her children, or to us grandchildren. Many of them became letters destined for the Red Book.

She would often sit there silently, a notepad on her thighs and a pen in hand, looking serious and focused. If you dared interrupt, she'd say "Shhhhh, be quiet, be quiet," and start writing. I loved watching her think and jot things down. I always told myself I would emulate her. Tà knew how to use silence and make the most of it. She thought, rephrased, wrote and acted. Her resulting messages were clear, lucid, and very effective. Her advice might sometimes have seemed obvious, but it really never was. Her tangible, practical, insightful words always arrived at the right time.

Grandmother wrote a whole series of reflections for us to keep in the Red Book, based on what she had witnessed and lived through, warning us off making trivial but common mistakes "to avoid trouble and unpleasant surprises." One fine day, she sent a handwritten note, a list from her notepad entitled, "Important Rules for the Grandchildren." She loved writing out rules in lists.

"Point one: Never delegate the signature for your own or your company's checks.

Two: Never sign IOUs.

Three: Never offer a guarantee for anyone.

Four: Never let friends who have become financiers persuade you to trust them with your savings. You stand to lose both money and friendship.

Five: Before embarking on a business that always involves capital, cover your back with an equal amount of secured, untouchable, undiscoverable capital.

Six: If you are enticed by people offering you honors, associations, or a seat on a board of directors, be prepared for any related liabilities.

Seven: Do not divulge your financial affairs to strangers. Prudence and diffidence are of vital importance to avoiding so many pitfalls.

Eight: Be cautious in everything: think before you act. God gave us a brain to use, not to gloss over everything, race around and act superficially.

Nine: During negotiations, after making a verbal agreement, attempt to confirm everything in writing, and request similar confirmation from the other party, i.e., your interlocutor.

Ten: These rules and recommendations do not prohibit giving love, support, and teaching to those around us who may need them. These are two different yet essential paths.

Eleven: Giving as much as you can is a basic tenet of life, responding to a precise divine plan, and therefore always a seed that germinates goodness.

Twelve (and final point): Unquestioned honesty must illuminate your life. It will give you the confidence to act; it will make your eyes shine with light, reflecting inner tranquility and allowing you to sleep at night. The sleep of the just, as the Gospel says. With love, Tà."

Sometimes, she would pick up her notepad in the early morning, immediately after waking up, when after a good night's sleep new ideas and concepts were at their clearest. As a little girl, I remember sleeping in the big bed with her a few times. Her bedroom was huge, packed with objects. I loved poking around, scrutinizing her collections and photographs. But woe betide if you touched anything or asked for too much information. Quickly and fearfully, I crawled into her big, scented, starched bed, careful not to say a word too many. The only words allowed were prayers, of which Tà was the sweetest teacher. We would recite a Hail Mary, an Our Father, the *Angiolin Bellin Bellino*, and then in an intimate tone and using simple phrases, Tà would give thanks to God and ask him to continue to protect us all. She would turn off the light and, until 7 in the morning when the clock radio roared into action, not a fly dared buzz in that huge room. Tà would get up, throw open the windows to breathtaking views, grab the breakfast tray outside the door and clamber back into bed with the newspapers, her notepad, and her ever-present magnifying glass. As she listened to the radio news, she carefully flipped through the *Corriere della Sera* and *La Nazione*, then wrote a few notes while sipping her tea with milk and saccharin. Meanwhile, she prepared the tub for a voluminous morning bath, scented with exquisite aromas. Her favorite fragrance was the Bien Être eau de cologne. Every moment was ripe for thinking. After the bath, she brushed her hair, put on a tiny amount of cream and entered the walk-in closet to carefully choose her outfit for the day. A colorful suit, a silk scarf and that inevitable string of pearls.

"You know, it doesn't take a lot to be stylish," she once told me. Indeed, her closets contained only essentials for always being well turned-out, nothing superfluous.

The phone calls began to come in at 8 o'clock from her grandchildren, friends, and children. Everyone knew that was the right time to catch her, even if it wasn't always the best time for her. It wasn't unusual to see her irritated, forced to talk on the phone as she tried to finish getting ready, impatient to grab her notepad and go through the orders for the staff in the house.

One of that series of morning notes became a letter to us.

"A company's importance and validity are measured by the value of the people who work there. We must get ready because the future is China and indeed all of Asia. By planning the company's growth at a slow and steady pace, you achieve more solid and long-lasting results. We need to train our young people without wasting time. If we make the right choices, we can grow culturally at the same time as modernizing, at all times safeguarding our DNA. This is critical. This is how to set in motion a great commercial apparatus, but it's essential to look after every aspect in detail."

Tà never missed an opportunity to reiterate her thoughts on globalization.

"Although it seems to be a contemporary concept, in vogue over the last two decades, I believe that the idea of globalization has always been a part of our company, ever since Salvatore's earliest days. In the 1980s, it became more manifest when Massimo and Leonardo started to expand our business further abroad, Massimo revitalizing and expanding our presence in the United States, Leonardo assessing it in Asia. When I say our philosophy has been to think globally from the start, it's because in this field as in so many others, Salvatore was a truly revolutionary thinker."

Tà still keeps in her office a page from a 1926 issue of *Japanese Daily News,* an article about Grandfather and his studies of the Japanese foot, to which he dedicated himself because he wanted to make sure he could offer a comfortable fit to Japanese women, whose feet are structurally different from Western women's. All the way back in the 1920s, Grandfather dreamed of Italian artisans making shoes for the whole world. So Tà was basically correct when she said that he was an early proponent of globalization. In the 1940s, he helped establish the idea of Made in Italy, and in 1958 he traveled to Australia to seek out new opportunities for expansion.

Tà wanted Massimo to pursue a career as a lawyer, and for a while he studied law. But in 1982, an opportunity arose that radically changed his life. Burt Tansky, then president of Saks Fifth Avenue, suggested to Tà that Massimo go to New York and enroll on Saks's Executive Training Program: six months' dedicated training for young buyers, introducing them to the professional world.

"Burt thought it would be good for Massimo, a chance to learn and understand the business from the other side of the desk. Even though I was less than happy he would be away from home for so long, I grew to like the idea. Massimo was excited about the prospect, and eventually convinced me. It turned out to be an outstanding decision for both him and the company. Just like Salvatore and me before him, Massimo fell in love with the United States. When he finished his classes at Saks, he would walk down Fifth Avenue to our store, spend a few hours working, and think about how to incorporate everything he was learning into our retail operations.

It was the perfect workshop. He returned to Italy with a clear proposal: to stay on in New York and expand the company's position and visibility across the United States. He presented an action plan, we approved it, and it continues to this day as Salvatore Ferragamo USA. A true motive for pride and the crowning achievement of Salvatore's dream."

Tà would travel to the United States at every opportunity to see Massimo in New York, always happy to soak up the city's energy and optimism.

The history of Ferragamo's distribution has an interesting aspect to it. In the 1980s, the company distributed 70% of its products to America and 30% to Italy and the rest of the world. Today, America accounts for 35%, Europe and Italy 30%, and Asia 35%. The past decades have seen enormous growth in Ferragamo operations around the world, leveraging the fantastic affirmation of Italian design and the company's decision to expand into the exciting new Asian market. Ferragamo initially had only a small presence there, for Giovanna's designs rather than shoes. In the 1970s, Japan placed very high import taxes on foreign shoes, making it tough to export products there. At

that time, Ferragamo had a showroom in Palazzo Strozzi dedicated to its ready-to-wear line. One day, Giovanna met a buyer
from a large Japanese store that every season increased its purchases. Ferragamo began to have a presence in Asia back then,
even if the real expansion came later, propelled by the vision of
Leonardo, whom Tà nicknamed "our icebreaker."

After developing the men's line, Leonardo opened a series of
men's boutiques in the 1980s that became very popular. In 1987,
he took a trip to Asia that broke through a new frontier, glimps-
ing an opportunity very few had seen before: tangible demand
for luxury goods on the continent. Shortly after that trip, he
opened Ferragamo's first office in Hong Kong, a single desk in
someone else's place, but that was all he needed to gain a foot-
hold in this new market. Through his insight, Ferragamo became the first luxury brand to establish itself in Asia, expanding
into China, Japan, Korea, the Philippines, Thailand, Malaysia,
Indonesia and India.

Tà was on the same wavelength.

"In my own small way, I made a contribution to our expansion in Asia. On one of my New York trips, a saleswoman at our
Fifth Avenue store came over to me and said, 'Mrs. Ferragamo,
may I introduce you to a very important client?' I replied, 'Of
course, with great pleasure.' As you know, I love personally getting to know our clients. The saleswoman introduced me to a
very tall, beautiful woman named Lady Harrison, wife of actor
Rex Harrison. She had fallen in love with one of our shoe styles.
In fact, it fit her so well and was so comfortable that as we chat-
ted about this and that, she asked if it was possible to reproduce
that same design in different colors. She wanted to be able to
wear these shoes in combination with various outfits. We hadn't
made custom shoes for a long while, but I could see that she
was really keen on this, and she had been so kind... Being a particularly good customer, I told her we would do it gladly. We
took an order for dozens of pairs of shoes created especially for
Lady Harrison, and she was enormously grateful. The very next
day, she sent me a letter in which she said she'd like to introduce
me to a friend of hers, a partner of one of the most important
entrepreneurs in Asia, Peter Woo, who was looking to invest in

a fashion house. So impressed was Lady Harrison at what we had done for her that she immediately wrote to Peter Woo, suggesting Ferragamo as a potential partner for his business. This simple exchange resulted in a hugely successful deal between our company and Peter Woo, who became a trusted colleague and partner and also a great friend of ours. Who knows what would have happened if I had said to Lady Harrison, 'Sorry, we don't make shoes on demand anymore.' The lesson is obvious. You must always be open to opportunities, because you never know where new business may crop up."

In October 2006, Tà sent us a letter to which she attached Peter Woo's speech from a dinner held to celebrate his 20 years of collaboration with Ferragamo. His words were a veritable chronicle of the company's early years in China.

"My friends, 20 years ago we held a very special dinner at the Mandarin Hotel to celebrate the start of a business relationship between my family and Ferragamo; 20 years ago, Mrs. Wanda Ferragamo attended that event to kick off the partnership. To mark this evening's event, I received a brief note from her that I wish to read out to you: 'Dear Peter and Bessie, our 20-year partnership could not have been happier or more satisfying. We look forward to continuity and success for many years to come, in the same perfect harmony as in the past. We send our most sincere best wishes to you and your entire family.'"

Once more, Tà had written just a few lines to great effect. Then the letter continued with Peter Woo's speech.

"Wanda is a wonderful, caring woman, so very dear to Bessie, myself and our children all these years, and it is my honor to consider myself her friend. Back in 1960, Wanda stepped into some very big shoes as the custodian of her husband's dreams. She had no idea how to run a business. Well, over the years, she has built up a major family enterprise... The rest, as they say, is history. Ferragamo is a preeminent brand among an elite group of Italian fashion houses whose business is still 100% in family hands. Ferragamo is a success story, one that we are delighted to be part of in Asia. Ferragamo LOVE LIVE posters are plastered up on walls the world over. Our team, led here by Balbina Wong, has done a great job over the years promoting brand integrity, building up a quality franchise and keeping our customers happy and satisfied. I thank the team for this, and Balbina for such outstanding results. I also cannot fail to mention Eileen Bygrave, who has contributed in so many ways to the success of our business. I must also thank the Ferragamo team, wonderful partners whose trust and vision are the cornerstone of this partnership's success. When we first began, we shared a dream. Alongside Hong Kong's continued prosperity, that dream has come true. I still remember the many hours I spent talking with Ferruccio and Leonardo about Hong Kong and China, at a time when many people were anxious about the future. We all agreed and we were all confident. We should be proud of what we've achieved—our China portfolio is top notch. Last year, on October 20, 2005, at the Forbidden City we celebrated our tenth year in China. What a memorable event that was: 20 years ago we started up a business relationship, which today has grown into such a strong family relationship. The family is here, too: Ferruccio, Leonardo, Giovanna, Fulvia and from the third generation, James, Emanuele, and Angelica. We extend a warm welcome to you as custodians of Salvatore Ferragamo's dreams, which we hope to share in for a long time to come. My family and I wish to thank you for your warmth and friendship over the years. Looking forward, we hope for the same continuity, success, and harmony our dear Wanda wishes for—indeed, I couldn't have put it better myself. We look forward to many more exciting, successful, and optimistic years to come. We are here to celebrate the future that awaits us."

I immediately understood the lesson Tà wished to convey through this letter, with its official tone. Peter Woo's words overflowed with genuine gratitude for a working relationship nurtured over the years by paying attention not just to business but also (and above all) to people. That was Tà to a T. She won people over to her side before winning anything else.

Tà pointed out that the company's growth and diversification in the 1980s and 1990s, and most notably its operational management strategy, had had to adapt to new scenarios. Both manufacturing and distribution had grown into large divisions, making it necessary to bring in many senior managers from outside the family.

"That was a major decision for us, one of several crucial changes to the company's structure, but we knew very well—and that's why we all decided on it together—how essential it was for the growth of our now-global brand and for its stabilization for generations to come. As always, big changes are followed by an adjustment period. I noticed this as I conveyed our values and ethics to the managers, and then let them get on with their jobs. However hard it was to make, it was the right decision, one that we took together and, I believe to this day, a good thing."

Massimo refers to the Sala Blu at Palazzo Spini Feroni as the "yelling room," because that's where meetings are held to decide on important company matters. (Rather than yelling, heated discussions would be a more accurate term...)

"We never force through any idea or proposal, or try to change anyone's mind. We spend a lot of time discussing each idea, considering its pros and cons. Slowly, we seek to throw light on every aspect of it, so that we can all reach a consensus. This way of proceeding has proven effective over time, and it explains why we always all want to be there when there's an important decision to take. We've never gotten to the point where we've had to vote, but that's not to say that certain proposals didn't take time to emerge from the Sala Blu."

Tà told me about one time when they were invited to Harvard University, where the family's decision-making approach was analyzed for the students. Andrall Pearson, a professor of Economics at Harvard, with whom Tà had mutual friends, contacted her to invite them along.

"They were so keen to understand how a famous shoe company, one that in 1960 had only ten stores, had managed to become an internationally famous luxury brand entirely run by the family, with more than 250 stores worldwide in 45 different countries. The invitation from Harvard made me rethink everything we had done. For the first time, I stopped to look back at what we had accomplished since Salvatore's death. I was so proud to see that by working together, we really had made his dreams come true."

Coincidentally, the Harvard campus is just a few miles away from the Thomas G. Plant Shoe Factory in Jamaica Plain, where Grandfather worked when he first went to Boston in 1915. From there, seeking his future he traveled on to California without a penny in his pocket. Almost a century later, Tà and Massimo traveled back to the same area as guests of one of the world's most prestigious universities, which was studying the results of the company Grandfather Salvatore founded.

"It felt strange sitting in those Harvard classrooms, hearing my children speak with scientific coldness tinged with warm admiration. The students were interested in the tiniest details of their personalities as they tried to work out how their management style affected the company's operations, how we were able to work together as a united team. They questioned us one by one. I was impressed with their preparation. And they were very impressed to find that none of the family members running the company had a college degree. They were intrigued when I told them that our approach to growth is to look at the point we want to reach as if through binoculars, so as to look even farther ahead. Once we've agreed on the destination, it doesn't matter if we take one route or another. We try and stay flexible, aiming all the while for the same goal. Other people may prefer magnifying glasses to binoculars, but that's a mistake. With magnifying glasses, you become obsessed with every little detail and lose sight of the big picture."

I have never met another person as attentive to detail as Tà, without ever losing sight of the big picture. She never tired of telling us it's not just being successful that's important, it's how you maintain that success.

"Why do you think, at the age of 90, I still go into the office from 10 to 6? It's not like you can rest on your laurels! There is still so much work to be done."

After that visit to Harvard, Tà sent us a letter in which, in the middle of the page, in bold, block capitals, she wrote, "Culture comes before economics."

She explained herself thus: "As valuable preparation for your working life ahead of you, this sentence is of paramount importance. Here's the thing. Take advantage now, in your youth, to make the most of your studies. There is competition in this world. Education and culture will help you rise to that competition and make you understand business life in all its ramifications. That's why I urge you to study, read, enrich yourself with notions and concepts. Professor Pearson at Harvard shared an illuminating anecdote with Massimo and me. Shortly before our visit, the University received a 10 million dollar gift from a former student (the figure is less important than the reason). The offer came with a note from an alumnus who wished to thank the University for the teachings he had received, without which he could never have had the success he went on to achieve in his work."

A Letter to Fiamma

As I hurried out of the house to go to work at the newspaper on an unusually cold and gloomy Buenos Aires morning, I glimpsed a letter from Tà in the mailbox. I slipped it into my purse so I could read it at my desk once I got to the newsroom, suspecting it might contain an interesting insight or two. To my surprise, when I opened it, I didn't find a letter from Tà, but one that Great-grandfather Fulvio had written to Fiamma when she married Giuseppe in 1969. Tà had treasured this letter over the years, and now it had come down to us to keep in the Red Book. Seeking some inspiration for that dreary day, I read it in one go while the computer booted up.

They were the words of a man of faith who believed in the institution of marriage by divine hand, as Tà did too. She rendered her marriage sacred, staying faithful to every vow she took, even more so after Grandfather Salvatore's death. With all the hubbub going on in the newsroom, I was unable to do much thinking about this latest letter, but I did find myself wondering about Aunt Fiamma, a very special, sunny, constructive and affectionate woman who passed away in 1998, exactly a year after I got married. She had attended the wedding even though her health was failing. I can still see her, smiling and enthusiastic in the front row as I turned round toward the congregation in a moment of emotion to seek comfort from my big family. In his letter, Great-grandfather Fulvio called Fiamma "his dearest granddaughter." She always did have a thought for everyone and time for us all. Her loss generated indelible suffering, and not just within the family.

"When she was riding her bike or strolling around Florence, everyone said hello, to which she responded with smiles and greetings," Tà recalled. "She gave a nickname to everyone she worked with, things like Cicci or Brindellone, and addressed each person in her own idiosyncratic way. She was always thinking of others, and never put on airs and graces. She couldn't, it just wasn't in her DNA. Journalists, artisans, or royal highnesses, it didn't matter, she had a frank relationship with everyone. Even Prince Charles, who was a good friend of Fiamma and Giuseppe's, and who went to stay with them in San Giuliano, held her in high esteem."

Aunt Fiamma loved having guests all the time. Behind the thick walls of the old Sicilian residence, at San Giuliano the air was perfumed not just with the citrus groves surrounding the beautiful house, but also by Fiamma's hospitality and curiosity for the world.

"When Prince Charles went to Sicily to visit San Giuliano, he came with a 9-person entourage, including his painting tutor. Prince Charles painted a lot of Sicilian watercolors during his stay. By that time, Fiamma was deep into her jam project. In some old closet, she had happened upon a fabulous recipe from her mother-in-law's cook. Everyone knows how to make jam, but this one had a secret ingredient: the addition of a small piece of sour orange, which lends the most amazing of flavors. With this little apercu and Giulia's hard work, mother and daughter started up a business that now sells around the world. Fiamma was unable to sit still. Having so many citrus groves and willing Sicilian women at her disposal, she came up with the idea of making homemade jams. She designed the labels, chose the jars, and equipped an old building on their property with kitchens in which to fill jars with orange, lemon, grapefruit, and tangerine jams. Those delicious jams burst with Fiamma's love for Sicily, something that Giulia inherited. Neither in Sicily nor Florence did Fiamma ever rest. She was involved in a thousand activities, from FAI (the Italian Environmental Fund) to the Florence Opera House, and despite working all day long she never neglected Giuseppe, Diego, Giulia, or Maria."

When I was a child, I used to go stay with my San Giuliano cousins in Florence, often getting lost in their palazzo on Via dei Serragli. I still remember Auntie's shrill voice echoing off the high walls when she returned from the office. "Diegooo, Giuliaaa, Mariaaa, Giniii" she would cheerfully call out. We would all jump up at once and go greet her. She was always in a hurry, yet always in a good mood. As soon as she got home, she would sit down by the phone and light a cigarette. A little later Chris, her butler, arrived with a glass of white wine, which she sipped between phone calls, each one an opportunity for her to wield her unmistakable laugh.

Aunt Fiamma's return home brought a wave of warmth to that immense house, whose formal atmosphere and size had left me awestruck. A smile was painted on her perfect mouth, always made-up in bright lipstick. She was so very sweet-natured, and at the same time active and determined: another fine example of a hardworking woman full of femininity.

Fiamma created the *Vara*, the famous low-heeled pump with a bow that became popular around the world and has remained a Ferragamo staple ever since. Even today, thirty years on, it is still one of the company's top products in terms of sales and image. It is such a classic, successful model because it completely caters to its customers' needs, which as it happens were Fiamma's needs too. The *Vara* is comfy to wear, elegant to look at, and is appropriate for both daytime and evening wear. We have never stopped making them, and they remain a tribute to her vitality to this day.

"Fiamma did so much for the company, for the family, for the style that sets us apart, and so much for our Museum and all that it represents. She wanted it to be a cultural and historical venue, not trivial, not commercial, but as special and precious as Grandfather's life had been, as his life warranted being interpreted and passed on. We will never forget the determination with which she fought for this, including against some strong and influential figures."

Our family's unity helped Tà overcome the pain of losing Fiamma, and then my mom as well... a pain I find myself unable to describe.

"I like to think we are different arteries feeding the same heart," Tà said, a quote that makes me tearful to remember.

On multiple occasions, people asked Tà how she managed to harmoniously keep her six children together within the same company. Her answer was always the same:

"I treated my children the same, without favoritism. First by paying them the same, then by differentiating positions in areas according to their interests to avoid conflict. Right from the start, for conflict avoidance I took the decision that dear as they are, no spouses should work at the company. I have treated all six of them equally in other realms as well. Everyone has their own account at the company: if they want a product, they have to buy it, albeit at a discount, using the account at their disposal. Nothing is free for anyone. Everyone has to pay. When they married, each of my children received a home and a property on which to earn a financial return. I hired an attorney help me avoid imbalances arising from changes to property values over time."

What Tà feared most were feelings of jealousy. Using her brilliant and enviable "common sense," she always tried her best not to create or arouse any jealousies around her.

"With my own eyes, I have seen how jealousy destroys entire families. I have struggled my whole life to treat each of my children equally, so as not to create wrong-headed feelings among them. As a mother and grandmother, my first concern has always been to know you are all happy. The first and most important thing a mother can give is love, and that includes physically. We should never hide the feelings we have for others. A lack of affection is detrimental to children. I have no regrets in any of this, I gave you all plenty of kisses and cuddles."

When I think back to the fuchsia-pink lipstick marks Tà used to leave on our cheeks when we were little... She grabbed your face with one hand under the chin and planted a firm kiss on your cheek. I was almost blown away by those outpourings of affection from this woman who could be as endearing as she was fearsome.

Certainly, when Aunt Fiamma passed away, and then my mother, Tà gave us all tangible affection and compassion.

Aunt Fiamma's funeral at Santo Spirito was attended not just by friends and relatives, but coworkers and people with whom she had shared the various aspects of her generous life. The homeless man from San Frediano whom she met every day on the street and respectfully greeted, helping him whenever she could, walked into the church clutching a flower. And I will never forget the words that Helen O'Hagan, a very close family friend, read at church—words that touch me more deeply today than ever. Written by British author Henry Scott Holland, they were inspired by St. Augustine. Read out in English, they sounded even more official:

Death is nothing at all. It does not count.
I have only slipped away into the next room.
Nothing has happened.
Everything remains exactly as it was.
I am I, and you are you, and the old life that we lived
    so fondly together is untouched, unchanged.
Whatever we were to each other, that we are still.
Call me by the old familiar name.
Speak of me in the easy way which you always used.
Put no difference into your tone.
Wear no forced air of solemnity or sorrow.
Laugh as we always laughed at the little jokes that we
    enjoyed together.
Play, smile, think of me, pray for me.
Let my name be ever the household word that it always was.
Let it be spoken without an effort, without the ghost of
    a shadow upon it.

Life means all that it ever meant.
It is the same as it ever was.
There is absolute and unbroken continuity.
What is this death but a negligible accident?
Why should I be out of mind because I am out of sight?
I am but waiting for you, for an interval, somewhere
    very near, just round the corner. All is well.
Nothing is lost.
One brief moment and all will be as it was before.
How we shall laugh at the trouble of parting
    when we meet again!

It was raining so hard that day in Florence it almost looked as if the sky was crying too. I was concerned not just for my cousins but for my mom as well: I had never seen her so desperate and distraught. Aunt Fiamma had died the day before and I had hotfooted it to Florence. I accompanied Mom to the Baroni store to buy cushions for the coffin, for Aunt's head to rest on. As we walked, she said, "I cannot believe it. I simply cannot believe I can live without the courage Fiammina gave me. She wasn't just a sister, she was like a mother to me. She was the best of friends..."

Being the eldest, Fiamma really was a kind of mother to her siblings. She had a truly special bond with my mother. They talked on the phone every evening, exchanging tips and opinions, not to mention clothes among the cousins. Aunt Fiamma would send suitcases full of clothes from Florence. When we opened them up at home we were all so overjoyed, not least because it was a chance for me to spend time together with my mother and my siblings, which always made me happy.

The day after the funeral, we flew together to Sicily, where, according to her and her family's wishes, Auntie would be buried. Mass was celebrated in a small chapel adjacent to their home at San Giuliano. From there, we walked to the cemetery.

"I'll never forget that walk," Tà said one day as we reminisced about Aunt Fiamma. "All the townspeople lined up, sorrowfully sharing in our grief as we passed the kindergarten Fiamma had supported for years, the little children silently looking on under the hot sun."

Today more than ever, I wonder how Tà survived that pain, or the pain that followed that one... Each time, I find myself coming up with the same answer: her Faith.

A few days after aunt Fiamma's death, Tà received a telegram from a family of artisans who had been very fond of her daughter: "Dear Mrs. Wanda, don't worry, don't let things get you down, because up there in Heaven the Angels will love the Marquise as much as we loved her down here on earth."

Not just words but Faith with a capital F, just like Tà's.

Magic Wanda

"Magic Wanda" was the title of an article, an interview in a 20-page special report published by *WWD* in 2006, dedicated entirely to the House of Ferragamo. I immediately thought how perfectly the name "Magic Wanda" fit Tà. The photo that ran alongside the article portrayed her standing in front of a big table in the Palazzo Spini Feroni meeting room, capturing that honest gaze of hers, arms folded, two large pearls in her ears and a string around her neck, in a blue suit with an elegant diamond brooch poking out from beneath a colorful scarf.

I stared at the photo for a long time, almost as if I wanted to have her close by, sitting in front of me in my untidy Argentine office, which she would no doubt have criticized. She looked beautiful and, even more, reassuring. I was also reassured by her interview, as ever full of gratitude toward Grandfather, the family, and the whole company. Always give thanks: another of Tà's great teachings.

Despite receiving a Cavaliere del Lavoro Honor and a host of awards from all over the world, the last being an Honorary

Degree from the Fashion Institute of New York, our magic Tà was actually a very reserved person who loved to listen more than be listened to, who loved to learn, who was keen to know rather than be known. Endowed with enviable curiosity, she met extraordinary people throughout her lifetime, particularly women, some of whom she cited in her letters for the Red Book.

"Salvatore was the shoemaker to the stars," she said, "but it was hardly just movie stars who wore his shoes. There were also queens, princesses, first ladies, businesswomen... I could write a whole book about these amazing encounters."

That book, sadly, is the one thing Tà didn't work on, although it could be argued that she did write everything down in her notes, letters, anecdotes and her story, revealing her to be an extraordinary woman on a par with, perhaps even greater than, the extraordinary women she met.

Tà had a true talent for the written word: she wrote to everyone, at every opportunity. "Dropping a few lines is always a good thing to do," she liked to say. The office houses over forty folders packed with the letters she wrote to ministers, businessmen, friends, children, grandchildren, and employees. Writing was her favorite way of communicating, and very effective she was at it, too. She was empathetic and sensitive and always managed to touch people's hearts.

Among Tà's many encounters, she recalled with great pride her meeting with the Maharani of Jaipur in 1985 at the first retrospective dedicated to Grandfather at Palazzo Strozzi. She was the daughter of the Maharani of Cooch Behar, one of India's most prominent and elegant women, with an insatiable passion for shoes, especially Salvatore Ferragamos. In the 1930s, she ordered over 300 pairs, some of which were the most amazing shoes Grandfather created: "True works of art impossible to replicate today, because that degree of luxury no longer exists in the world," was Tà's succinct opinion.

One day, two small bags arrived at Palazzo Spini Feroni for Grandfather from the Maharani.

"When he opened them, Salvatore was astonished to see they were full of pearls, diamonds, rubies, gems, and precious stones. The bags were accompanied by a note requesting him to make three pairs of shoes incorporating these gemstones into the design. I still remember his amazement and pride. The first pair he made was a green silk shoe with a spiral of pearls climbing up from the heels. For the second pair, he used black velvet and a diamond buckle; the third pair was, perhaps, the most jaw-dropping pair of shoes Salvatore ever created: a wedge-heeled, high platform shoe the Maharani could wear under a sari, its entire surface decorated with an intricate pattern of diamonds, emeralds, sapphires, and pearls set in brass. Copies of these shoes are in our Museum. Although the jewels are obviously crystal reproductions, they still exemplify life at an Indian royal court."

Many royal women chose Grandfather to custom-make shoes for them. As a child, I would spend hours looking through period photographs trying to spot the queens and princesses whose names were written on the shoe lasts. The story of the three queens is among the most famous.

"One evening, at dinner Salvatore told the children that three queens had visited him that day. I will never forget the excitement on our children's faces as they listened to him in silence. That morning, the Queen of Holland, the Queen of Greece, and the Queen of Romania had all visited their father at the office. After Salvatore's death, Princess Beatrice of Holland, Queen Juliana's daughter, walked into the store and, with great discretion, almost unnoticed carefully chose some shoes. I am still surprised by such humility. If only they were all like that!"

Once she proudly told me about the two times Queen Elizabeth of England invited her.

"Once in London, another time in Rome. Two wondrous occasions, but the one at Buckingham Palace will forever stay etched in my memory. That dinner was in March 2005, in honor of President Ciampi's state visit. I was invited to represent the Italian fashion industry, and also because Salvatore had made the Queen her engagement shoes.

It was the most formal event I have ever attended. The invitation came with a separate document that detailed protocol. My first concern was my appearance: which dress to wear, what shoes, the jewelry... It certainly wasn't the first time I'd attended a gala dinner, and I thought that by now I was ready for anything, but an invitation to Buckingham Palace was something special. I decided to wear a black dress with gold and cream detailing by Mary McFadden, an American designer, two strings of pearls and matching earrings. Dressed in white, the Queen wore a magnificent diamond and pearl tiara. She was truly majestic, her manners and her person. The dinner was served in the palace's main ballroom. Never in my life—and I've been to a lot of dinners—have I sat at such a gorgeously laid table, decorated with roses that looked fresh out of a painting, and gold candelabras running the length of the table. After being introduced to Her Royal Highness and the other guests, I was escorted to my seat but told not to sit. First, there was a grand procession of royal ladies and their husbands, then the guests of honor, the Queen, President Ciampi... Truly unforgettable."

Il Giornale published an article about Tà's attendance at the gala dinner, and, of course, she sent it to us for the Red Book. "It was such a thrill driving down the wide boulevard that leads to Buckingham Palace, draped end-to-end with Italian and British flags." In her inimitable style, speaking to a journalist from the Milanese newspaper, Tà said: "The important thing is to have constructive relations with the whole world, and thus respond to a divine plan." I recognize her patriotic spirit and her open-minded, international mentality in those words.

When Her Royal Highness and the Duke of Edinburgh came to Rome, they invited Tà to a gala dinner at the Palazzo del Quirinale. "I was seated next to Prince Philip, and warned that he was generally a nice person, but could sometimes be in a bad mood and therefore difficult to entertain. I was seated to his left, Mrs. Ciampi to his right. Apparently, the Prince was in a good mood. He was even cracking jokes! Provocatively, he asked Mrs. Ciampi how old she was. She calmly replied to him, 'I'm eighty years old.' He replied, 'Me too.' Then he turned to me and said, 'How about you, ma'am?' I quickly replied, 'Me too!' Prince Philip burst out laughing, 'So, this is the 80-year-olds club!' From then on, we enjoyed an easy-going, entertaining conversation on the English aristocracy."

As well as high nobility, Tà was also fascinated by the great American families.

"American ladies have always been Salvatore Ferragamo's most loyal customers. To name one, Nancy Reagan. I was fortunate enough to meet her when she and President Reagan visited Venice in 1987, at a luncheon held in their honor at Palazzo Grassi. Before lunch, some of us were taken to a private room to be introduced to the President and his wife. When I walked in, Mrs. Reagan took me to one side and confessed she was a huge Ferragamo fan. Such a lovely thing to say. President Reagan was a most agreeable man. A few years later, our friend Fred Ryan arranged for Massimo and me to meet him at his Los Angeles office, on the fiftieth floor of a magnificent building with views out over the city. With a delightful smile, the President said to me, 'So what can I do for you, Mrs. Ferragamo?' I didn't have anything to ask him for, so I replied, 'Nothing President, absolutely nothing.' He was speechless. 'I just want to thank you for the work you're doing for world peace and for encouraging Gorbachev to join you in that.' So strong was Reagan's personality and charisma, you could feel it in the room. I was happy to have met him and had the opportunity to talk with him. I met Hillary Clinton in Florence in 1999 during a conference at Villa La Pietra, the former home of Sir Harold Acton, today owned by New York University. During her stay, she visited Palazzo Spini Feroni to look around the Museum. I accompanied her and showed her one pair of shoes in particular, which were special because they were made from the skin of a fish known as a sea leopard. Many years earlier, Salvatore had received a letter from the King of Norway in which he wrote: 'You are a genius, you have so many ideas... Is there anything you can do with this skin?' Apparently, there was an abundance of sea leopards in Norway at the time, and the King was looking for a way of recycling their skins as a business opportunity. Salvatore did indeed find a way to process them, making them flexible enough for shoemaking. I enthusiastically shared this story with Mrs. Clinton, concluding: 'The king was so happy, Salvatore was happy, everyone ended up being happy!' She looked me straight in the eye and said, 'Everyone except the sea leopard!' This time, it was I who was left speechless... Although I only spent a little time with her, I hold Barbara Bush in great esteem. She came to our

Rome store on Via Condotti, usually a pedestrian street, in a gleaming, long black limousine. A crowd of curious onlookers awaited her. She waved to them, walked into the store, picked out a few pairs of shoes and left."

Immediately after the attack on the Twin Towers in 2001, Massimo, Chiara and the children went to their country home on Long Island. Tà called Massimo and advised him not to return to New York right away because it was dangerous, but Uncle replied that he wanted to go to the office, that it was necessary to resume normal life. By no means reassured, Tà wrote a letter to Mrs. Bush: "You probably don't know who I am, but since we are both mothers, we may consider ourselves proud of our sons who during these horrific days have continued to work for the good of the country and the people, yours as President, mine as a manager." Tà enclosed a photo of Massimo's kids on their terrace in New York holding the American flag. Mrs. Bush wrote her a very kind thank you letter. "Of course I know who you are. You are legend." Tà was so flattered. She never felt or believed that she was a legend, but thanks to her letters, that was what she became to one and all.

It didn't matter who the recipient was, Tà always managed to get a reply, and often to achieve significant results. One person she wrote letters to on multiple occasions was Mariastella Gelmini, Italy's Minister of Education, who was a favorite recipient because education was so dear to Tà's heart. In one letter, Tà wrote:

"Dear Minister, I am honored to correspond with you, but I would be even more honored if, next time you come to Florence, you visit our Museum, where we have a collection of every original model of shoe made by Salvatore Ferragamo, my husband, between 1930 to 1960, the year of his death. I am pleased to send you my husband's autobiography, which he wrote two years before we were parted. Our country has quite a number of autobiographies written by illustrious self-made entrepreneurs, both Italian, such as Leonardo Del Vecchio, Angelo Rizzoli and others, and Italian-American, for example Lee Iacocca and Mario Cuomo. I have often thought how useful it would be to distribute these books in schools, as an example to young Italians who have little idea of the sacrifices required of self-made men to achieve their success and found great companies. We have a major archive at our company headquarters. After studying the anatomy of the foot, my husband filed as many as 400 patents for shoes alone, using this work to revise the shoemaking process in order to achieve a perfect fit. Forgive me if I've gone on a bit, but my husband's work is still valid and applicable today. I do hope that we have the pleasure of seeing you at our offices in Florence. Until then, cordial greetings and best wishes for all success in your work and life. Wanda Ferragamo."

A skilled communicator for the company's benefit, Tà was driven by a genuine desire to uplift younger generations by providing encouraging examples and positive stories. As Pope Francis said (and as the ancients well understood), "Education is not the filling of a pot but the lighting of a fire." Sometime before that letter, Tà had sent Minister Gelmini a newspaper clipping of an article about a case of racism. As always, we grandchildren received copies of her letters.

"Dear Minister Gelmini, I am sending you a newspaper clipping I wish to bring to your attention. I was deeply saddened by this case of 13-year-old children who beat up and almost broke the nose of a Cuban boy who was out skateboarding. As a mother, I was struck by the thought that these violent kids had not been taught, either in their families or at school, that skin color means nothing. We are human beings and we need to respect each other. Because they all work, the mothers of today see little of their children. Kids come home from school and don't see their parents. They get on their mopeds and go cause trouble in bars, etc. You, Mrs. Gelmini, are a person we all respect and admire in Italy. You must forgive me if I take the liberty of offering a suggestion to a person like you, who occupies a position of such great responsibility and prestige, but I believe we should encourage human and moral education for all children of this age. If I were in your place, I would invite to the Quirinale (a beautiful place where I have been many times for pleasant occasions) groups of 100–150 professors from every region. Assisted by psychologists and scholars, you could talk to them, ensure that they feel the full responsibility of, firstly, teaching civic education, respect for others, and conduct worthy of a civilized and culturally rich country. Such basic education for the young should be instilled as early as possible, I would say from the age of 6 or 7, and be reinforced as they grow older. Our children should not see a Black child as an enemy but as a brother. Indeed, they must learn to help the weakest. You must encourage these kids to understand the pain of the mother who, through no fault of his own, saw her badly beaten child return home. This wickedness must be erased from children's soul. Teachers can do so much. Now that both parents are busy working, the teacher's job is twice as important as it was in the past. My suggestion to invite the teaching staff may seem somewhat eccentric, but I am sure that teachers would feel honored by your welcome, celebrated and gratified by the beauty of those rooms unknown to many. Do not judge me as presumptuous, because it is true that teachers can do so much: kids absorb so much of what they are told. My best wishes for your continued success. I salute you and thank you for everything you are able to do. A mother from Florence."

I read this letter several times on the day I received it, before filing it away in my Red Book. Those breathless words conveyed Grandmother's sincere desire for moral education, revealing her determined character and ability to dream, her humility and shrewdness, but above all her love and constructive attitude toward her country.

When my son Leo was born, Tà shared an anecdote with me.

"A French noblewoman asked a cardinal, 'Monseigneur, à quel âge il faut commencer l'éducation de mon petit fils?' The cardinal replied, 'Madame, combien d'années a votre fils?' She replied, 'Il a quatre ans.' The cardinal retorted: 'Madame, vous avez déjà perdu quatre ans.' You see Ginevra, the important thing is to be able to foster a child's sense of responsibility at all times. That's the most important thing there is, even more so than academic achievement, because it is the compass that will truly help them achieve the goals they set for themselves in life."

Tà was fascinated by the Montessori method. She believed that children are able to understand everything and do things independently from a tender age. The principles she naturally applied to our parents were a limited number of clear rules, and a general respect for others.

Another story Tà loved to tell was that about Mr. William and Mrs. Lila Wallace, the creators of the *Reader's Digest* and great friends of hers.

"When they were young, they were impecunious but smart and full of creativity. He had served in World War I as a volunteer and was wounded on the French front. Stuck in hospital, he would read the papers. Realizing they were too verbose and hard to understand, he racked his brains for months until he came up with a great idea: to condense and distribute succinct, digested reading matter to people who don't have the time to read all the newspapers, such as American businessmen and others. And that's how *Reader's Digest* was born! After major publishers turned down his idea, the couple decided to launch a subscription drive themselves. William wrote a letter to students, teachers, professors, and college and university alumni asking them to send one dollar 'blind' to start a monthly magazine with the characteristics he described. As soon as they sent out the letters, the Wallaces went off on honeymoon. When they returned home, they found whole bundles of responses and raised nearly $5,000. Their adventure had begun. Later that publication became international, the monthly magazine translated into almost every language. In just a few years, they became the owners of a world-spanning company. We met Lila when she came to Florence in 1953 or 1954. Almost as soon as she checked in to the Grand Hotel, she came to our Via Tornabuoni store and commissioned Salvatore to make a whole collection of shoes for her. Her beauty and elegance were beyond my ability to describe them: people used to turn and stare as she walked by. They invited me to their country house near New York, where I once again appreciated Lila for who she was: a smart journalist who combined great sophistication with a deep interest in everything happening in this world. She and her husband were good friends of ours for many years."

Lady Diana was another person dear to Tà's heart.

"I have an intense memory of the 'sad princess.' She was so beautiful! Tall, with those big, blue, winning eyes, so strong yet so fragile. I met her through my former colleague, Gabriella Di Nora after she moved to London to work at Harvey Nichols, where she was in charge of VIP shopping. For many years, we made shoes and bags in-house especially for Lady Di. She would sometimes ask us to make a pair of shoes for her in three days. It was next to no time, but you couldn't say no to Lady Diana! Besides, she was so well-mannered. She sent us thank you letters that we loved to receive. I met her several times. The first was at a lunch at Palazzo Vecchio in 1985, when she was on an official visit to Italy with Prince Charles. The last time was at an antiques fair in London in June 1990, when I invited her to come to Capri. Then tragedy struck. It was an honor to have been invited to her funeral. The silence, flowers lining the streets, the people's love, the church overflowing with crowds. It was all so moving."

When asked if she ever had an ideal client, Tà was generally at a loss. But I can safely say that Audrey Hepburn most certainly held a special place in her heart. They were close friends and greatly esteemed one another.

"She was such a dear woman, so beautiful, inside and out! We became friends in 1954, when she visited Palazzo Spini Feroni with Anita Loos, the author of the film *Gentlemen Prefer Blondes*. Anita had been a good client of Salvatore's since her Hollywood days. Audrey was becoming famous at that time with *Roman Holiday*, which became an iconic film for a whole era. I've seen all Audrey's movies, but I loved that movie in particular because it showed our beautiful Italy at its best. Once Salvatore invited Anita and Audrey to dinner at Il Palagio. I was obviously very excited about the idea. I wanted everything to be absolutely flawless for their visit, so I took care of everything, down to the last detail, from the menu to the flowers to the tablecloths, everything! I'll remember that evening forever. When they arrived at our home in Fiesole, our butler was unable to contain his surprise. He knew we had important guests coming for dinner, but when he saw Audrey he was so overwhelmed he could barely serve properly: he only had eyes for her. At one point, he dropped a spoon onto her shoulder. It clattered to the ground, making a tremendous din. I was mortified, but Audrey remained impassive, as if nothing had happened. She didn't even turn her head, showing how well-mannered and sensitive she was. She wasn't just a great actress, she was a great lady. Fiamma and Giovanna were also thrilled to meet her, because she was their idol. You cannot imagine how many times they asked me to take them to see *Roman Holiday*. When they behaved well, at school and at home, Salvatore and I would reward them by inviting them to come and meet our most famous clients. They were entranced by Audrey. She was such a sweetheart…"

Grandfather created many shoes for Audrey Hepburn, in particular a pump she adored and wore all the time. That shoe is today a permanent model in the Ferragamo Creations collection: "She had a beautiful size 38 foot. The last shoe we custom-made for her is now on display at the Museum."

In his biography of his mother, Audrey's son Sean Ferrer wrote that shoes were crucial for her, the foundation of an ethic based on quality. Audrey said that beautiful shoes made it possible to wear simple clothes. She considered Salvatore a friend and thought he was the finest shoemaker of all time; she also knew how upset he became at the sight of tortured or damaged feet. Audrey was fascinated by the fact that the philosophers of antiquity claimed the feet were the cradle of the soul. This was why she thought Grandfather did the most beautiful job in the world: dressing people's souls. He was indeed convinced that feet talked to him.

"Our fabulous friendship was crowned when our company and the Audrey Hepburn Children's Fund put on a fund-raiser for a new Audrey Hepburn Children's House at Hackensack University Medical Center in New Jersey, which treats more than a thousand abused children every year. We raised a portion of these funds by putting on an exhibition about Audrey, which toured the world for a good two years. She was such a sweet, warm person… Even though we didn't see one another for long periods of time, when we ran into each other again it was as if we'd met up the day before. Once, we were both honored at the Waldorf Astoria in New York. She was accompanied by her great friend Hubert de Givenchy. When it was my turn to speak, I expressed joy at being in such good company, alongside Audrey and Countess Jacqueline de Ribes, and remarked on how their style and femininity should serve as an example to every woman. I told the spoon story, and everyone in the room laughed and applauded, agreeing that I had captured Audrey's grace in my speech. When we opened our Beverly Hills store in 1991, we held a dinner for six hundred people to benefit UNICEF, to which Audrey dedicated her final years as a peace ambassador. Such a wonderful evening... Audrey was at my table with Nancy Reagan and James Stewart. She did such incredible work for UNICEF, visiting countries beset by the tragedies of hunger and childhood diseases. The last time I saw her was the following year, in New York. She had just got back from Somalia, in the throes of civil war with many people starving. I complimented her on her work. 'These people are so unfortunate, I simply must do everything I can to help,' she told me. She was most definitely not doing it for the publicity. She truly felt it was her mission... and a sacred mission at that. She began feeling ill after that trip to Africa, suffering from strange stomach pains. I could see in her eyes that something wasn't right. Shortly thereafter, she informed me that her doctor had diagnosed cancer. She took refuge in her Swiss chalet at Tolochenaz, living out her final days with views out over her garden and the mountains she loved. She was so very brave, behaving with surprising dignity. She was only 63 years old when she died, almost the same age as Salvatore. Another very great loss for me. Audrey and Salvatore had something in common: they both deeply understood that outer beauty, whether it be in clothes, shoes, or appearance, can only exist in combination with inner beauty built on solid principles and good character."

I think of Tà's stories every time I wear a pair of "Audrey shoes." I have them in a variety of colors and they are among my favorites. In Buenos Aires, people used to stop me in the street and ask me where I bought them. Discreet and refined, they make me feel neat and tidy (Tà's magic words) and allow me to dream of the refinement of days gone by. This elegant, comfortable and versatile shoe is not just a design, it is a receptacle of deep human values and a genuine love of beauty. When I look down at my feet shod in those shoes on, they always look great.

Tà's friends included Dora Dalla Chiesa, the General's first wife, who like Tà was originally from the Irpinia region.

"General Carlo Alberto once asked if I would invite Dora to stay with me as he shuttled from Turin to Rome as part of his job fighting terrorism. Nanny Bea took her for a tour while I was at work. She told me she was extremely thrifty, a culture of austerity no doubt absorbed from the family she grew up in, and then from her husband. Dora was an amiable, outgoing and beautiful woman in love. Sadly, she smoked and drank coffee all day long, because she was so apprehensive about the General. The day before she died of a heart attack, collapsing on the couch, her spectacles on and a book in her hand, the doctor who was looking after her examined her and found no impending danger... I spoke at length with the General, a man tenderly in love who wanted to talk to everyone about her. Truly a man from another age, the General! I once asked him how he spent Christmas, and as if it were the most natural thing in the world, he replied: 'With my men at the barracks, of course!' He made do with very little: a bed and a small room. They were a couple that proved how man and woman 'train' one another. Dora's love for her husband was not just love, it was a kind of dedication to a cause. Although they were very different, there was something in Salvatore I associate with the General: dedication to a cause (in Salvatore's case, building the company) combined with great moral rigor. Carlo Alberto Dalla Chiesa's relationship with Dora was a true love story. The General was concerned because he knew the risks that came with his job had, in the long run, taken a toll on Dora's body and health. He couldn't wait for his granddaughter, named Dora in his wife's honor, to be born. He was killed by the Mafia before she came into the world."

On a visit to Florence, in Tà's office before lunch, I noticed a beautiful blue glittering bracelet on the table. I stared at it with curiosity. Tà immediately came over, picked it up and excitedly told me the story behind it.

"I had this made to mark the union between European countries, delighted that, alongside the current wave of globalization, the European Community is finally a reality. In 2008, Finland's ambassador to Rome, a woman, invited me for a lovely event that brought together 19 ambassadors' wives at her official residence for a luncheon in my honor. She presented me as an example, as a woman who, widowed with six children, had become a successful businesswoman. Even if, I know, I'm not the only one in such a situation, I was obviously honored."

As she said this, Tà clasped the bracelet around my wrist, rather brusquely pushing up the sleeves of my sweater. "*Mamma mia*, this huge sweater on such beautiful arms... Here it is... Take it with you to Argentina, as a representative of Europe." Satisfied, she pushed up both sleeves, all the way up to the elbow to show off that beautiful bright blue bracelet.

"I went to that ambassadors' luncheon with Giò. Everyone was invited to tell their story. I learned that when abroad, ambassadors' wives play an important role supporting and representing their husbands. Many said they'd had to quit their jobs; others, that they had to leave their children behind in another city to finish their studies. Indeed, life offers all of us a goal to reach, a mission to accomplish. I was thrilled to hear the names of all of the European Community countries the ambassadors and their spouses represented in Italy. I gave each one of them a bracelet. They were delighted."

Unfortunately, I no longer have that bracelet. It may have gotten lost in my various moves. Perhaps it will turn up somewhere one day. At the time, I certainly didn't ascribe it the value I would today. Thinking about that shiny, glittering bracelet, I'm surer than ever that Tà was indeed "Magic Wanda!"

16.

Triple-Eared Wheat

Tà often told us about Grandfather's passion for botany. In Viesca, he succeeded in crossing two types of wheat, obtaining a hybrid with three ears. News of his discovery was published by a number of journals. The Count of Frassineto, a Florentine nobleman who owned a number of local farms, complimented him. Believing that Salvatore had discovered a formula that would triple flour production, they began making big plans for the future. In actual fact, that experiment turned out to be a complete accident. The following year, with the new harvest, the wheat ears were two-headed again, and that was the last they heard from the Count of Frassineto.

Thinking about this story, I cannot help associating that third head on the ear with third-generation fragility. Over the past two decades, since the grandchildren grew up and began working, we have repeatedly been warned about the problems family businesses have when the third generation takes over. Lengthy meetings with advisors from Ambrosetti Consulting, readings and essays of all kinds on companies that had failed when the third generation was at the helm... All this resulted in a very strict family pact, revised and corrected several times, that set out accurate procedural rules at the company. It's no coincidence that only three of us grandchildren went to work at the Salvatore Ferragamo company. By personal choice, timing, or lack of the necessary requirements, many of the rest of us opted for a different path.

One thing is for sure: our third generation benefited greatly from Tà's attentiveness and constructive attitude, helping us to understand our common interests by being aware that a problem for one is a problem for all. She was the perfect, impossible-to-replicate coordinator of all this.

I was not by any means the only one of us who enjoyed wonderful chats with her and benefited from her advice. Every time I went back to Italy, I always wound up in the Sala Musica at Palazzo Spini Feroni, where Tà had lunch when she was in the office, generally with other members of the family. I remember one sultry July day, taking Ottavia and Leo there when they were kids. Uncle Leonardo and his daughter Mariasole were already there. After a scrumptious rice and spring vegetable timbale and tasty eggplant flans, Silvano brought in a plate of exotic fruit and ice cream for the kids, who then happily entertained themselves for a while in the vestibule, drawing with crayons Tà had put out for them beforehand. In the meantime, Uncle ran off to a meeting and Mariasole and I remained at the table with Grandmother, who, as usual, almost as if intuiting the question in our eyes, quickly came to the point.

She called in Silvano. Asking him to come closer, she whispered something in his ear. The somber and responsive blue-uniformed Silvano reappeared a few minutes later carrying a framed white picture. I immediately recognized it as a letter she had recently sent us for the Red Book.

"You remember I sent this to the Florence newspaper *La Nazione*, commenting on that news item about some boys trampling a Crucifix? I shall read it out to you now. I believe these words, and I think you will find them empowering."

In a solemn tone, moving her hand rhythmically as she always did when reading something out loud, she began:

"Children, how I pity you! With your absurd and sacrilegious gesture, your offense to the Cross, you trample on Love in all of its aspects, as indispensable to life, as essential and living a part of life itself, as is Love for a child, for parents, for a sick person in need of care and affection. You trample on generosity and sacrifice built of Love, self-denial for the good, and forgiveness. Through your evil act you destroy the symbol of the heavens, because Jesus Christ is Love. A friend of mine was mugged in Paris once; she fell, hurting her elbow. The first thing she should have done was call the police. But no, she went to church to ask Our Lady to forgive the thief because, to commit such a deplorable act, he must surely have been in great need. My friend's example is a gesture of Love. Your case, however, is different; it springs from the wickedness of an empty soul. My father used to say that it is impossible to smile with an empty soul. Well, fill the emptiness of your soul with Love, and you will be fulfilled and happy. Remember always, Love comes from Christ represented on that Cross you so savagely destroyed. Though, you should understand that you have not defeated and will never be able to defeat Love, for, as a living part of life, it is indestructible."

With a resolute gesture, Tà put the framed letter down on the table. She looked up at us and asked, "Understand? There's nothing to question. Follow Jesus always, and everything becomes abundantly clear." She fell silent.

Mariasole and I looked at one other, bewitched. Neither she nor I dared say a word. Over lunch we had talked about Faith, about different "beliefs," unaware of our grandmother's attentive ear. As ever, she heard everything, she understood everything on the fly. That same Faith that was such a cornerstone of her life, without which, as she said, so many things would not have happened.

"The key to achieving all these outcomes," Tà continued, "is to understand that, others aside, we must derive satisfaction from what we have achieved by looking at the normally inflexible but honest judge that is our conscience. That must suffice for us. Thankfully, there are so many positive examples around, so many young people full of good qualities, eager to better themselves, and so many attentive parents. Take care of your children when they are teenagers. Kids have to live their own experiences, make their own mistakes, but you must always keep a line of communication open. That's the only true guarantee of the bond between parents and children. Now, if you'll excuse me, I have to get back to the office, I have a lot of things to attend to," she said, spelling the end of our talk. After calling for Silvano a few times, she hurriedly said her goodbyes, and with that look on her face that was all-seeing, that left nothing to chance, she left.

Tà sent us many letters on the topic of our moral, spiritual, and professional upbringing. She often gave us examples of "little things" that concealed great truths. To Tà's mind, small, seemingly insignificant events in everyday life were actually the result of a network of relationships that each of us weaves, as important as major events that constitute veritable turning points in our own personal stories.

"One thing's for sure: a society that fails to combine well-being with moral rigor is not a strong society, capable of renewing itself and building a future. I truly believe that dialog between parents and children is one of the most fundamental things in the world, the basis on which family harmony is forged... And this applies all the way up to state level."

She also sent us her concerted, enlightening and, as was so often the case, unconventional thoughts on the concept of consistency, another cornerstone of her world.

"A word that encompasses so many meanings, for a luxury fashion house consistency means being aligned with a certain lifestyle, conduct and upbringing, an understated elegance achieved by training the people who help us in our tasks and our business. Of course, dependent upon the level you live and the activities you conduct, this definition applies to so many other areas too. Always remember what it means to be consistent: fulfilling one's obligations and performing duties that reflect what we do and who we are, all the while respecting the founder of the company, whom we must always recall with love and gratitude."

One day, I asked Tà if anything truly frightened her.

Without hesitation, she answered, "Loneliness. And also witnessing a decline in our products, which after all lie at the heart of everything. The loss of our identity after all the energy and effort we've put into it."

Tà expressed her concerns to us in a letter. She was a firm believer in the importance of our family's identity, which she saw reflected in what she called "the gentleman's philosophy": respect for others, style, and modesty in living one's own life. Even if they did not work for the company, she distributed her letters to all of her 23 grandchildren, keeping everyone informed about what was happening at the firm. One of her "circulars" about the Chinese market went like this:

"In interviews, Louis Vuitton, Chanel, and Hermès have said how closely they wish to focus on this market. We were smart to go in first, but I feel like we're getting a little bit complacent, failing to carefully consider how to move forward. I've read that in China, girls keen to advance themselves, keen on European and Western fashion, make big-ticket purchases at brand-name stores. All this prompts me to deduce that we must not rest on our laurels or we'll fall behind. On the contrary, we must pay close attention to all areas of this receptive market, ensuring that we supply it on a daily basis, especially the most sought-after sizes, and keep on adding new elements. We must constantly be on the alert, our eyes and ears open, to ensure the right retail marketing. We must carefully choose creative designers, fashion coordinators (to keep ugliness at bay), merchandising 'as God intended it,' stay abreast of developments in the fashion world, and find buyers who are already capable and responsible before we hire them. That means presenting them with a collection and seeing what shoes, dresses, bags, silk products, bijoux, and small leather goods they choose, revealing their taste and orientations. It has been my direct, lived experience that what aspiring employees say when they first show up is not at all what they know how to do. Unfortunately, we might end up having them around for a while, along with whatever damage they cause."

Tà strongly defended the value and history of our products. She insisted so much on training sales personnel in her priorities of product and customer.

"Ferragamo has good customers because it's our philosophy to look after them. I'm sure they keep coming back to us because they know we believe in our products and in their quality. I also wish to encourage you to be vigilant about how you go out into the world. You must always be the unfailing representatives of our identity. I will never stop noticing how you present yourself, how you dress, your style, and your demeanor."

At Christmastime, how we dressed as little kids was imperative. Tà always wanted us to wear identical outfits: boys in suits and ties, girls in an inevitable burgundy velvet dress with a white embroidered collar. She had an entire collection of these dresses in Florence, one or two in each size, for each age. We all hated them because they were so heavy, uncomfortable and often itched when worn, plus it was impossible to find a matching petticoat. Ten o'clock in the morning on December 25 was the burgundy dress time. Our mothers would take us to the guest room changing area at Il Palagio where, from one year to the next, our clothes were carefully stored away in mothballs and cellophane.

I cannot recall a single Christmas without that weight on me. Today, I can think back at it with tenderness: that touch of elegance repaid the torture of wearing it. When we arrived, we'd find all the cousins in their underwear, white socks and patent leather shoes, while Mom and my aunts impatiently searched high and low for the right-sized dress for each of us.

This was the worst and most frustrating moment of the year for me: I was the tubbiest of all the grandchildren, so those tiny velvet dresses squeezed me on all sides. One year, they had to sew me into one; another, they had to give me a larger size that hung down below my feet, making it impossible for me to walk. And if those velvet dresses weren't enough, there was also an entire supply of turquoise taffeta to fall back on. There really was no way out.

"Only now do I realize how much you hated them, but you all looked so pretty in the same dress, singing and reciting Christmas poems. I happened upon the first of those dresses in Paris, and then had my seamstress make ten more just like it."

After all the dress palaver, on Christmas Day we all walked to mass in Maiano, where in a thick Tuscan accent the unforgettable Don Giulio celebrated mass in a sea of friendly faces. The highlight of the day was the return to Il Palagio for Christmas lunch. So many times Uncle Massimo dressed up as Santa Claus and came in through the dining room window with a sack of presents. I remember tables heaped high with gifts and surprises of every kind and provenance, decorated with all the passion and energy Tà put into everything. But as we grew up and multiplied, exasperated by the number of gifts and with a natural aversion to waste and consumerism, Tà imposed the rule of one gift per person, to be drawn by lot: for many years, a fun, practical, and inexpensive solution.

"When I was growing up, we didn't have Christmas trees. That wasn't a tradition in southern Italy. What we did have was a very strong tradition of nativity scenes," Tà once told me as she stood by the characters in her wonderful Neapolitan crib. "Only when I moved to Florence did we buy a Christmas tree for the first time. And I remember you all, one at a time, opening presents under the tree. Such a bonding moment for me. I have always kept a close eye on your unity and harmony as cousins. Those of you who lived in Milan, I really wanted your moms to take you to Roccamare in the summers so you could all be together. I wanted you to learn our family values and bring you closer together. I'm so glad I was able to do that."

Christmas in Florence was always a wonderful celebration, as were the long summers at Roccamare, of which I have the fondest childhood memories. We were and still are a real gang of 23 cousins, now with spouses and on average three children each. I can understand Tà's satisfaction at seeing us all together, especially because we all get along. Only now do I realize what great efforts she put into this achievement.

With the family growing bigger and bigger and the business greatly expanded, a major change was in the air. After much consideration, in June 2011 Salvatore Ferragamo went public and listed on the stock market.

"A step change in our history, a solution that chimes with the modern world and safeguards the future for you all, ensuring quality as you make your Grandfather's and my dreams come true. Every morning, I wake up with gratitude and optimism and look out my window at the city of Florence, my home for 70 years now. Then I look up at the sky. Even when it's cloudy, I look for a corner of blue and say a prayer. I know it will be heard. When people ask me why I never remarried, I answer that at times I have regretted not doing so. It wasn't always easy to make decisions on my own, to not share that burden with someone by my side. I know that your Grandfather, to whom I dedicated my life, would have been happy for me to have a man to dispel my loneliness, a man with a heart and a head who would not have interfered in my relationship with my children. Unfortunately, I never met anyone like that. There was no-one else like your grandfather."

Reflecting on these words of Tà's, I am reminded of a letter she wrote in July 2011, thanking Salvatore Ferragamo's employees after the company listed. I was in Argentina at the time, on the verge of returning to Italy for my summer holidays. I was sent some press cuttings from Florence, accompanied by photographs showing family members and managers on the steps outside the Palazzo della Borsa in Piazza Affari, Milan. I regretted not being there with them to witness this event, but Tà's words, as always, carried a deeper meaning.

"As we list on the stock market, I feel a need and a duty to share this important, historic step for our company with you all, and to thank you for helping to make it possible. Opening up to the stock market will make the brand stronger and better appreciated as we pursue the goals we have always set ourselves and that, thanks to all your help, we have so far been able to achieve. The commitment we all have shown in the areas we're involved in must maintain the excellence for which Italy is best known and esteemed around the world: a legacy that is true and tangible and that, through all of our efforts, we must hand down to future generations. Now more than ever, our task is to maintain the prestige and quality of Ferragamo's products worldwide, proud of its totally Italian origin, exceeding rather than dashing the expectations of savers who invest and believe in us, in our products, in what we are today and what we will become tomorrow. The trust the market places in us must make us proud and drive us to exceed our own expectations. Today, we all look to the future with the same determination and spirit that has guided us all these years, dedicating renewed strength and energy to the work we do every day."

As soon as I arrived in Italy, I personally thanked Tà for her words. Despite the distance, she had made me feel part of an incredible family, made up not just of family members but of so many people, many of whom I have never known, who have dedicated themselves to the company with such commitment, as if they too were part of the family. Tà had so much trust—perhaps Faith—in the family and all these people.

Things have changed a lot since then, but the desire to keep this great dream going remains as strong as ever.

Thank You, Tà

This is the epilogue I would never have wanted to write.

Mom and Tà are no longer with us.

I wrote the first draft of this book ten years ago, initially as a gift to Tà for her ninetieth birthday.

I had ten copies printed and packaged in a print shop in Buenos Aires: one for Tà, one for my mother, and the others for my siblings and a handful of other recipients. I had despaired at not finding a printer willing to supply me with so few copies, but in the end, I persuaded a publisher friend of mine, Dudu Von Thielman, to help me out. She introduced me to Andres, a printer whose workshop was on a cross-street off Calle Cordoba. I put myself in his hands, shuttling back and forth through those burning streets, irked that he couldn't source the right paper or a less glossy cover. Back then, importing *papel* was just one of the problems Argentina had to face.

In the end, we got there. On December 17, 2011, I stuffed the copies into my suitcase and left Buenos Aires in time to reach Florence on the following day for lunch to celebrate Tà's birthday.

I landed in Rome early in the morning, and took the train to Florence. I was so excited. As the train streaked through the Tuscan hills and approached the city, I tried to imagine Tà's face as I handed her *her* book.

The only person who knew about the gift, Mom, was eagerly waiting for me at the station. Every time I left for or came back from Argentina, she was bright-eyed and overcome with emotion. Such a tender memory, even more intense today.

She accompanied me to the stationery store at Parione, where we had the book packaged in a beautiful burgundy box, the same color as the cover, wrapped in elegant Florentine paper, and tied with a satin bow. Then we headed to the office, but before joining the rest of the family in the dining room, we went to Tà's room to give her the book.

As soon as I walked in, she threw me a questioning look. Then, she melted into an affectionate greeting. She seemed almost intimidated by my birthday wishes and the beautiful package. "But you didn't have to give me anything, I don't deserve it..." she said, not meaning it at all. As she opened it, she took care not to ruin the paper, carefully folding it away with the satin bow. When she saw her own image on the book cover, she seemed at first not to understand. Then she immediately asked who the publisher was. I explained that it was a gift from me to her.

She enjoyed browsing through the book, dwelling longest on the photographs, until it was time to go to lunch. With *her* book under her arm, Tà walked ahead of us at a brisk pace to join my uncles, aunts, and cousins who were waiting to congratulate her.

The dining table was decorated with a composition of flowers emerging from a cabbage: a surprise from Silvano for Tà's birthday that did not go unnoticed.

"See how Silvano expresses himself in all the beautiful things life gives us?" Tà said, a phrase she had used in a dedication to him for his personal "red book"—he too had received one, titled *Silvano's Tables*. It was an album in which the faithful butler, by now an expert table decorator, was instructed by Tà to put photos of his creations, indicating the events for which he made them. This beautiful table would also be documented and archived in that book.

What a wonderful day. Everything was perfect. Grandmother was smiling, still lively despite her age; my mother was full of energy, and all mine that day; my comforting and numerous family was there, the table at Palazzo Spini Feroni once again confirming the care Tà lavished on everyone and everything.

That weekend, I stayed at Tà's home in Fiesole. We spent a chilly afternoon reading the book together, all in one go. Tà never overdoes it with the heating: "*Mamma mia*, how expensive it is, and to think I grew up without any heating at all!" After succeeding in coaxing a Callas CD to play on the living room stereo, she sat down next to me on the couch.

"That woman's voice is so incredible. There's such a weight of suffering in it, so much pain she had to convey. She is truly unsurpassed. I met her once in Florence, before she went on stage, and afterwards many times in New York. I have listened to her voice countless times..." she said. When the stereo skipped, irritated, Tà got up to start it over again. "*Madonna Santa*, one day I'm going to smash this thing to bits!" After slapping one of the speakers, she sat back down beside me, the gas heater on full blast, a white plaid on her thighs, and focused back on the book.

We asked her time and again to write a book... How it would have delighted us to hear her tell her story herself, in her smart, practical, witty way of writing.

Anyway, she loved *her* book and that was, for me, one of the best afternoons we ever spent together.

As soon as I got back to Argentina after the Christmas vacation, the first thing I found on the table by the front door was a letter from Tà. She hadn't even given me the time to get home...

"My dearest Ginevra, welcome back home to Buenos Aires! We were happy to have had you stay with us for a few days. Next time, we must spend some time in Viesca too. You have no idea how soothing and relaxing the air is there. Other people have felt this, not just me. I even had a study done on it a while back. We can talk about it at length the next time we meet. I am unable to find the words to thank you for all you have done for me! You have shown such affection, respect and consideration, and I'd like to tell you how much I appreciate it! At the end of the day, all I ever did was my duty, and that is never enough to thank

Salvatore, who gave us all so much. I'd like to take this opportunity to remind you to always talk to your kids, naturally, to the extent they are able to absorb at their age. I get so disheartened by all the young people, 14 or 15 years old, to whom no values are passed on. When they get home in the afternoon after school, their mother is out working to make ends meet, and when she gets home she has to cook, clean, iron... after a day's work, lacking the strength to do anything else. If I were in politics, I would create a ministry just for young people, to look after a whole host of things, first and foremost their upbringing. I look forward to receiving your notes on that Bible class. I am always so happy to hear from you. Hugs to you, Ottavia, Leo and Andrea. Yours, Tà."

I was back home but felt neither distant nor alone thanks to that letter that, as always, brought me the comfort I needed.

Two years later, I left Argentina and returned to live in Italy. Even now, I get a lump in my throat when I think about that time, one that was particularly strange for me. Spending 11 years in a different world had radically altered me, uprooting me from my country, from the city where I was born and raised. Almost as if they were oxygen, I missed the light, the space, the freedom and simplicity that marked my life in Argentina, a country that had welcomed me with open arms, consoling me for all that distance from my family.

Back in Italy, I gave up my job as a journalist, which had been how I had lived through those sunny days in Buenos Aires, between the *La Nación* offices in the Microcentro, then alone in my home office on the roof of the French building where we lived, surrounded by plants and a city vegetable garden. I slowly realized that those moments had become memories of a daily routine I would never experience again. My children spoke Spanish, the language in which, for a little while longer, we grounded our thoughts and expressed our feelings. That language and its literature introduced me to a world of words and emotions that truly spoke to me. In Milan, I suddenly felt like a stranger. I must admit, it took me a while to readjust. Perhaps I still haven't fully adapted, which is why I try to get back to the southern hemisphere whenever I can.

Certainly, upon my return to Italy, I would never have thought that shortly afterward I would lose the most important women in my world: first my mother, then Tà. I was fortunate enough to have had them in my life for a long time, even if work kept them busy all the time. Every now and then, when the grayness of Milan made me melancholy, I would go to Corso Matteotti to greet my mother in her office, to visit this creative woman in her own element. She was always in the midst of a cloud of smoke, a cigarillo in her mouth, working until the evening on some new project or other after dispatching her day's work. She never stopped. A legacy of "always making and producing something, at all times," something Tà and Grandfather Salvatore passed on through the family DNA.

After taking a master's degree at Bocconi, I started working on the family farm in Maremma, where among other things, we breed horses. My visits to see Tà became a more regular occurrence. I'd travel from Grosseto to Florence, stay at her place overnight or lunch with her at the office, and then continue on to Milan. Lucid and constructive to the end, these were such special moments for me to enjoy her during the last years of her long life.

The sweetness and enthusiasm with which Tà received me the last time I ever saw her provide the most beautiful memory she could have left me. It was September. I arrived at Il Palagio after spending the day in the saddle for a race. "Still doing these horrible horseback rides..." she scolded before I even mentioned it, coming over to give me a kiss. I sensed the thinness of her skin and a certain weakness in that gesture into which she usually poured such energy. She then went to sit back down in her home office, dressed in white linens, combed and bejeweled, her pink lipstick on her now lean mouth, elegant despite being on her own at the house that day.

She asked me a few superfluous questions, I showed her a few pictures of the kids on the iPad, and then, sullenly, in an unusually fragile tone, she asked me about Mom. "How long has she been gone, now?" she asked, as if she had lost track of time, but I knew perfectly well that she had counted every single day during those six months of inconsolable suffering.

She had glided silently away, my Mom, one sunny April holiday when she would usually have been outdoors somewhere, enjoying her innate desire to be in nature whenever she could. She left as discreetly as she'd lived her life, a silent, protective, generous, determined, and reserved tiger as colorful as the scarves she designed.

I didn't stay for dinner at Tà's. She told me she was tired and wanted to retire early. She walked me to the door, and with another kiss bade me goodbye. I watched her walk back into the house from the car, and that was the last time I saw her. A few days later, she went to join my Mom.

"Florence, even to you I owe a final farewell..."

Tà's wonderful letter to Florence has been displayed since December 21, 2021 at Palazzo Vecchio on a pedestal, printed in two languages, to celebrate the hundredth anniversary of her birth. In the Cortile della Dogana, at the visitors' entrance to the historic palazzo, everyone may now read her words of gratitude to the city that embraced and hosted her throughout her life.

In July 2019, the Piazzetta Salvatore e Wanda Ferragamo was unveiled, reachable on foot just over Ponte Vecchio toward the other side of River Arno. I go there for a cappuccino every time I'm in Florence, and think back on all Tà's great stories and teachings.

I open the Red Book at random and search through Tà's letters for answers that no longer arrive today. As I write this, I hear the jingle of a silver angel on a chain around my neck: Tà's final gift, so full of meaning, which she would have given us at Christmas. Only, she passed away before. It was found in her office, wrapped for every one of her granddaughters, yet again granting us eternal protection. A final gesture of love, the value that always inspired and guided her, as she told us in a brief letter from July 2009.

Love is the supreme good in our lives:

1. What is it that keeps us going through fatigue? LOVE
2. What is it that keeps us moving forward? LOVE
3. What is it that gives us the strength to endure contrariness and offense? LOVE
4. What is it that makes us work to honor those who are no longer with us? LOVE
5. What makes us pass on to our children all the best and wisest things we can for their future? LOVE
6. What offers us the joy of giving? LOVE
7. What is it that makes us hold a child and wish them all good things in this world? LOVE
8. Who imprinted this feeling in our hearts? He who gave flowers their fragrance, fertilized the earth, and heaped colors onto fish and butterflies to create a living, heart-beating world. He's God, infinite good, goodness within goodness, light within darkness, and peace within the spirit.

Wanda and Salvatore
Ferragamo walk past
Palazzo Spini Feroni with
Audrey Hepburn, 1954

Wanda and Salvatore
attending a social event,
1950s

Wanda Ferragamo at
Viesca, 2006

The silver angel, the final
gift by Wanda Ferragamo
to her granddaughters,
2018

Wanda Ferragamo with work
colleagues Roberto Gaggioli,
Angela Bongi, Marisa
Balestrieri and accountant
Giuseppe Anichini, 1969

Wanda and Fiamma Ferragamo
on the terrace of Palazzo Spini
Feroni, 1967

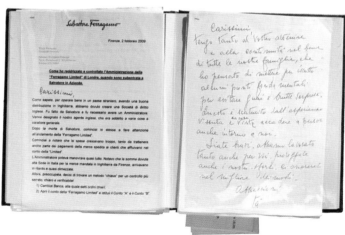

Wanda Ferragamo in her office,
early 1980s

The Red Book open to the pages
containing the letter "How I tidied
up and oversaw Management
of Ferragamo Limited in London
when I took over from Salvatore
at the Company"

Four generations of Ferragamo
women, 2014

Wanda Ferragamo receiving an
Honorary Degree in Fine Arts from
the Fashion Institute of Technology (FIT)
of the State University of New York on
May 22, 2007. Pictured with Joyce F. Brown,
president of FIT

The Ferragamo family,
early 1980s

The Ferragamo family on the roof of Palazzo
Spini Feroni, 1983: Fiamma, Wanda, and
Fulvia (foreground), Giovanna, Leonardo,
Ferruccio, and a model (background)

The Ferragamo family gathered in the Sala
Consiglio of Palazzo Spini Feroni, 1980s

The rose named after
Wanda Ferragamo

The ten large terracotta
pots given by Wanda
Ferragamo to the Château
du Clos Lucé in Amboise,
France, the last residence
of Leonardo da Vinci

Wanda and her little grandchildren

Wanda with her twin grandchildren,
James and Salvatore, 1972

Wanda with her grandchildren
Angelica, James, Diego
and Salvatore, Palazzo Spini
Feroni, 2004

The Ferragamo family at the opening of the store on Fifth Avenue in New York, 2003: Diego Paternò Castello di San Giuliano, Giovanna, James, Angelica Visconti, Fulvia, Massimo, Ferruccio, and Wanda

Wanda Ferragamo with her six children, 1990s: Fulvia, Massimo, Fiamma, Ferruccio (standing), Leonardo, and Giovanna (sitting)

Wanda Ferragamo with Peter Woo at the gala dinner organized for the opening of the Ferragamo store in Hong Kong, 1989

Wanda and Fiamma Ferragamo at
Palazzo Spini Feroni, 1980s

Wanda Ferragamo meets Kathy
Bates in the Ferragamo store in
Los Angeles at event celebrating the
opening of the exhibition *Salvatore
Ferragamo. The Art of the Shoe
(1898–1960)* at Los Angeles County
Museum of Art, 1992

Wanda Ferragamo with actor
Gregory Peck at a gala dinner held
at Palazzo Spini Feroni for the
inauguration of the Salvatore
Ferragamo exhibition at Palazzo
Strozzi, Florence, 1985

Wanda Ferragamo with Chinese
actress Zhang Ziyi at the 2004 Milan
Fashion Week

Wanda Ferragamo and fashion
designer Roberto Capucci
at a Pitti Uomo event in 1992

Wanda Ferragamo with Audrey
Hepburn at the Rodeo Drive store
opening in Beverly Hills, February
14, 1991

Wanda Ferragamo meets
Princess Diana at a charity event
at Grosvenor House Hotel in
London, June 13, 1990

Wanda Ferragamo with movie and
theater director Franco Zeffirelli, 1983

Wanda Ferragamo with Tanaka Ikko at press
conference called for opening of Salvatore
Ferragamo exhibition at the Sogetsu-Kai
Foundation in Tokyo, 1998

Wanda Ferragamo with President
of the United States Ronald Reagan
and his wife Nancy, 1987

Wanda Ferragamo with Marisa
Berenson at the opening of the
Ferragamo store on Rue du
Faubourg Saint-Honoré, Paris,
December 1996

Wanda Ferragamo and her
daughters Fulvia, Giovanna, and
Fiamma with Ray Charles at the
March 1997 fashion show

Wanda Ferragamo at the opening event of
*I protagonisti della moda. Salvatore
Ferragamo 1898–1960*, the first retrospective
exhibition dedicated to Ferragamo, held at
Palazzo Strozzi, Florence, 1985

The family with Neiman Marcus at the
inauguration of the retrospective exhibition
dedicated to Salvatore Ferragamo at the
Los Angeles County Museum of Art, 1992

Wanda Ferragamo speaking on the occasion
of receiving the New York University
Honorary Degree in Commercial Science,
May 16, 1996

Wanda Ferragamo meets Pope John Paul II
in Rome, 1986

Wanda Ferragamo with Gina Lollobrigida at
the gala dinner organized by Prime Time
Promotions with Salvatore Ferragamo on
the occasion of the 12th Christmas Concert
in the Vatican, December 18, 2004

Wanda Ferragamo is received by Queen
Elizabeth II of England at Buckingham
Palace, March 15, 2005

Wanda Ferragamo receives an
Order of the British Empire from
British Ambassador Patrick
Fairweather, June 7, 1995

Wanda Ferragamo receiving the
Tiberio d'Oro award in Capri, 1969

Wanda Ferragamo with President of
the Italian Republic Francesco
Cossiga after receiving the Honor
of the Ordine dei Cavalieri del
Lavoro, October 22, 1987

President of the Italian Republic
Carlo Azeglio Ciampi confers
Ordine al Merito dei Cavalieri di
Gran Croce on Wanda Ferragamo,
March 8, 2004

Wanda Ferragamo receives Honorary
Degree in Humane Letters from the City
University of New York, May 22, 1986

President of the Italian Republic Oscar
Luigi Scalfaro with Wanda Ferragamo at
Italian Quality Award, Quirinale Palace,
Rome, July 1, 1997

Prix Léonard de Vinci, awarded to Wanda
Ferragamo on September 23, 2011. The award
was established by the Saint-Bris family and
the Les Hénokiens Association, which attends
to and promotes family-based companies with
more than a hundred years of history

Mela d'Oro for fashion, technology, and design, 26th Marisa Bellisario Prize, awarded to Wanda Ferragamo for her great contribution to luxury-quality Made in Italy products, June 20, 2014

The Minerva Lifetime Achievement Award under the High Patronage of the President of the Italian Republic conferred on Wanda Ferragamo, 2004

Fiorino d'Oro, awarded by the City of Florence to Wanda Ferragamo as an example of a modern and courageous entrepreneur, October 4, 1996

Tà's Red Book
The life of Wanda Ferragamo

Edited by
Laura Bosio

Design
Leonardo Sonnoli

Layout
Angelo Galiotto

Copy editors
Emanuela Di Lallo
Mariangela Palazzi-Williams

Translation
Conor Deane, Adam Victor, and
Oona Smyth for *Scriptum*, Rome

Photo credits

Archivio Elisabetta Catalano,
© Photo ELISABETTA CATALANO, pp. 267 top, 269
Archivio Foto Locchi, Florence / © ARCHIVIO FOTO LOCCHI, pp. 136 bottom, 137 top, 138, 139 top, 264 top
© Museo Salvatore Ferragamo, Florence, cover, pp. 123, 124, 125 center and bottom, 126, 127, 128, 129, 130, 133, 134, 135, 136 top, 137 bottom, 139 bottom, 140, 141, 264 bottom, 265 top, 266, 268 bottom, 270, 271, 272 top and bottom left, 273, 274, 275, 276, 277, 278, 279, 280, 281, 282 top. Photo Arrigo Coppitz, pp. 131, 265 bottom, 267 bottom. Photo Guglielmo De Micheli, p. 125 top. Photo Silvia Montevecchi, pp. 132, 282 bottom, 283
© Roberto Quagli, p. 272 bottom right
© Simon Watson, p. 268 top

The publisher is at the disposal of rights holders regarding any unidentified iconographic sources.

This volume was printed by Electa S.p.A.
at Elcograf S.p.A., Via Mondadori 15, Verona, in 2022

Electa uses PEFC certified paper that guarantees
sustainable management of forestry resources